SAN FRANCISCO'S INTERNATIONAL HOTEL

In the series

Asian American History and Culture

edited by Sucheng Chan, David Palumbo-Liu, Michael Omi, K. Scott Wong, and Linda Trinh Võ

Antonio T. Tiongson Jr., Edgardo V. Gutierrez, and Ricardo V. Gutierrez, eds., *Positively No Filipinos Allowed: Building Communities and Discourse*

Sucheng Chan, ed., *Chinese American Transnationalism: The Flow of People, Resources, and Ideas between China and America during the Exclusion Era*

Keith Lawrence and Floyd Cheung, eds., *Recovered Legacies: Authority and Identity in Early Asian American Literature*

Rajini Srikanth, *The World Next Door: South Asian American Literature and the Idea of America*

Linda Trinh Võ, *Mobilizing an Asian American Community*

Franklin S. Odo, *No Sword to Bury: Japanese Americans in Hawai'i during World War II*

Josephine Lee, Imogene L. Lim, and Yuko Matsukawa, eds., *Re/collecting Early Asian America: Essays in Cultural History*

Linda Trinh Võ and Rick Bonus, eds., *Contemporary Asian American Communities: Intersections and Divergences*

Sunaina Marr Maira, *Desis in the House: Indian American Youth Culture in New York City*

Teresa Williams-León and Cynthia Nakashima, eds., *The Sum of Our Parts: Mixed-Heritage Asian Americans*

Tung Pok Chin with Winifred C. Chin, *Paper Son: One Man's Story*

Amy Ling, ed., *Yellow Light: The Flowering of Asian American Arts*

Rick Bonus, *Locating Filipino Americans: Ethnicity and the Cultural Politics of Space*

Darrell Y. Hamamoto and Sandra Liu, eds., *Countervisions: Asian American Film Criticism*

Martin F. Manalansan, IV, ed., *Cultural Compass: Ethnographic Explorations of Asian America*

Ko-lin Chin, *Smuggled Chinese: Clandestine Immigration to the United States*

Evelyn Hu-DeHart, ed., *Across the Pacific: Asian Americans and Globalization*

Soo-Young Chin, *Doing What Had to Be Done: The Life Narrative of Dora Yum Kim*

Robert G. Lee, *Orientals: Asian Americans in Popular Culture*

David L. Eng and Alice Y. Hom, eds., *Q & A: Queer in Asian America*

K. Scott Wong and Sucheng Chan, eds., *Claiming America: Constructing Chinese American Identities during the Exclusion Era*

San Francisco's International Hotel

Mobilizing the Filipino American Community in the Anti-Eviction Movement

ESTELLA HABAL

TEMPLE UNIVERSITY PRESS
Philadelphia

Temple University Press
1601 North Broad Street
Philadelphia PA 19122
www.temple.edu/tempress

Paper edition published 2008
Cloth edition published 2007
Printed in the United States of America

∞

The paper used in this publication meets the requirements
of the American National Standard for Information Sciences—
Permanence of Paper for Printed Library Materials, ANSI Z39.48-1992

Library of Congress Cataloging-in-Publication Data

Habal, Estella, 1949–
San Francisco's International Hotel : mobilizing the Filipino American
community in the anti-eviction movement / Estella Habal.
p. cm. — (Asian American History and Culture)
Includes bibliographical references and index.
ISBN 13: 978-1-59213-446-5 ISBN 10: 1-59213-446-7 (paper : alk. paper)
1. Older people—Housing—California—San Francisco.
2. Eviction—California—San Francisco. 3. Filipino Americans—
California—San Francisco. I. Title.

HD7287.92.U55S24 2007
362.6'3—dc22 2006035024

2 4 6 8 9 7 5 3

CONTENTS

ACKNOWLEDGMENTS

I BECAME INVOLVED in the struggle to save the International Hotel soon after I arrived in San Francisco in 1971, and it seems that I have never left that struggle, even since the eviction of the elderly tenants in 1977 and the building's demolition in 1979. Now, with the resurrection of the International Hotel in 2005, I am still deeply involved. I played a key role working with the tenants in the anti-eviction movement, behind the scenes, as a member of the leading Filipino organization, the Katipunan ng mga Demokratikong Pilipino (KDP), or Union of Democratic Filipinos. I worked so quietly with the elderly members of the International Hotel Tenants Association that many of the thousands of people who also participated may never have known my name. Nonetheless, I was there. I observed all that happened, and I developed close, family-like bonds with the "manongs."

I have carried the memory of the I-Hotel for decades. After many years as a mother and an activist, I decided to tell the story of the anti-eviction movement as one of its participants. Writing a historically informed memoir has been very difficult, particularly because of the hurt involved, but it has also been deeply satisfying. The effort to save the International Hotel was one of the most extensive grassroots movements in San Francisco's history and a major moment in the development of the Filipino American community. I hope that this book will illuminate this turbulent, transformative period in our history. I have to acknowledge that I owe a great debt to the many individuals and organizations who participated in the anti-eviction movement, and I hope that this small effort does justice to their sacrifices.

I especially thank the tenants of the International Hotel, almost all of whom are now dead. Without those "manongs," as they were known, there would have been no struggle to save the International Hotel, and there would have been one less testament to the endurance and courage of the Filipino pioneers who first came to the United States in the early twentieth century. I was able to draw on the knowledge and experience of tenant leaders such as Frank Alarcon, Felix Ayson, Etta (Moon) Chung, So Chung, Luisa de la Cruz, Joe Diones, Claudio Domingo, "Tex" Llamera, Nita Rader, Joe Regadio, Frankie de los Reyes, and Wahat Tompao.

When I participated in the International Hotel anti-eviction movement, I worked closely with Emil de Guzman and Jeanette Lazam, the two other members of the KDP I-Hotel team. I conducted countless conversations as well as formal interviews with both of them over the course of many years; without their help, I would not have been able to piece together our responses to the complex, day-to-day events of the anti-eviction movement. De Guzman, who was the leader of the tenants' association at the time of the eviction, has participated in the International Hotel movement since its inception in 1968, and he has stubbornly "kept the faith." I owe a lot to his inspiration, as well as to his deep knowledge of the movement.

Al Robles, poet and oral historian of Manilatown, and the activist Bill Sorro offered crucial insights and analysis, and they remain stalwarts in the development of the new International Hotel. I also thank all of the others who offered their time for interviews, including Ben Abarca, Liz (Abello) Del Sol, Fred Basconcillo, Chris Braga, Luisa Castro, Frank Celada, Harvey Dong, Lillian Galedo, Bruce Occena, Carl Regal, and Maxi Villones. Fran (Finley) Peavy, one of the key leaders of the hotel's "internal security team," contributed important information, and Peter Rubin described his experiences on the Support Committee. Sidney Wolinsky and Gilbert Graham, two of the lawyers who defended the hotel in the courts, assisted me with interviews and explained the complicated legal issues.

The Manilatown Heritage Foundation (MHF), which manages the International Hotel Manilatown Center in the newly rebuilt International Hotel, played a key role by gathering, preserving, and digitizing valuable archives of the struggle, including letters, flyers, meeting notes, posters, position papers, memoirs, and more. Several personal archives have now been collected within the MHF archive. They include invaluable material collected by Luisa Castro, one of the early activists in United Filipino Association, and by Steve Friedman, an activist in the period just before eviction. Especially important were archives of the KDP gathered by Abe Ignacio and the late Helen Toribio. I was also able to use archival material collected by Ed Ilumin, Edith Witt, and David Prowler, who were all members of the San Francisco Human Rights Commission staff at different times during the anti-eviction struggle. In particular, I drew heavily on an unfinished manuscript by David Prowler that recounts the history of the movement, which he wrote a few years after the eviction. Prowler also supplied handwritten notes he kept during the events of 1977, including the eviction.

Chester Harman played a key role during the anti-eviction movement as an activist with the Northern California Alliance and as a housing consultant. He has contributed to the MHF Archive letters from Mayor George Moscone, housing studies, handwritten minutes, journal notes, a vast collection of newspaper clippings, and much more, all of which I have found crucial for writing this book. His contributions as a writer can be seen throughout my account, particularly his important study of urban development, *City for Sale: The Transformation of San Francisco.*

I was also assisted by several master's theses and dissertations, particularly those by Teri Lee, Carole Levine, and Vivian Tsen. The audio recordings of Norman Jayo, who produced radio reports of the International Hotel, particularly during the night of the eviction, were especially helpful. The film *The Fall of the I-Hotel,* by Curtis Choy, also aided me as an important visual document of the eviction.

Also valuable were materials in the Amy Schecter Files at the International Longshoremen's and Warehousemen's Union Library; at the Bancroft Library, University of California, Berkeley; at San Francisco City Hall; in the San Francisco Room, San Francisco Public Library; in the Special Collections of the Green Library, Stanford University; and the University of California, Los Angeles, Asian American Studies Center.

Nancy Hom, formerly of the Kearny Street Workshop, assisted me in gathering photographs generously donated by Tom Drescher, Chris Fujimoto, Bob Hsiang, Jerry Jew, and Calvin Roberts. Calvin Roberts graciously donated his time to assist me in preparing the photographs for publication.

My husband, Hilton Obenzinger, offered professional editorial consultation throughout the course of this project. I would not have been able to master this book's complex writing task without his guidance and constant personal support. Max Elbaum also provided perceptive editorial consultation.

This project began as a dissertation in history at the University of California, Davis, and I acknowledge the members of my dissertation committee for their guidance: Chairman Clarence Walker and Lorena Oropeza of the History Department; Michael P. Smith, of the Human and Community Development Department; David Sweet of the University of California, Santa Cruz, History Department; and Gordon Chang of the Stanford University History Department. I also recognize the support of, and guidance from, the late Professor Roland Marchand of the University of California, Davis, History Department. I am especially grateful to David Palumbo-Liu of Stanford, who offered advice on how to transform the dissertation into a book, and to Janet Francendese of Temple University Press for her patience and persistence.

My husband, Hilton, and my children—Anthony Alonzo, Don Alonzo, Kalayaan Nagtalan, and Isaac Obenzinger—supported me while I spent too much time away from them working on this project. Three of my children grew up in and around the International Hotel, and all of them understood the importance of the hotel to our history. My youngest son, Isaac, now works at the International Hotel Manilatown Center. Still, during the movement and the writing of this book, my involvement meant that they did not receive all the attention they deserved, and I owe them my deepest gratitude and love.

While all those I have thanked have contributed important materials and shared their experiences and viewpoints, I take responsibility for this history's opinions and analysis, as well as for any of its shortcomings.

Yet this is not the end of my gratitude, just as it is not the end of the International Hotel. The new International Hotel, rebuilt decades after the eviction in 1977, is a project that involves many people who deserve recognition, particularly the activists in the Chinatown community, as I describe later in the book. As part of the resurrection of the International Hotel, the Manilatown Heritage Foundation was formed to commemorate the legacy of the struggle and all of the accomplishments of the Filipino American community. I express my gratitude to the young activists involved in the MHF, those future leaders of the Filipino American community who will continue to remember the International Hotel.

ACRONYMS

AAPA	Asian American Political Alliance
ACC	Asian Community Center
BAC	Bay Area Council
BAGL	Bay Area Gay Liberation
BART	Bay Area Rapid Transit
CAC	International Hotel Citizens Advisory Committee
CANE	Committee against Nihonmachi Eviction
CCDC	Chinatown Community Development Center
CCHC	Chinese Community Housing Corporation
CIO	Congress of Industrial Organizations
CPA	Chinese Progressive Association
CPP	Communist Party of the Philippines
CPUSA	Communist Party of the United States of America
CRC	Chinatown Resource Center
EOC	Economic Opportunity Council
EOP	Equal Opportunity Program
IH, I-Hotel	International Hotel
IHSHI	International Hotel Senior Housing Inc.
IHTA	International Hotel Tenants Association
ILWU	International Longshoremen's and Warehousemen's Union (now called the International Longshore and Warehouse Union)
IWK	I Wor Kuen
KDP	Katipunan ng mga Demokratikong Pilipino (Union of Democratic Filipinos)
KSHC	Kearny Street Housing Corporation

KSW	Kearny Street Workshop
LRS	League for Revolutionary Struggle
MHF	Manilatown Heritage Foundation
NCA	Northern California Alliance
NCRCLP	National Committee for Restoration of Civil Liberties in the Philippines
NPA	New People's Army
PAA	Pilipino American Alliance
PACE	Philippine [Pilipino] American Collegiate Endeavor
RU	Revolutionary Union
RCP	Revolutionary Communist Party
SIPA	Search to Involve Pilipino Americans
SPUR	San Francisco Planning and Urban Renewal Association (now called the San Francisco Planning and Urban Research Association)
TOOR	Tenants and Owners in Opposition to Redevelopment
UC	University of California
UCLA	University of California, Los Angeles
UFA	United Filipino Association
UFW	United Farm Workers

CHRONOLOGY OF LEGAL AND POLITICAL EVENTS

1968 *October:* Tenants receive eviction order to leave the International Hotel by January 1, 1969. The UFA represents the tenants.

November 27: Tenants hold a protest march to oppose the eviction to make way for a parking lot. A news conference is held at Tino's Barber Shop.

December 3: Assemblyman John Burton works out a deal with Walter Shorenstein, landlord and president of Milton Meyer and Company, to suspend action.

December 5: The San Francisco Human Rights Commission strongly opposes the eviction and requests a full discussion of the issue with residents and hotel owners.

1969 *March 16:* A suspicious fire kills three I-Hotel tenants and guts the third floor.

March 20: Tenants testify at a Human Rights Commission hearing to housing experts, structural engineers, architects.

March 20: The Ford Foundation offers guarantee of up to twenty-five thousand dollars a year in rental to the owners for the period of the lease. (Milton Meyer and Company collects one thousand two hundred dollars a month in rent.)

March 20: Students join tenants in their fight, refurbishing the hotel.

March 26: At a complaint hearing, Filipino tenants tell the city's Department of Public Works that "they will not leave the hotel if ordered to do so, and if the hotel is demolished, it will be done 'over our bodies.'" The director of the Department of Public Works orders the owners to bring the hotel up to code.

March 27: Sid Wolinsky of San Francisco Neighborhood Legal Assistance files a legal suit on behalf of two tenants who were burned in the fire, charging that demolition of the hotel violates the residents' constitutional rights and will destroy the Filipino community. Shorenstein is accused of using his influence as a Recreation and Parks Commissioner to bring about the eviction, demolition, and displacement.

April 18: Tenants stage a protest at Mayor Joseph Alioto's Earthquake Party. Mayor Alioto is publicly embarrassed.

April 23: Tenants call a press conference to protest harassment by Milton Meyer and Company for shutting off electricity, refusing routine maintenance, and telling tenants they must move. Fire damage is not repaired.

May 5: Mayor Alioto proposes a three-part plan as a solution.

May 8: Federal Judge George B. Harris dismisses the suit to save the I-Hotel because "no federal questions [are] involved."

May 10: I-Hotel tenants present signed petition to Mayor Alioto rejecting his three-part plan.

May 23: The Center for Community Change of Washington, D.C., gives fifty thousand dollars from the Ford Foundation to the UFA for restoration and renovation and rent money to lease the I-Hotel.

June 1: Tenants hold an Eviction Day Party; the city obtains an extension to July 1.

June 18: A lease agreement is reached. The lease will run for three years, from July 1, 1969, to June 30, 1972.

September: The UFA appeals broadly to the community for help in refurbishing the hotel. College students join in.

1970 *February:* UC Berkeley students make a pubic appeal and print a broadside on the tenants' behalf that says, "Save the International Hotel: I Am Old, I Am Poor, I Am Tired, I Don't Want to Move." The broadside publicizes the community organizations Manilatown Information Center, Wei Min She, I Wor Kuen, Everybody's Bookstore, Asian Legal Services, and Chinatown Co-operative Garment Factory.

1972 *Spring:* The IHTA is founded.

May 23: Tenants and supporters demonstrate at Shorenstein's headquarters in the financial district to demand a new lease agreement with the IHTA.

June 30: The lease agreement ends; month-to-month rental begins.

June 30: The UFA disbands.

1973 *July 3–4:* The KDP is founded.

October 31: Four Seas Investment Corporation buys the I-Hotel from Milton Meyer and Company.

1974 *September 24:* Four Seas orders eviction.

October 24: Tenants and supporters demonstrate at Four Seas headquarters. The San Francisco Lawyers Committee for Urban Affairs files a suit on behalf of the tenants seeking damages and an injunction against their scheduled eviction.

November 8: Four Seas files a complaint of unlawful detainer (illegal habitation of the building) against the IHTA.

1975 *January 17:* Four Seas applies to the city's Central Permit Bureau for a demolition permit.

March 3: Supervisor John L. Molinari proposes an ordinance regarding the issuance of demolition and alteration permits throughout the city for multifamily dwellings.

March 10: Four Seas receives a demolition permit.

April 24: The Board of Permit Appeals upholds Four Seas' permit.

1976 *January 15:* Four Seas' demolition permit expires.

February 23: Building Inspector Alfred Goldberg refuses to cancel the demolition permit. The IHTA appeals to the Board of Permit Appeals.

April 30: Superior Court Judge Ira A. Brown directs a deadlocked jury to render a verdict for the plaintiff, Four Seas. Attorney Gilbert Graham appeals the directed verdict to the State Court of Appeal.

July 27: The State Court of Appeal turns down the appeal of the lower court's eviction order. The case is appealed to the State Supreme Court.

July 27: Undersheriff James Denman states that he will not enforce the eviction order while the tenants are appealing it in court.

July 29: Mayor George Moscone presents a proposal to the Housing Authority calling for nonprofit ownership of the I-Hotel. The State Supreme Court stays the Superior Court's eviction order, postponing the decision.

September 3: The State Supreme Court rejects the appeal and lifts the stay of eviction.

October 21: The Housing Authority approves Moscone plan.

November 2: The Board of Supervisors rejects Moscone plan to allocate 1.3 million dollars of federal community-development funds toward the I-Hotel. Instead, the board votes to use the money to upgrade police services in Hayes Valley and other high-crime areas. Moscone vetoes the board's vote.

November 15: The Board of Supervisors upholds the mayor's veto of money to upgrade police services by a vote of 6–5.

November 30: The Board of Supervisors votes to support Moscone plan, 6–4.

December 3: Judge Brown issues a new order to evict the tenants. Sheriff Hongisto is ordered to carry out the eviction by December 15.

December 14: Judge Brown denies the stay request brought by the sheriff and the IHTA. Judge Brown brushes off claims that the Sheriff's Office has insufficient manpower to carry out the eviction.

December 20: Sheriff Hongisto and Undersheriff Denman are charged with contempt of court for refusing to carry out the eviction.

December 23: The Housing Authority votes unanimously to condemn the building, employ eminent domain, and resell the I-Hotel to the tenants' nonprofit organization.

December 23: By a 6–4 vote, the Board of Supervisors directs the Housing Authority to use 1.3 million dollars in federal community-development funds to implement the Moscone Plan.

December 28: Judge John E. Benson denies Sheriff Hongisto's motion for a mistrial. Hongisto testifies that his failure to evict the tenants was not "willful" and therefore not a violation of the court order.

1977 *January 7:* Sheriff Hongisto attempts to serve the eviction notice. Only first-floor businesses are successfully served.

January 10: Sheriff Hongisto and Undersheriff Denman are convicted of contempt of court, and each is sentenced to five days in jail and fined five hundred dollars for failing to evict. Under Judge Brown's latest order, tenants must be out by 5 P.M. on January 19.

January 11: Under the contempt-of-court order Sheriff Hongisto successfully posts eviction notices.

January 11: The San Francisco Housing Authority loses a court petition for immediate possession of the I-Hotel for use as low-cost public housing. The case is appealed to the State Court of Appeal.

January 12: A mass demonstration of 2,500–3,000 supporters is held.

January 16: A mass demonstration of 7,000 supporters is held to protect tenants and defy eviction.

January 17: Judge Brown stays the latest order of eviction because Police Chief Charles Gain tells him that automatic weapons and gasoline have been spotted at the I-Hotel.

February 1: Tenants and supporters rally at City Hall. Four Seas petitions a writ of mandamus to the Superior Court.

April 29: Sheriff Hongisto begins serving five days for contempt of court in the San Francisco county jail in San Bruno.

May 27: Superior Court Judge Charles Peery rejects the Housing Authority's case for eminent domain.

June 3: Judge Brown signs the fifth eviction order, to be completed by July 6. Brown declines another request for a stay while Gilbert Graham, attorney, appeals Judge Peery's decision.

June 3: Joe Diones is ousted as chairman of the IHTA. Emil de Guzman is elected to replace him.

June 12: Mass demonstration of 1,500–2,000 supporters march four abreast in front of the I-Hotel to prevent eviction.

June 12: Tenants and supporters barricade doors; activate telephone tree; and get security, medical, and media teams ready for a siege.

June 15: The State Court of Appeal stays the eviction order. Tenants ask the court to stay the eviction order until the eminent-domain appeal is considered. The Housing Authority appeals the eminent-domain case in State Court of Appeal.

June 16: The I-Hotel is placed on the National Register of Historic Places.

June 20: The IHTA and housing consultants present a new eminent-domain plan to Mayor Moscone. He refuses to review the new plan, stating that he is optimistic that the State Court of Appeal will rule in favor of his plan.

July 1: The State Court of Appeal lifts the eviction order.

July 6: Moscone directs the Housing Authority to file a stay-of-eviction order at the State Supreme Court.

July 12: The State Supreme Court temporarily halts the eviction order until it decides whether to hear the case on its merits.

July 27: The State Supreme Court lifts all legal barriers to immediate eviction of the tenants, even though the appeal on eminent domain has yet to be reviewed in the State Court of Appeal. A panel of six justices, with Chief Justice Rose Bird and Justice Stanley Mosk dissenting, refuse to hear a petition asking them to block Judge Brown's eviction order until the appeals are heard. The action also dissolves the State Supreme Court's stay-of-eviction, ordered July 12.

August 2: Proposition A seeking end of district elections and Proposition B recalling the mayor and all elected officials are defeated.

August 4: The tenants are evicted from the I-Hotel.

September 1: The State Supreme Court refuses to block the demolition permit. Five justices refuse to grant a hearing, even though the Board of Permit Appeals wants to revoke it. However, the city notifies Four Seas that a stop-work order exists.

September 3: Tenants move to the Stanford Hotel, where the IHTA sets up an office in room 123.

November 4: Supporters and former tenants file a 2 million dollar claim for damages against the City of San Francisco.

November 8: Proposition U, a policy statement asking voters whether the city should buy the I-Hotel, bring it up to code, and turn it over to the Housing Authority for low-rent housing, is defeated.

December 8: Four Seas files a 1.3 million dollar damage claim against San Francisco, alleging that the city had denied it use of the I-Hotel since November 3, 1976.

1978 *February 22:* Four Seas is fined five hundred dollars and placed on two years' probation for demolishing the I-Hotel without a valid permit. Fred Grange, boss of the wrecking crew, is sentenced to fifteen days in jail, fined five hundred dollars, and placed on two years' probation.

September 1: The State Supreme Court refuses to block the demolition permit.

1979 *January:* Four Seas continues demolition of the I-Hotel.

Fall: Four Seas completes demolition of the I-Hotel.

October: Mayor Dianne Feinstein establishes the International Hotel Citizens Advisory Committee.

1980 San Francisco Planning Commission and Board of Supervisors approve I-Hotel Block Development Plan for public–private mixed-use project.

1983–84 Negotiations are carried out with Four Seas for a mixed-use project.

1984–86 The project proposal is further developed, and negotiations continue between Four Seas, the CAC, and the city.

1986 *June:* Four Seas withdraws the proposal.

1988–93 Three other proposals by private developers are considered; each is withdrawn due to financial infeasibility.

1994 Pan-Magna, the hotel's new owner, agrees to sell the I-Hotel site for community use to the San Francisco Archdiocese of the Catholic church. The sale is finalized 1998.

The MHF is formed.

The U.S. Department of Housing and Urban Development awards an 8.3 million dollar grant to develop the site for low-income housing.

The KSHC, a nonprofit subsidiary of the International Hotel CAC, selects the Chinese Community Housing Corporation (later, the Chinatown Community Development Center) to develop affordable housing at the I-Hotel site. The MHF co-sponsors the plan to design commemorative and cultural elements for the building.

The San Francisco Mayor's Office of Housing allocates 8.7 million dollars toward the new senior housing.

2005 *August 26:* A grand opening celebration is held for the new International Hotel and International Hotel Manilatown Center.

"Coming Home to a Fresh Crop of Rice"

"WE WON'T MOVE!" thousands chanted on August 4, 1977, as police on horseback clubbed their way to the front door of the International Hotel at 848 Kearny Street.[1] The hotel was the last remnant of the ten-block Manilatown neighborhood that stretched along Kearny Street between San Francisco's Chinatown and financial district.

After hours of attacks by police swinging batons, the "human barricade" of thousands of nonviolent demonstrators who had massed in front of the building relented. People inside the building sat on the floor, locked arms, and prepared for passive resistance. In the early-morning hours, sheriff's deputies rousted each tenant from his room, and the elderly Filipinos and Chinese were led out the door with only the clothes on their backs. Each tenant was accompanied by at least one young activist who served as caretaker and eyewitness to possible police brutality. As the frail tenants emerged from the front door, thousands who had stayed up through the night cheered in support and wept.

When the Sheriff's Department evicted the I-Hotel tenants, it was the culmination of a conflict that had had lasted almost a decade. Starting in 1968 with a core of elderly first-generation Filipino immigrants, the anti-eviction movement quickly grew to incorporate radicalized Asian American youth, particularly Filipinos. The first generation of Filipinos in San Francisco's Manilatown planted the seeds of activism when they resisted eviction from their home and community, and their example inspired Filipino college students and other young people to become activists themselves.

I was one of those young activists, and I played a key role in the anti-eviction movement as a member of the leading Filipino radical organization at that time, the Katipunan ng mga Demokratikong Pilipino (KDP), or Union of Democratic Filipinos. Before becoming involved in the I-Hotel struggle, I had participated in the emerging Filipino American identity movement in Los Angeles as a founder of Search to Involve Pilipino Americans (SIPA), one of the first Filipino youth organizations formed during the upsurge of the late 1960s.[2] I moved to San Francisco in 1971 and became involved in the activities surrounding the International Hotel, including those that led to the formation of the KDP.

I was a member of the three-person KDP I-Hotel team that collaborated with the elderly tenants to lead the struggle, and in this book I tell the history of the anti-eviction movement as a direct participant. I was not there for the entire struggle, but I was present for much of it, and for a time I worked as the bookkeeper for the tenants' association. During the crucial period leading up to the eviction, I was a full-time cadre assigned by the KDP. There was such a swirl of events, so many activities happening simultaneously, that even when I was directly and deeply involved I could not keep track of it all. Consequently, I draw on many resources in addition to my firsthand experience to tell this story. They include expanded interviews with the two other members of the KDP I-Hotel team, Emil de Guzman and Jeanette Lazam, and interviews with other participants; newspaper clippings, official documents, letters, meeting notes, and internal memos; and many other sources.

I tell the story of the anti-eviction movement from its inception, focusing on the role of Filipinos. At the same time, the story of the International Hotel intersects with the origins of the Asian American movement and the upsurge of the New Left in the 1960s and '70s. It is also, importantly, a story of how the people of San Francisco resisted the destruction of affordable housing and the expansion of "downtown" corporate interests. I tell these stories to a certain degree, but I pay particular attention to how the International Hotel helped to shape a distinctly Filipino American consciousness.

As broad as the movement became (and as intertwined as it was with other narratives), the I-Hotel provided a distinctly Filipino experience characterized by a unique intergenerational bond. The struggle to keep the Filipino immigrants, affectionately known as the "manongs" (a Filipino term of endearment for elder brother or uncle), in their homes for almost a decade created deep ties between these impoverished pioneers and the college-age Filipino activists who came to their aid. For the youth, the I-Hotel invoked an active recovery of the past, the honoring of injured forefathers; for the elderly tenants, it meant recognition and a glimpse of the promise of American democracy that their generation had long cherished. In the course of resisting eviction, working and personal relations grew, and a family consciousness rooted in Filipino values of respect for the elderly developed.

For the young people, this sharply contrasted with the narrowly youth-oriented expressions of the mainly white antiwar and counterculture movements. There was no "generation gap" among Filipinos—at least, not between the very old and the very young (although many of the youth felt a serious rift with their own parents). The left-oriented elderly—many of whom were seasoned veterans of the labor movement—joined with the newly radicalized youth to create an identity through political struggle. In the process, a coherent, self-conscious narrative of Filipino experience in America took shape that had not been known before. The youth created a common history with the manongs that helped to galvanize the Filipino American community and to give the young activists a new sense of identity and purpose.

The International Hotel was also crucial for the development of the Asian American movement that had emerged during the student upheavals at the University of California (UC), Berkeley, and San Francisco State in 1968–69. Students felt compelled to "Serve the People" in their own communities, and the I-Hotel, right on the edge of Chinatown, was a magnet for Chinese as well as Filipino activists. Storefronts in the I-Hotel would eventually house offices and community projects of the Asian American left, and they, too, would face eviction. With a community arts center, a Filipino American newspaper, a radical bookstore, two Chinese community centers, and, above all, the International Hotel Tenants Association (IHTA), the hotel was the place where activists organized themselves and developed long-lasting ties to their communities.

The anti-eviction movement eventually expanded to include an extraordinarily broad range of constituencies throughout San Francisco and the Bay Area, including civil-rights activists, labor unions, religious leaders, the antiwar movement, and the growing gay community. A large segment of San Francisco's population had strong sympathies with the need for available, affordable housing, in contrast to the needs for corporate expansion. Homelessness was not yet a massive phenomenon, but many residents of the city feared that they could be denied housing altogether, which gave the International Hotel movement a broad appeal. Eventually, saving the I-Hotel won considerable support from the mayor, city supervisors, and other major politicians. Even the sheriff went to jail rather than carry out the eviction—until he acquiesced to the courts.

Much was at stake in the I-Hotel battle: It was a fight for housing rights versus private-property rights; for a neighborhood's existence versus extinction and dispersal; and for the extension of democratic rights to the poor and working class. It was also part of a resistance to urban policies that aimed to transform San Francisco according to the master plans of commercial and financial interests. By the start of the anti-eviction movement in 1968, "Manhattanization," or the high-rise expansion of the financial district in downtown San Francisco, had already been under way for more than a decade.[3] The focus of the transformation was the downtown area, which city planners expected to expand upward with numerous high-rise office buildings (such as the TransAmerica Pyramid, just two blocks away from the I-Hotel), and outward into adjacent neighborhoods. Manilatown had stretched along ten blocks of Kearny Street, north from Market Street to Columbus Avenue and along the eastern edge of Chinatown, and was one block west of the financial district. Consequently, the neighborhood stood in the way of "progress," and many of the single-resident-occupancy hotels that made the core of the community had already been demolished. Over the course of the 1950s and '60s, the neighborhood had been chipped away, except for the very last block where the International Hotel stood.

The will of the tenants backed by mass action characterized the entire movement, and the plight of a few old, once forgotten men became a constant factor in San Francisco city politics. At certain times, particularly between 1975 and 1979, the fate of the International Hotel became a major issue in the electoral arena, and the anti-eviction movement helped to shape a left–liberal coalition that successfully challenged the status quo in city politics. "The attack on the I-Hotel produced some of the most dramatic confrontations in the city's history," writes the urban historian and anti-eviction activist Chester Hartman.[4] Historians like Hartman regard the anti-eviction movement as a significant event in San Francisco's history. When the eviction finally occurred, it had a profound effect on the city as a whole, particularly because it was linked to two other catastrophes that marked San Francisco at the end of the turbulent 1970s, each of which dealt a blow to the left–liberal upsurge.

The eviction on August 3–4, 1977, was a major setback to anti-corporate neighborhood activists who saw housing and neighborhood preservation, particularly of minority communities, as key issues in preserving the working-class, progressive character of the city. On November 18, 1978, the People's Temple mass suicide at Jonestown, Guyana, decimated an entire cohort of African American community activists, and the tragedy traumatized many progressives who had been allied with the People's Temple leader, Reverend Jim Jones. Then, only nine days later, on November 27, 1978, Mayor George Moscone and Supervisor Harvey Milk were assassinated, eliminating two of the main personalities of the new political alliance. Moscone and Jones, who had been appointed as a housing commissioner, were both major players in the International Hotel battle.

Despite the 1977 eviction, the International Hotel movement was never entirely defeated, and it grew to legendary importance to the communities involved. For more than two decades after the demolition of the hotel in 1979, the site remained an empty hole along Kearny Street. It gaped like an open wound for Filipino Americans, a reminder of both discrimination and defiance that marked our history in the United States. But the fact that the hole was not filled with a parking lot or office building also became a positive symbol. No commercial project could be built on the site without a significant housing component because of pressure from the Filipino and Chinese communities and other city activists.[5]

Even as it stood empty, the International Hotel site remained a "hot potato" in city politics. With the destruction of Manilatown, Chinatown community groups adopted the site as their own. There had been many attempts in San Francisco's history to remove the Chinese from the valuable real estate of Chinatown's central location, and keeping the site from being absorbed into the financial district as an office building was critical for preserving the entire community.[6] Several agencies and groups combined their efforts, and after several failed attempts, they succeeded in a plan to build on the entire block that the old I-Hotel shared.

Completed in 2005, a new International Hotel now stands on the corner of Jackson Street with the same address as the old hotel: 848 Kearny Street. After decades, the anti-eviction movement can celebrate a victory. Although the old building and its tenants are gone, the new, rebuilt International Hotel is devoted to low-income housing for the elderly and disabled.

The International Hotel Manilatown Center is located on the ground floor of the rebuilt hotel. The Manilatown Heritage Foundation (MHF) was founded in 1994 to assist in the development of the center to preserve the history of San Francisco's Filipino community and to pay homage to the tenants who fought the battle to save the International Hotel through educational programs, exhibits, and cultural performances. The International Hotel Manilatown Center now plays a role in celebrating Filipinos as an ethnic minority in the United States. The memory of the tenants is preserved; their photographs are displayed throughout the new building; and new generations have a space to learn about and participate in their history, along with the history of the first Filipino community. The new International Hotel is a reminder of what should never have happened—a victory of profits over human rights—and of what did occur: a celebration of community power. Its presence contributes to a memory of resistance and a narrative of identity for Filipino Americans today.

The International Hotel anti-eviction movement is a significant—and living—memory in San Francisco's history, as well. Tens of thousands of people came to the support of the tenants during the anti-eviction battle, working on media and legal committees, helping to provide nighttime security to prevent arson and other mischief, forming medical teams to aid the tenants and injured supporters, organizing countless demonstrations, and joining the human barricade around the building. Most progressive people who lived in San Francisco during the anti-eviction movement participated in one way or another, and many have vivid, poignant memories of their involvement. The International Hotel was a formative experience for many, just as the 1934 San Francisco General Strike was for an earlier generation, and the anti-eviction movement's memory still evokes passion among its veterans.

When I began this project, I cried for a week, unable to write anything intelligible because it was such an emotional experience to remember the deep bonds with the tenants and the great pain of the eviction. At many points, I had to put the project down. Many of the elderly died during the struggle or soon after, and I had to cope with feelings of guilt and remorse. Trauma has a way of making you forget, because forgetting is one way to cope with hurtful events. But once the process of forgetting has created enough distance, it can also create the conditions for the past to be seen with new eyes. At such a point, remembering becomes even more necessary, particularly when so little has been done to bring the story into the public arena. Rather than a history of irretrievable loss, this is now a history of redemption, a healing of an old wound, and the passing on of a legacy. Telling the International Hotel story plays a significant role in transforming a sense of defeat and humiliation into an experience of collective strength.

The new International Hotel represents many things to Chinatown, the housing movement, and San Francisco. But the Manilatown Center also makes it a way for new generations of Filipinos to remember the manongs, the vanished neighborhood in which these pioneers once lived, and the unity of Asian American communities. As the longtime International Hotel activist Al Robles writes in a poem, the new International Hotel is "like coming home to Manilatown after a fresh crop of rice."[7]

IN CHAPTER 1, "Manilatown, Manongs, and the Student Radicals," I relate the history of Manilatown and early Filipino immigration to the United States. I describe the life of the manongs as they faced hard labor and migrant conditions, how anti-miscegenation laws and harsh labor policies restricted their community mostly to men, and how they developed political skills as labor-union activists. Chapter 1 tells how Kearny Street became a refuge from racial violence where the manongs could survive among friends in a hostile world.

As the tenants began their first protest against eviction in 1968, Filipino and Asian American students were protesting the Vietnam War and were swept up in rebellions at San Francisco State College and at UC Berkeley, to demand that more minority students have access to higher education; that Third World studies be created to educate minorities about their histories and conditions; and that education relate to the needs to communities. Chapter 1 describes how Filipino and Asian American students reached out to the International Hotel to "serve the people" and "find our roots," and how contact with the elders inspired the students and made them aware of the manongs' unknown history of discrimination and resistance. The student radicals were a generation of Americanized Filipinos who had been cut off from their Filipino heritage, and they rediscovered their past and the situation back in the Philippines. As part of this awakening, the students revered the manongs as an oppressed people, and a bond across generations developed as they began to recognize the effects of racism. The tenants' resistance to eviction and the upsurge of student radicalism converged to become a powerful force.

In Chapter 2, "A Home or a Parking Lot? Human Rights versus Property Rights, 1968–69," I recount the initial organizing of the tenants, particularly the formation of the United Filipino Association (UFA) to represent them. Mayor Joseph Alioto presented various plans to relocate the tenants, which they rejected. A suspicious fire killed three tenants in 1969, which galvanized the tenants and their student supporters. A lease was finally negotiated with the landlord, Milton Meyer and Company, preventing eviction at least until 1974.

The third chapter, "Peace with a Lease: Renewal and Revolution, 1969–74," describes the outpouring of student support to repair the hotel after the fire. When more students gravitated to the hotel, they developed community organizations and rented the storefronts in the I-Hotel. Chapter 3 also discusses the intergenerational bonds that blossomed, as well as the gender dynamics that developed between the old bachelors and the young women, creating a unique situation. One of the storefront groups was Kalayaan International; Chapter 3 relates how this group developed into the KDP, a transnational, revolutionary organization that addressed both the democratic rights of Filipinos in America and the fight against the Marcos dictatorship in the Philippines. The chapter examines the new wave of émigrés or nationals who joined Filipino Americans in constructing a new community identity. During this time, the Chinese storefront organizations were inspired by Maoist politics to become revolutionary communist organizations. As the lease drew to a close, the UFA disbanded, and the IHTA was formed.

In Chapter 4, "The Tiger Leaps: Fighting the Four Seas Investment Corporation, 1974–77," a new landlord enters the picture: Four Seas Investment Corporation, owned by Supasit Mahaguna, a shadowy businessman from Thailand. Four Seas did not renew the lease and once again attempted to evict the tenants. Chapter 4 describes how the tenants mobilized support and entered into a series of court battles to prevent eviction. Moscone had vowed to support the I-Hotel before his mayoralty campaign, and when he was elected, he offered a plan to save the hotel in which the city's Housing Authority would use its power of eminent domain to buy it and then sell it to the IHTA. Critics dubbed it the "buy-back plan." Divisions erupted among the tenants and supporters over the plan, which opponents criticized as a trick to force the tenants to abandon the hotel when they could not afford the 1.3 million dollars required. Support for the plan primarily came from the IHTA's chairman, Joe Diones, and the KDP.

In the fifth chapter, "'*Makibaka!* Dare to Struggle!' The IHTA and the KDP, 1977," I recount how the tenants led the mass movement and how their political consciousness grew to take up their cause as a struggle that benefited all people. I describe the increasing isolation of Diones and the Moscone plan and the untenable position of the KDP's I-Hotel team because of its tactical support for the plan and for the embattled and increasingly unstable Diones. After growing threats of violence from Diones, the KDP moved to oust him, and Emil de Guzman was elected as the organization's new chairman. Despite rumors that the young activists had staged a takeover, the IHTA maintained its organizational integrity. Chapter 5 describes how the three of us on the KDP I-Hotel team worked to develop strong, respectful bonds with the tenants, despite disagreements. I also discuss the problem of the "invisibility" of Filipinos other than the tenants. The chapter analyzes the "dual program" of the KDP and the pressure to go in conflicting directions, especially with the rise of new immigrants in different social sectors.

The sixth chapter, "People's Power versus Propertied Elites, 1977," paints a picture of how the broad support for the I-Hotel developed through the operation of three coalitions in conjunction (and sometimes in opposition) to each other. I analyze the fluctuations of the left–liberal alliance and how the KDP's efforts to build ties with public officials were often undermined by ultra-leftists who rejected any relationships with politicians. City politics heated up with Propositions A and B to repeal the newly approved reform of district elections for supervisors and to recall every one of the city's elected officials. As the courts ruled against the city's use of eminent domain in the Moscone plan, housing consultants working for the IHTA presented a new plan that addressed the court's complaints. By this time, however, it was too late. Moscone and other liberals had been alienated and decided to withdraw their support for the I-Hotel after the two propositions were soundly defeated on August 2. The coalition made preparations to resist eviction.

In Chapter 7, "The Fall of the I-Hotel: Eviction and Demolition, 1977–79," I recall the intense trauma of the eviction night of August 3–4, 1977; of how supporters on the "human barricade" nonviolently resisted baton-swinging police on horseback; and of how Sheriff Richard Hongisto swung a sledgehammer to open the doors so that deputies could bring each tenant out. I describe the immediate aftermath: finding emergency shelter and then, later, housing the tenants at the Stanford Hotel. Chapter 7 recounts how the IHTA fought on, campaigning for a ballot initiative, Proposition U, to support the tenants. Finally, after unsuccessfully opposing demolition, the IHTA dissolved. Mayor Dianne Feinstein appointed the International Hotel Citizens Advisory Committee, with former tenants and Chinatown activists, and began the decades-long battle to rebuild the I-Hotel.

Finally, in the conclusion, "The Rise of the I-Hotel, 1979–2005," I recount the protracted effort to rebuild the International Hotel and the legacy of the hotel for the Filipino American community. The chapter reprises the history of the Asian American left and the KDP and discusses how former activists have taken on leading roles in their communities. I describe the founding of the Manilatown Heritage Foundation and the opening of the International Hotel Manilatown Center as an expression of community power and an exhibition and performance space for recovering the history of the first Filipinos and to celebrate all the contributions of Filipino Americans.

CHAPTER ONE

Manilatown, Manongs, and the Student Radicals

While still across the ocean,
I heard of the USA.
So thrilled by wild imagination,
I left through Manila Bay.

—Philip Vera Cruz,
"Profits Enslave the World"

Refuge on Kearny Street

Manilatown cannot be found on any maps of San Francisco, although it was a very real place. The neighborhood was built from the human results of the annexation of the Philippines, the establishment of colonial relations, the drive for cheap labor in the United States, and racial segregation. When the struggle to save the International Hotel began in 1968, few knew about its elderly tenants or the Kearny Street community of Filipinos. Manilatown was invisible to most San Franciscans, except to those who made their homes there. Only when the tenants forced the public to pay attention to the last remaining block did the outlines of what had already been lost become clear.

San Francisco's International Hotel has had several incarnations. The original International Hotel was built in 1854 on Jackson Street; it moved to 848 Kearny Street, bounded by Jackson and Washington streets and Columbus Avenue, in 1873.[1] The sixty-one-year-old building that the tenants began defending in 1968 had been built in 1907, after the original hotel was demolished in the 1906 earthquake and fire.

In its very earliest days, the I-Hotel was a luxury accommodation in the city's center that catered to visiting dignitaries. It took on its Asian character when it began to house Japanese naval officers at the turn of the century.[2] With the triumph of the United States in the Philippine–American War (officially 1899–1902, although resistance lasted far longer), Filipinos began coming to America as subjects of their new colonial ruler. As "American nationals," or wards, of the United States who were neither aliens nor citizens, they could immigrate freely. Filipinos came to a segregated society, however, and by the time they began to occupy rooms at the I-Hotel in the 1920s, the neighborhood and the fortunes of the hotel had changed.

In 1968, the International Hotel was a workers' hotel with 184 rooms.[3] The three-story structure had residential units on the two upper floors and commercial and community space on the ground level and in the basement. Twelve stores, including billiard halls, filled the ground floor, and a well-known nightclub, the "hungry i," was housed in the basement in the mid- to late 1960s. The street-level shops and commercial establishments served as gathering and eating places for tenants of the I-Hotel and similar hotels in the area.

The I-Hotel had more spacious rooms, as well as more generous light wells on each side of the hallways, than the average rooming houses built for Chinatown's largely male population.[4] Chinatown's residential hotels ranged in size from very small (6–8 rooms) to very large (150–200 rooms); residents of an entire floor (usually 10–12 rooms) shared a bathroom and kitchen.[5] At the I-Hotel, a large communal kitchen accommodated most of the tenants' needs, and each floor had two hallway bathrooms. Some tenants kept electric burners to heat water and cook in their rooms, but most preferred to eat at the inexpensive restaurants downstairs or in Chinatown, just across the street.

From the 1920s to the mid-1960s, the neighborhood of the I-Hotel housed the first Filipino community in San Francisco. In 1968, the neighborhood came to be known as "Manilatown," but during its heyday, Filipinos referred to it as "Filipino town" or simply as "Kearny Street." Most white San Franciscans thought the area was part of Chinatown.[6] Since Filipinos were racially categorized as Asians, white Americans assumed that Filipinos would be housed adjacent to the Chinese.[7] The neighborhood was formed around a spine of Chinatown, Kearny Street, and the numerous residential hotels on that street or adjacent to it. Before World War II, Filipinos could rent rooms in the hotels as long as they stayed within an area bounded by Columbus Avenue to the north and California Street to the south. After World War II, the most rigid segregation began to loosen, and the line extended even farther south, toward Market Street. Until then, Columbus Avenue had been the major dividing line: Beyond that boundary, no Filipino could rent a room. Even as discrimination eased, though, only certain hotels regularly accepted Filipinos, such as the Antwerp, Bell, Palm, San Joaquin, Stanford, and Yulanda. Thirty-seven hotels housed up to 30,000 Filipino workers in Manilatown's heyday in the 1920s and '30s.[8]

In his 1946 classic *America Is in the Heart,* Carlos Bulosan describes his and other Filipinos' experiences of bitter violence and harsh discrimination in the 1920s and '30s. Bulosan, like many of his generation, would roam the streets, as a friend later revealed: "He would walk about Kearny Street in San Francisco near the Filipino pool halls and restaurants in 'Manilatown' and physically immerse his dream of America in that incongruous part of humanity, as if in so doing he hoped to find the truth about his own salvation, the salvation of his own people, the salvation of America."[9] Bulosan's dream of America—the dream of democratic rights and dignity, of fair play and opportunity—could be nourished in Manilatown because the neighborhood evolved as a respite filled with comforting cultural meanings. It held out hope for three-way salvation: for the individual, for the people, and for the promises of American democracy. As in other American ghettos where minorities—"that incongruous part of humanity"—were forced to congregate, the manongs carved out a place of their own.

From the 1940s to the early 1960s, the Kearny Street neighborhood was a bustling community with businesses that served the needs of Filipino working men. The hotels housed skilled and unskilled Filipino workers, from farm workers to domestic servants and culinary workers, from merchant seaman and sailors to war-industry workers and military personnel, and from migrants to retired workers. Several Filipino barbershops on Kearny Street, and numerous cafes and restaurants, dotted the area alongside bail-bond offices and the Hall of Justice. As early as 1918, the Santa Maria Restaurant, owned by brothers from the Visayan region of the Philippines, stood on Jackson near Kearny Street. Many stores and restaurants opened during the late 1940s and '50s. New businesses such as Bataan Drug Store, Bataan Restaurant, and Bataan Pool, named for the World War II battle in which U.S. and Filipino soldiers fought to save the Philippines from Japanese control, seemed to reflect pride and optimism. Facing the I-Hotel were businesses such as the Santa Maria pool hall, a bar called the Alcatraz, the Mango Cigar Smoke Shop, and various cafes and restaurants: Bagong Sikat, Blanco's, the Manila Cafe, PI Clipper, and the Sampaguita. Around the corner, on Pacific Avenue, was a nightclub, the Corregidor.[10] In 1982, Jess Esteva, publisher of the Filipino community newspaper *Mabuhay Republic,* remembered, "When I came here in '45, there were 27 Filipino restaurants all the way up Kearny Street to Columbus. Now there are one or two, that's all. And all the hotels in the area were full of Filipinos. No more."[11]

Despite the proliferation of businesses in Manilatown, few Filipinos were able to become businessmen or professionals. Even in 1960, the majority of Filipinos still occupied lower-income and lower-status sectors of the working class. Only 4 percent held professional status.[12] Filipinos who ran businesses usually leased the properties from white owners.

Some Filipino businesses operated alongside Chinese businesses and catered to the needs of Filipino patrons.[13] By the time Filipino immigrants began arriving in the United States, the Chinese and Japanese already had ethnic businesses that could easily adjust to accommodate a Filipino clientele. Chinese and Japanese grocers, for instance, merely added Filipino foods to their retail list. Since much of Filipino immigration coincided with the Great Depression, newcomers could not gain the economic means to establish businesses. Racial discrimination restricted the retail market even further. Filipino businessmen and merchants barely gained a foothold; those who did clustered on Kearny Street, and they constituted the heart of the Filipino community.[14]

Filipinos developed complex relations with their Chinese neighbors. San Francisco's Chinese quarter was no different from other segregated communities, which meant, among other things, that it was afflicted with social problems such as gambling, prostitution, saloons, opium dens, and crowded living conditions. Although whites owned many of the illegal businesses, they regarded the Chinese as particularly prone to vices such as drug dealing and gambling and as preferring overcrowded housing and unsanitary living conditions. White people frequented the area because their shady activities drew no notice. Filipino businesses adjacent to Chinese businesses often provided cover—for instance, bookies planted themselves in the back rooms of Filipino businesses, where they could operate unmolested. Local city officials, looking the other way, participated in these dealings. In the back of his cafe, one man recalled, his father had told him about numerous "friendly" visits by the local sheriff.[15] In the shadow of the Hall of Justice, just a block away from the International Hotel, these illegal activities were tolerated, if not promoted.

For thousands of Filipino workers, the Kearny Street neighborhood was a way station, a home base for a mobile workforce, a largely male population, most of them from the barrios and farms of the Ilocos and Visayan regions of the Philippines.[16] The men worked in seasonal jobs on the farms of California's Central Valley, Washington State, and Oregon and in Alaskan salmon canneries. During the off-season, usually the winter months, they migrated to the cities to find jobs as culinary helpers, domestic servants, and hotel workers. In California, Filipinos followed the agricultural work cycle: In March, they began general farm work; fruit and vegetable harvesting followed from May to September; and by October, they began drifting into cities, reaching the highest population in January.[17]

Urban life was attractive and varied as an interlude from the drudgery of farm work and the harsh conditions of the fish factories.[18] The seasonal workers congregated in the Filipino centers in major cities, such as Kearny Street in San Francisco, the International District in Honolulu, Chinatown (now known as the International District) in Seattle, and Bunker Hill in Los Angeles. Filipinos flocked to the cities to experience the varieties of urban life; many also tried to continue their education. They gathered in Kearny Street to find relatives and town mates, to seek companionship, and to enjoy aspects of Filipino cultural life.

In his 1948 book *I Have Lived with the American People,* Manuel Buaken describes the Filipino restaurants and other businesses as a refuge—a "wholesome atmosphere"—from the ugly realities of racial beatings, low wages, and exploitation. A Filipino restaurant, he wrote,

> is not only a place to dine, but a place to meet friends, and a place to loiter and relax a while after days or weeks of strenuous and often unpleasant menial, domestic labor. Here is a place where the pressure of racial differences is relaxed. Here is a place where one hears and speaks one's own dialect without hostile or curious glances. Here is a place to meet those who, like yourself, are struggling to go to school and

> to learn, but must work so hard that no leisure is left to learn the important things that America has to teach. Here is a place to feed your body and to relax your mind and feel at home.[19]

Many Filipinos preferred to live and work in the cities because the conditions on the farms were horrible. Housing in the rural camps was in the style of military barracks, with rows of single beds or cots, whereas hotels in the cities offered single-occupancy rooms—a luxury by comparison.[20] The population of Filipinos in the San Francisco Bay Area varied widely according to the season, with estimates ranging from 2,500 in the summer to 30,000 in the winter in the 1920s and '30s.[21]

Buaken documented the rural and urban cycles, describing the dynamic of failing to find a city job, then leaving the city to work in rural areas. Unable to find employment in Los Angeles, he traveled to Stockton's "Little Manila," the principal Filipino center in the West, which he found filled with other Filipinos searching for work, many of whom were being bilked out of what little money they had by crooked gamblers.[22] In the cities, Filipinos were restricted to domestic-service work as janitors, valets, kitchen helpers, pantry men, dishwashers, and busboys. In 1930, about 25 percent of the Filipinos (11,441 men and 336 women out of 45,200) on the U.S. mainland were service workers. Of this total, 7,154 men and 232 women were located in California.[23]

The poet and activist Al Robles interviewed many manongs—those itinerant workers grown old. Their testimony, such as Robles's account of Mariano Amoite, reveals a common story:

> Filipinos lived at the various hotels scattered around Kearny Street—from the Shasta, to the St. Paul, to the Clayton, to the Justice, to the Ampara Hotel. They kept their rooms, as small as they were, they stayed. Some of them, like Mariano Amoite, lived in the hotel for about 50 years. He worked in the farm areas but kept up his room in the city. . . . He's 80 years old, and was one of the first to come to the I-Hotel to live. Then he went off to Walnut Grove to pick walnuts and then to Concord to pick pears and then off to Salinas. . . . Now he lives at the Justice Hotel in a small room. He spends some afternoons sitting in the sun around Portsmouth Square. Many manongs can be seen playing checkers in the park. Manong Amoite worked all his life on the farms. His social security pension is $60.00 a month.[24]

Having worked in the fields for a lifetime, surviving one form of victimization after another, Manong Mariano wanted the comfort of a single room and to play checkers in the park.

Manilatown and the needs of Mariano Mariano and others like him were generally invisible to the broader population. Because Filipinos were tucked within Chinatown, few outsiders distinguished them from the Chinese. Despite their large number, Filipinos lacked a political voice; their occupations as migrant farm workers, seamen, sailors, and domestic servants left them rootless and with even less power than the Chinese.

Early Filipino Immigration

The colonial relationship between the United States and the Philippines dates to 1898, when Spain ceded the islands to the United States after its defeat in the Spanish–American War. However, Filipinos had declared independence from Spain on June 12, 1898; when they discovered that their independence had been usurped, they fought the Americans just as fiercely as they had fought the Spanish. The Philippine–American War took the lives of between 250,000 and 1 million Filipinos. The independence movement was defeated in 1902, but significant resistance lasted at least until 1913.[25]

Filipinos began to arrive in the United States only a few years after the United States seized control of the Philippines. By 1903, a few hundred Filipinos had begun to study at U.S. universities and colleges.[26] The Philippine territorial government had chosen the students, called *pensionados,* to become future leaders and bureaucrats for the colonial administration, and their studies were subsidized by the U.S. government. Welcomed by the white population on many American campuses and at conferences and religious functions, the *pensionados* were offered as evidence of America's "benevolent assimilation."[27] Sometimes called "fountain-pen boys" because they characteristically carried briefcases and fountain pens, most *pensionados* returned to the Philippines after finishing their studies to take up posts in the colonial government or education system. News of their successes fueled immigration by many self-supporting students and a large number of mess boys who, after a period of enlistment in the U.S. Navy, would take their discharges in American ports.

Filipinos began to arrive in Hawaii in 1906, recruited by the Hawaiian Sugar Planters' Association as plantation workers (*sakadas*). By 1935, there were 120,000 Filipinos in the territory.[28] By contrast, the census reported only 5,603 Filipinos in the mainland United States in 1920.[29] However, by 1923 Filipinos had begun to travel in larger numbers to the mainland to fill the demand for cheap labor, primarily in the agricultural valleys of Salinas, San Joaquin, and Sacramento, California. The Chinese Exclusion Act of 1882 had ended most Chinese immigration long before, and the Japanese, already restricted by the Gentlemen's Agreement of 1907, were effectively excluded by the Immigration Act of 1924. As a result, Filipinos were recruited as the third wave of Asian labor.

Filipino men made up an extremely exploitable workforce, laboring primarily as migrants without families. Filipinos were used as "stoop labor," or unskilled field hands, on large farms, particularly for lettuce, asparagus, sugar beets, and carrots. Asparagus-farm work, which was designed for gangs of single men without family attachments, was particularly onerous. More than 6,000 Filipino laborers were used in asparagus farming in the 1930s.[30] Their wages were lower than those of white workers in the fields, because wage levels were based on racial considerations.[31]

Filipinos arrived in the United States as steerage passengers from Manila or from Honolulu. The majority of the influx (about 56 percent) into California in 1923–29 came from Hawaii to seek better economic opportunities.[32] In 1924, Filipinos led a sensational but unsuccessful strike for higher wages on the plantations of Hawaii that caused many of them to be blacklisted and forced them to come to mainland cities.[33] San Francisco and Los Angeles were the main arrival points for Filipino immigrants on the West Coast. By 1930, 45,208 Filipinos lived on the U.S. mainland, 30,000 of them in California.[34]

Because Filipinos, as nationals or wards of the United States, were not subjected to the existing immigration laws that targeted aliens, they were able to come into the country in large numbers. However, despite their official "in-between" status—neither American citizen nor legally alien—Filipinos were effectively treated as aliens. They were ineligible for citizenship; they could not vote or hold public office; and they were subjected to the discriminatory legislation that affected other "aliens." For example, 4,000 Filipinos worked in the Merchant Marine, but most of them were discharged in 1937 when Congress passed an act requiring that 90 percent of the crews be American citizens.[35]

White society treated Filipinos as aliens incapable of assimilating to American cultural and political mores. At the same time, however, Filipinos were educated to think otherwise: Under the American system of public education instituted by colonial rulers in the Philippines, Filipinos were taught that they, too, had a stake in the values and ideals of a democratic society.[36] Returned *pensionados* reported economic opportunities in the United States, but they also promoted the notion that Americans cherished freedom and democracy that Filipinos, as nationals, could also claim as their own. These expectations led people to emigrate, and it was the tension between expectations and harsh reality that caused many to become active as labor organizers when they arrived.

Between 1934 and 1946, the number of Filipinos in the United States decreased overall, due largely to the Tydings-McDuffie Act of 1934, which called for Philippine independence in ten years' time and reduced the quota of Filipino immigrants to fifty per year. Most support for independence among non-Filipinos flowed from racist motivations to exclude Filipinos from participating in any aspect of American life rather than from principled support for national self-determination. Leaders of the anti-Filipino movement did not stop with excluding new immigrants: They called for the deportation of Filipinos already living in the United States. Under the Filipino Repatriation Act of 1935, the U.S. government paid for the transportation of Filipinos back to the Philippines while forbidding their reentry into the United States. This opportunistic law did not apply to Filipinos in Hawaii, however, because the demand for Filipino labor there was too high. Only 2,190 people returned to the Philippines under the program.[37]

Many Filipinos in the first generation of immigrants, particularly those who had come directly from the Philippines rather than from Hawaii, hoped to continue their education in the United States and return to the Philippines with professional degrees. Many were self-supporting students who ended up working at low-wage jobs all their lives, unable to fulfill their dreams of completing their education.[38] These immigrants were enticed by American colonial schoolteachers and missionaries and by the early glowing reports from *pensionados,* as well as by the sales pitches of passenger agents from steamship companies. But economic exploitation, poverty during the Great Depression, and World War II dashed their hopes.

Philip Vera Cruz, who became a second vice-president of the United Farm Workers (UFW), recalled his experiences in 1926 when his family sold a parcel of land and borrowed from relatives to send him to the United States:

> I came to the United States because my main objective was to continue my studies. The reason why I was motivated to go to school was because we use to have American teachers and they told us that there were many poor students in the United States who were working their way through. So I was willing to work for my education. I thought I could come and do the same thing.[39]

In his poem "Profits Enslave the World," Vera Cruz describes the great anticipation and bitter disappointment of those who came:

> *But beautiful bright pictures*
> *Were half of the whole story. . . .*
> *Reflections of great wealth and power*
> *In a land of slavery.*[40]

Regardless of their ambitions and efforts, Filipinos faced the migratory work pattern of the agricultural laborer and eventually succumbed to its grueling cycle. "I was a hungry stray dog," Vera Cruz writes in the poem, "too busy to keep myself alive."

Filipino pioneers like Vera Cruz participated in the labor movement, directing their main efforts at winning higher wages and decent working conditions among agricultural, cannery, and service workers. The traditional hierarchical and deferential relations between members of the Filipino middle and working classes were absent in this first group of immigrants. Among the manongs, deference to leaders was based on the actual practice of winning battles and concessions from farmers and employers.

Racism in the labor movement prevented Filipinos from joining most unions. "Blood unionism"—that is, organizing only along racial and ethnic lines—became an alternative. Although blood unionism usually met with defeat, it was often the only choice for minorities. One positive aspect of blood unionism was that it helped to identify leaders within the Filipino community. But successes in the days of blood unionism were few.[41] Some unions did accept Filipinos, such as the Brotherhood of Sleeping Car Porters led by A. Phillip Randolph, and, most notably, some left-leaning Congress of Industrial Organizations (CIO) unions. Filipinos were also welcomed into the Communist Party.[42]

Racial Violence and Gender Imbalance

As the number of Filipinos grew, white violence increased, especially after Filipinos began to organize and stopped being regarded as compliant, and therefore "desirable," workers. Between 1928 and 1930, racial violence against Filipinos rose to a peak, with riots occurring in small California agricultural towns such as Exeter, Watsonville, and Stockton; in Yakima, Washington; and in Hood River and Banks, Oregon. Economic competition, especially during the Depression, and racism intersected with white men's sexual anxieties to fuel intense violence against "oversexed" Filipino men.[43]

Agricultural business saw greater profits from Filipino migrants if they excluded "nonproductive" family members, saving the expense of housing, feeding, clothing, and educating them. Such hiring policies created a predominately male-only society. Filipino cultural traditions required women to be accompanied by male chaperones—usually husbands, fathers, or brothers—when traveling. However, patriarchal values, hostile living conditions, and a "sojourner" mentality of migrants who plan to return home were only partial reasons for the imbalance. Labor-recruitment practices and legal restrictions were the most important factors.[44]

Severe gender imbalances in the Filipino population affected the community for generations. Some 84.3 percent of the immigrants were men under thirty who came to the United States without parents, wives, or children. In California, the ratio of male to female Filipinos in the 1930s averaged 14:1. Only 18 percent of the Filipino men on the U.S. mainland were married, most of them with wives in the Philippines.[45] The few who did have families with them had brought them from Hawaii.

U.S. law categorized Filipinos, along with the Chinese and Japanese, as the "Mongoloid" race, despite their protests and feelings of difference. "Mongoloids" could not marry whites or become citizens. In 1933, a Filipino challenged California's anti-miscegenation law, claiming that Filipinos were not Mongolians. He won the case, but the state legislature quickly amended the law to include the so-called Malay race in the restricted category.[46]

The cycle of social instability seemed perpetual. Migratory life was not suitable for families, and the various Filipino enclaves in which one could settle down were rife with gambling and prostitution. Married men did not want to bring their wives from the Philippines to that environment. The more fortunate who found partners willing to raise families under such conditions married women out of the group, including fellow farm laborers of Mexican, Japanese, or Native American heritage; Native American women in Alaska; or white women who worked in domestic service or as taxi dancers. (White women who entered such marriages in states that did not have anti-miscegenation laws were usually ostracized from the white community.) These families had difficulty maintaining strong roots in Filipino cultural practices and values.

Lack of women meant that the men would not settle with families to create permanent communities. Thus, the majority of the first generation of Filipinos remained in male-only communities through most of their lives. Severe immigration restrictions and exclusionary laws also created a "bachelor society" in the Chinese community, and a common bond developed with aging Filipinos that became evident in the anti-eviction struggle. Only after the relaxation of immigration restrictions in 1965 did the ratio change. By 1980, Filipinas constituted more than half of the Filipino population.[47]

Racial segregation was enforced by extralegal methods such as individual and mob violence, as well. Chinese and Filipinos could not venture even a few blocks from their enclaves for fear of verbal abuse and beatings. When Filipinos attempted to find housing outside the Chinatown area, they were often told that apartments had already been rented, or they were simply and flatly turned down. Filipinos were restricted from the "more respectable" quarters of the surrounding white communities. Signs saying "No Filipinos or Dogs Allowed" were common.[48]

Sexual fears often intertwined with white racial aggression, creating explosive situations. Fred Basconcillo, a Filipino born in San Francisco, recalls an episode of racial violence instigated by sexual relations that left an indelible mark:

> During the war in 1942 or 1943 my sister and I went to the movies at the Warfield Theater on Market Street. As we were walking down towards the Ferry Building to take the Geary Street car, right there a few feet down from Geary and Market, there was a big commotion there. The crowd had a woman down against the curb—it was a white woman and they were stomping on her head. A rope went over the handle of the big statue called the "Mechanic's Statue"—it looks like a guy on a winepress. They lynched a Filipino there. I looked up and saw it was one of my father's friends. I remembered seeing him down near Kearny Street. The reason why they lynched him was that they caught him with a white woman.[49]

The violence of this incident is underscored by the fact that it took place during a period of increased friendship between Filipinos and Americans because of their alliance against the Japanese during World War II. The Kearny Street area was a safe haven for Filipinos, but only a few blocks away, if a Filipino was seen in the company of a white woman, he could be lynched. Manilatown became a home partly as an act of survival and partly as an act of defiance.

When Filipino families began to arrive in the United States after World War II, permanent neighborhoods in urban areas increased. By the 1960s, almost three-fourths of the Filipino population lived in the cities.[50] During World War II and afterward, Filipinos followed the migration patterns of other minorities who were drawn to the cities for greater economic opportunities. As with other minorities and women, some Filipinos got skilled and semiskilled jobs in war industries in the Bay Area.[51] At the same time, many of the early Filipino immigrants joined the armed forces during the war, determined to show Americans that "they were men, not house boys," as the historian Ronald Takaki writes.[52] When they returned from fighting in the Philippines, these veterans felt a sense of entitlement from the U.S. government. They were allowed to become U.S. citizens beginning in 1943. Many of them reunited with the wives they had left behind or married "war brides" they had met during their service, and they were permitted to bring their families with them from the Philippines to become naturalized citizens.[53]

After the war, modifications in immigration policy contributed to changes in the community. The 1934 Tydings-McDuffie Act, designed to exclude Filipinos, had changed their status from nationals or wards of the United States to "aliens ineligible for citizenship" while promising independence to the Philippines. When independence came in 1946, the quota for non-exempt Filipino immigration was raised from fifty to one hundred per year.[54] But veterans, who were exempt from the quota, were allowed to bring their families with them to the United States. In 1948, the U.S. Congress established the Exchange Visitors Program as a Cold War propaganda measure intended to educate professionals from other countries about American democracy and then to return them to their homelands. Under the program, which lasted into the 1960s, thousands of Filipina nurses came to the United States, and many of them attempted to stay.[55] In 1952, the McCarran-Walter Act eliminated the racial bar to citizenship and established occupational preferences for immigration, although it maintained quotas and instituted exclusion on the basis of "subversive" politics.[56]

Filipino families who arrived in San Francisco after World War II generally did not move to Manilatown. As better housing became available due to some easing of segregation, many of the new immigrants located in areas where other minorities already lived. Many moved to the city's Fillmore District, a primarily African American neighborhood, and particularly to the enclave within the district known as Japantown, which had been vacated as a result of Japanese internment during World War II. Still, before 1965 Filipino immigrants trickled in slowly and were mainly servicemen and sailors recruited into the U.S. military and their wives and children. Single and married servicemen and merchant sailors who had left their families in the Philippines often chose to live at the I-Hotel between assignments and to send money home to their families. Thus, the hotel remained an economic necessity. Many in the first generation of Filipinos stayed in labor camps in rural areas, while others retired in urban areas such as Kearny Street. Their fixed incomes and small pensions left them living in poverty.[57]

The Immigration Act of 1965 liberalized immigration restrictions and resulted in a growing stream of new Filipino immigrant families.[58] They rented small apartments in San Francisco's mainly white working-class South of Market area and largely Latino Mission District rather than in Chinatown or Manilatown. Meanwhile, the mostly male-only community of Filipino pioneers continued to live at the I-Hotel because of its cheap rent and the culture of the surrounding Filipino businesses. Manilatown increasingly became an enclave of elderly bachelors living out the remainder of their lives in familiar surroundings and among old friends. Many of the new immigrants were not even aware of their existence.

Life in the International Hotel

By 1968, Manilatown had been reduced, but it had not disappeared. For the manongs, the I-Hotel and its immediate environs constituted a vibrant community that supported them spiritually as well as materially. In many ways, the physical shelter, or "bricks and mortar," of the hotel was secondary to the total living environment. As a 1973 report by the U.S. Senate's Special Committee on Aging stated, "The number of supportive services available is as vital as the convenience of location. The atmosphere of activity and interchanges is more important than square footage or closet space."[59] The hotels, eating establishments, pool halls, barbershops, and stores in Manilatown provided community and familiarity in a hostile world.

For the elderly, keeping their homes and community made sense because there was no other available low-income housing for them in the city. These were close-knit communities that supported each other during hard times. Moreover, many of the manongs were fiercely independent and disdained the notion of accepting welfare or other people's care in nursing homes. Social-welfare workers found that they could not help the Filipino men in Manilatown when services became available to poor communities under President Lyndon Johnson's War on Poverty program in Chinatown: Pride prevented the aging bachelors from seeking help, and, as one reporter was told, it was "downright crazy" to believe that the government wanted to help them live better lives.[60] Many aging Filipino men did not return to the Philippines for fear that they would be deemed failures if they went back without large sums of money, or they were simply unable to pay the expense of traveling. Many of the single immigrant Chinese men in the hotel, including those who were married and had wives in China, were similarly unwilling or unable to return.[61]

The International Hotel's tenant population reflected the combination of U.S immigration laws that had limited the entry of women and children and hiring practices that encouraged single men to work as farm laborers and in other menial jobs. In 1968, the hotel housed retired farm workers, cannery workers who still traveled to Alaska and returned when the season was over, domestic and service workers who could not afford to live anywhere else, and seamen. The hotel provided not only housing but also an economic center. For example, many seamen who used the hotel as a permanent home paid rent while they were out to sea, storing their possessions securely at the hotel and using the hotel managers as bankers to keep their money safe.

The I-Hotel also served as a social network and cultural center. If you needed to find someone, you could ask at the barbershop or the billiard hall and, often, be told where the person you were looking for worked. During the anti-eviction movement, Ness Aquino, the UFA's first president, described the I-Hotel as "much more than a hotel. . . . [I]t is a center, the only one in the area, which provides a recreation room for the senior citizens and a place for them to come in off the street."[62] For these reasons, living in the rundown residential hotels was not only an economic necessity; it was also a choice.

Al Robles, the poet and a long-time friend and chronicler of the old-timers, told me many stories about the manongs and the bustle of shops and stores around Kearny Street in the 1950s and '60s: "Next door was Tino's Barber Shop and next door to that was Bataan Drug Store, the Bataan Pool Hall, the Bataan Restaurant. Mr. Muyco and his wife, Margaret, took over Lucky's Pool Hall. That pool hall has a history all the way up to now. The Filipino boys all know each other. We are drawn together. We all come from the same place. We feel at home here."[63]

Many of I-Hotel's elderly Filipino tenants had been political and social leaders in their youth; others grew into leadership roles as the efforts to stop the eviction called for people to step forward. Although they spoke with thick accents, they were appreciated for their keen political sensibilities and public-speaking abilities by the many students and supporters who came into contact with them. Outsiders sometimes misinterpreted the situation, believing that the elderly men were being misled by young students into taking radical political positions.[64] In reality, during the struggle to save the I-Hotel, the tenants constantly astonished their supporters. This group of elderly men had worked all their lives; they had experienced social and emotional anguish due to the sexual imbalance in the population; and they were ostracized by white society. In addition, their own people sometimes despised them or regarded them with shame because of their dire poverty, lack of formal education, and embarrassingly Filipino ways (thick accents, ethnic foods, traditional music, and so forth).

Yet the tenants in the I-Hotel struggle constantly astonished the youth and the various supporters who came to know them. They were totally capable of exercising leadership; they were experienced and fearless.[65]

Some of the manongs learned their leadership skills through labor-union participation. Pablo Valdez, a San Francisco trade unionist, came to the United States in 1928 as a student, but after years of unemployment and low-wage jobs, he became active in the CIO and joined several unions—"learning the ins and outs and the functions of the trade union movement," he said. "In 1937, I joined the Culinary Union, which includes cooks, bartenders, dishwashers, busboys, waiters and waitresses. I stayed in that union for almost 33 years until I retired."[66] The unions, along with the military, educated the manongs in political action, service, and leadership.

Antonio Gramsci's definition of "organic intellectuals" describes how certain ordinary workers can become "the thinking and organizing element of a particular social class [who] function in directing the ideas and aspirations of the class to which they organically belong."[67] The tenant leaders of the I-Hotel anti-eviction movement functioned in this manner to mobilize their cohorts for rallies, meetings, and social gatherings. All of the elderly tenants were working-class people, and many of the Filipino tenants had been involved in labor struggles during the Depression years. Valdez, for example, became a member of the KDP. He drew on his experience and training in the labor movement to give me guidance in speaking with the other manongs about political issues. Many of the elderly Filipino tenants had also fought in World War I and World War II. Their experience as veterans gave them a militant quality matched by their years as organizers and members of the labor movement during the Depression.[68]

Tenants who persisted until the eviction were tough, and they knew the broad contours of the struggle, particularly as they helped to formulate the demands: that human rights such as the needs of the elderly come before private-property rights; that affordable housing be available for the poor and for working people; that the financial interests that stood against community efforts to preserve the Manilatown and Chinatown area needed to be opposed by a group of tenants that could resist intimidation, joined by a mass movement of supporters. Tenant leaders such as Felix Ayson, Claudio Domingo, and Wahat Tompao initiated important discussions among other tenants and helped to organize and mobilize meetings, gatherings, and demonstrations. Their advanced age, frailty, heavy accents, lowly status, and brown skin fooled many into thinking they would be compliant toward those in power or would become tools of the students who sought to help them. But no one could pull the wool over their eyes. They were educated in the world and in struggle, whether as military veterans, as self-taught intellectuals, or as union organizers. They were perceptive, shrewd, and able to mesh with the youth who came to their aid. And they were willing to fight.[69]

"Find Our Roots": The Youth Rise Up

In 1968, the same year that the elderly tenants of the International Hotel began to resist eviction, Filipino American students in the Bay Area were swept up in rebellions at San Francisco State College and the University of California, Berkeley. As part of developing "Third World consciousness," Asian American students who protested the Vietnam War in the streets and marched in Third World strikes demanded that the universities be accountable to their communities. The political atmosphere on college campuses was "to get involved in the community," or to "Serve the People," a slogan taken from Chairman Mao Tse-tung's Cultural Revolution. It was fortuitous that the elderly tenants' resistance arose at exactly the same juncture as the student awakening. When they saw that the elderly tenants were protesting eviction, Filipino American students immediately gravitated to Manilatown.

Jovina Navarro explains the impulse of the students engaged in the strikes at UC Berkeley and San Francisco State this way:

> Third World students would no longer be lied to. No longer would they be passive participants of the miseducation process. The seven-month strike at San Francisco State, that led to the arrest of over 300 students (a total of 18 Pilipinos; 13 in just one day), is a concrete manifestation of Third World students' determination to have an education where they could learn the true history of their ancestors. For Pilipino Americans, the educational system was guilty of many injustices. Examples are the omission of the contribution of Pilipinos in the building of America as a nation; the perpetration of negative stereotypes, calling Pilipinos "gogos" and "monkeys," and describing them as "uncivilized" and "unassimilable"; the creation of myths and historical distortions like the Philippine–American "special relations," and much more.[70]

Students demanded that the universities recruit and admit Third World people, provide access to more support services, and increase hiring of Third World faculty and staff. Students regarded the link between academy and community as seamless, and classes were often conducted in the community. They demanded that education be "relevant" to the people's needs.

As part of this program, Asian American students from Berkeley conducted classes in a basement storefront of the International Hotel. Emil de Guzman, a key student organizer in support of the tenants, was introduced to the hotel through one of these classes. Organizers appealed to the students to help the tenants as a part of their education as activist intellectuals. "Involvement in this struggle is by no means a one-sided affair," students active in the I-Hotel movement explained in a 1970 broadside. "The student will benefit just as much, if not more. The mere participation in nitty [gritty] social action is more than any textbook could ever offer."[71]

The Third World Strike at San Francisco State was the first student strike in the San Francisco Bay Area, and the longest lasting. African American, Native American, Chicano, Latino, and Asian American students demanding self-determination were successful in establishing the first School of Ethnic Studies in the nation. Their demands that education be involved in peoples' needs had particular resonance because the students had organic links to their communities. San Francisco State was primarily a commuter college of working-class students, and the Filipino students who had been swept into the activism knew their communities well. With this grounding, the Filipino students took active roles on the front lines of the Third World Liberation Front, the coalition leading the strike at Berkeley.

In the spring of 1968, Filipino students formed the Philippine–American Collegiate Endeavor (PACE) at San Francisco State. They organized counseling and tutorial programs, high-school recruitment drives, newsletters, dances, ethnic studies curricula, and community outreach. PACE members expressed a Third World consciousness, a sense of self-determination and humanity, and opposition to racism. In its statement of goals and principles, PACE declared:

> We seek . . . simply to function as human beings, to control our lives. Initially following the myth of the American Dream, we worked to attend predominantly white colleges, but we have learned through direct analysis that is impossible for our people, so-called minorities, to function as human beings, in a racist society in which white always comes first. . . . So we have decided to fuse ourselves with masses of third world consciousness, which are the majority of the world's peoples, to create, through struggle, a new humanity, a new humanism, a New World Consciousness, and within that context collectively control our own destinies.[72]

As part of their community outreach and action programs, PACE members at San Francisco State were among the first in the community to respond to eviction notices posted at the International Hotel. One student described the tremendous outburst of support and how the energy swept him into the I-Hotel struggle: "We had 120 Pilipinos out there, senior citizens, residents of that building. We picketed down Montgomery. . . . These were elderly people, retired veterans. I got appointed to the board of that association. And it was then becoming an issue that totally involved me, and I was a student."[73]

Bruce Occena became radicalized through the Third World Strike at UC Berkeley. He also became involved in the I-Hotel struggle during its early days. Like the students at San Francisco State, Berkeley students proposed a Third World college that would focus on "contemporary problems of urban and rural living of Third World peoples. Therefore, its primary goals are to produce students having knowledge, expertise, understanding, commitment and desire to identify and present solutions to problems in their respective communities. Thus the mission of the Third World College is to focus on contemporary living and produce scholars to address the problems that accompany it."[74] Filipinos helped to found the Asian Student Union, which later became the Asian American Political Alliance (AAPA), in which Asian students formed study groups that focused on specific problems of Asians in America, protested the Vietnam War, and consciously built the Asian American movement.[75] Asian Americans felt a particular solidarity with the Vietnamese because of the racist manner in which the war was being conducted and their direct experience of anti-Asian discrimination. They attempted to raise the consciousness of the antiwar movement away from what they believed to be the narrow appeals of (white) self-interest to understanding the war as racial violence of an imperial power.

Filipino youth saw the potential of raising their fists in "Yellow Power" because they realized that unifying as Asians meant strength in greater numbers. They joined Asian contingents of larger protests against the Vietnam War, and they joined with others in Asian American alliances in common community projects. Soon, however, Filipino American students formed their own organizations and service centers. As Occena remembered, Filipino American students sought each other out, formed Filipino clubs, and began working on community projects such as the International Hotel movement. At UC Berkeley, a core of ten to fifteen Filipino students formed the Pilipino American Alliance (PAA).[76]

Who Were the Filipino American Students?

Bruce Occena's father was part of the early migration of Filipinos seeking education in America. He stayed and married a white woman. Many of his fellow Filipino students were children of farm-working families and came mainly from working-class valley towns in the San Fernando, Salinas, and Stockton areas. Others were children of U.S. veterans of World War II who had married war brides and brought their families to the United States. Frank Celada, another early student leader in the I-Hotel movement, came from this background. Most of these students, including Occena, participated in the Equal Opportunity Program or went to college through special admissions as disadvantaged students.[77] Once Filipino American students of the era realized that they were working class themselves, they felt validated and proud to uncover the histories of those "forgotten" men, the manongs.

When I became involved with the Filipino identity movement in 1968, I discovered that other students had fathers who were World War II veterans who had become citizens as a result of fighting in the war. The soldiers, who often married war brides much younger than themselves, and their families flourished in small Filipino communities in and around U.S. Navy and Army bases, such as Seaside, adjacent to the Fort Ord army base, and similar communities near bases in Alameda, Vallejo, and San Diego, California. As noted earlier, the families of these Filipino veterans were allowed to enter the United States on a nonquota basis.[78]

My father was a sergeant-major in the U.S. Army stationed at Fort MacArthur at San Pedro and then at Fort Ord on Monterey Bay. Fathers in the military were better off than men in the bachelor communities, although the veterans were still working class. While he was in the army, my father had earned a degree in electrical engineering, and he was able to benefit from certain military privileges, such as the use of military-base discount stores (PXs), health care for our family, and the ability to accumulate retirement income. The GI Bill allowed my father's cohort to buy homes and continue their education. Modest as these privileges were, they were sources of a relatively comfortable income and a great deal of pride. These veterans were able to take advantage of the loosening of racial restrictions and enhanced opportunities in employment and education during and after World War II. After leaving the military, my father worked for Douglas Aircraft. Defense-industry jobs previously had been denied to minorities and women.[79]

My father and other veterans were allowed to enter the United States as a small gesture of gratitude for their service in defeating Japan. These veterans came as "settlers" to the United States rather than as "sojourners" who expected to return to their homeland. Many, like my father, came with nuclear families and established small Filipino military communities in places like Fort Ord and the adjacent town of Seaside. They were not compelled to live in isolated agricultural labor camps or rundown urban areas, as the manongs did.[80]

Many parents of the student activists embraced American culture while denigrating their Filipino cultural characteristics and language. English was the official language of the Philippines; as a result of the American colonial educational system, most Filipinos spoke at least some. Knowledge of English was a point of pride and a marker of status; an "embarrassing" Filipino accent was considered a liability and a reason for discrimination. As occurs in many immigrant communities, most American-born Filipino children were not taught their family's native language out of fear that it would hamper their English-language skills and thus their chance to get ahead. For parents, survival meant teaching the children to be all American, even linguistically, and "English-only" practices were enforced, although Tagalog or one of the many other Philippine languages might have been spoken at home between the parents. Even with their broken English, most Filipinos were still proud they were from the most Westernized nation in Asia. Filipinos relished the fact that they, as immigrants from an American colonial outpost, could assimilate into U.S. culture more easily than other immigrants. Linguistic assimilation would be a key part of economic and cultural integration and mobility. After three hundred years of Spanish rule and about a half-century of American occupation, Filipinos were also among the most colonized people in Asia, which allowed them to identify readily with their colonial masters. But young people were beginning to find out that assimilation was meant for white immigrants, not racial minorities, even if they had no accents.[81]

Postwar prosperity and the Cold War mentality affected Filipino American families just as they did the majority of families in the United States. Although most Filipino American families were working class, they identified with the goals and aspirations of Middle America. The youth swept up in the Filipino identity movement were generally from this comfortable sector, and clashes increasingly took place between parents, who tended to be conservative, and their radicalized children. There was a noticeable generation gap, which included different attitudes toward the manongs.

Many parents were surprised and dismayed that their children were rallying to the manongs' cause. Liz Abello Del Sol, a student youth organizer from UC Berkeley, recalls that her plans to live at the I-Hotel in late 1969 shocked her parents. Her immediate family—her father, a Filipino machinist who had married an Indian woman from Oakland, her sister, and herself—lived in comfortable but modest conditions. She remembered her parents' saying that the International Hotel, situated on the "Kearny Street block," was an "unhealthy place for a young girl." To her parents, the Kearny Street block was a recreation spot for disreputable people and not a good place to live.[82]

In general, the post–World War II Filipino community was unsympathetic to the plight of the manongs. Perceived class differences, although not that large in reality, impeded support for farm workers in rural areas and poor tenants in urban areas. Parents of the youth considered manongs lowlifes who had gambled their earnings and pursued an unsavory lifestyle. With most of white society, they shared the middle-class attitude that this was a problem of individuals' bad behavior, which deserved to be punished. Many parents of the radicalized youth withdrew from the manongs as a result of political pressure, as well, since many of the manongs continued to be active in the labor movement, complained about discrimination, and remained close to communists during the McCarthy era. Government repression purged many of the manongs from unions, while within the Filipino community, leftists were pushed out of leadership roles.[83]

Activist Filipino youth of the 1970s rejected the community organizations of our parents and their forms of "validation" of a Filipino identity. We viewed those forms, such as organizations based on regions in the Philippines, as conservative and narrowly defined and as hindering the community's progressive development; we regarded such organizations as expressions of colonial mentality. In the radical upsurge of 1968, we began to realize that we were not middle class; that we were actually from working-class backgrounds, although we were more privileged than the manongs, and we formed our own organizations.

Students unearthed Bulosan's *America Is in the Heart,* first published in 1946. Through his vivid description of cruel conditions, exploitation, and resistance we learned about the militant organizers of the past. "Thus it was that I began to rediscover my native land, and the cultural roots there that had nourished me, and I felt a great urge to identify myself with the social awakening of my people," Bulosan wrote about his developing consciousness as a worker in the United States.[84] We passed around old copies of the book, and when it was reissued in 1973 by the University of Washington Press, *America Is in the Heart* became a "must read" for all Filipino students who wanted to know about the struggles of the manongs. Through Bulosan, we learned that the elderly and the young people shared internationalist perspectives, common experiences, and a rediscovery of the Philippines. We also identified with the manong generation, who had fought against racism and exploitation in the 1930s and afterward as part of a greater "proletarian solidarity." Philip Vera Cruz of the UFW articulates this internationalist perspective:

> When it comes to the farm workers movement, I see it as part of the movement that is taking place in the whole world. We think that we are a part of the struggle and that struggle is part of us. That's why we participate in demonstrations. . . . It's the same struggle all over the world, many fronts of the same struggle. As a member of the Farm Workers, and as a worker, I hope that a new system will arise in the future.[85]

At the same time, we uncovered the social, economic, political, and historical processes in the Philippines that fueled immigration to the United States.

Inspired by the Black Panthers' call for Black Power and self-determination, we voiced our own slogan, "Find Our Roots," to form a Filipino identity movement. Students in colleges and some high schools demanded classes that included Filipino American history and the Tagalog language. The slogan also provided a positive link between us and our immigrant parents who struggled for a better life for their children. Filipinos and other minorities who began to identify themselves as integral to the Third World created their own, ethnic-based identity movements with a "Third World" quality, linking the U.S. movements for racial equality with current struggles in their countries or with a mythical past that belonged only to the indigenous and uncolonized native. In areas where the Filipino community was small or absent, the sense of kinship with other Third World people led youths to join African American, Mexican, or other Asian groups. When I became politically aware while attending Long Beach State University, for example, I first joined the United Mexican American Students.

As student activists joined the strikes at San Francisco State and UC Berkeley, Filipino American youth also began to look to the Philippines, as other Third World activists looked to their homelands, for cultural meanings, icons, symbols, and values. It was an exciting moment to consciously reject what we considered to be colonized models from Spain and America. Instead, we sought out the "authentic" Filipino in the precolonial "Indio," the Spanish name given to the indigenous peoples of the Philippines (as well as those of the Americas). In many ways, we believed that the Filipino identity movement revived the critique of the Filipino first raised by Jose Rizal, who valued precolonial virtues over the values and lifestyle of the Spanish. Rizal's nationalism included the Indio as a model for enduring Filipino characteristics, such as honesty, generosity, and loyalty to kin and family.[86] In this rush of nationalist sentiment, some students even donned traditional native dress as everyday street wear, similar to the way African Americans donned dashikis and the Afro hairstyle.[87]

Filipino American students adopted Philippine revolutionary slogans and heroes, highlighting the role of U.S. imperialist domination in preventing full decolonization. We began to shed what we considered to be our "colonial mentalities," with decolonization as the goal. The struggle in the Philippines against neocolonial, imperialist domination also gave the Filipino American students a place in the pantheon of Third World liberation movements. We saw our struggle as part of a worldwide anticolonial upsurge of historic proportions. As small as the Filipino community was in America, we were participating in a world-historical process that gave us a sense of importance.

Students searched for the downtrodden and the poor; we sought out what we called the indigenous Filipino, the oppressed worker, and the masses. In the United States, Filipino American students romanticized heroes such as Bulosan and his generation of farm workers as well as Alaskan cannery workers (called *Alaskeros*), union organizers, and service and domestic workers. Other figures were revered, such as Lapu Lapu, the indigenous leader who had beheaded Magellan, the conqueror of the Philippines. Andres Bonifacio, the proletarian leader of the Katipunan who fought against Spanish oppression, was venerated instead of Emilio Aguinaldo, the first president of the Philippine republic, who was considered a traitor to the Philippine revolution because he had surrendered to U.S. imperialist power.[88]

On a more personal level, Filipino American youth did more than read about racism and discrimination in the pages of Bulosan. We learned firsthand from Filipino farm workers who had been instrumental in organizing the UFW's Delano Grape Strike of 1965 and the boycott that later became famous. Some of the first actions of the San Francisco and Berkeley strikers were to come to the aid of the UFW. We felt proud of our leaders, such as Larry Itliong and Philip Vera Cruz, organizers of the grape strike. Pete Velasco, third vice-president of the UFW and an organizer of food caravans from the San Francisco Bay Area, Los Angeles, and San Diego, became well known among all students, not just Filipinos. In the Bay Area, young activists worked with Pablo Valdez and Mario Hermoso, who had been labor organizers in the 1930s. We learned directly from the manongs how the first Filipino immigrants had been exploited and racially oppressed in a system that profited from their labor and then abandoned them, to be forgotten, in "Manilatowns."

While we accepted our acculturation in American society, we hungered for a more "authentic" connection to national identity. All of these needs were met through association with the manongs. While American society was caught up in youth rebellion and the generation gap, Filipino youth articulated this rebellion in a unique way: We rebelled by venerating the elderly "bachelors," rejecting the conservatism of our parents and favoring the radicalism—and the broken English—of the manongs.

Veneration of the Manongs

In fashioning their identities through activism, Filipino American youth consciously valorized the first generation's experiences of economic and racial exploitation by popularizing "*manong*," an Ilocano term that means elder brother. In doing so, the youth applied an aspect of Filipino culture that confers respect on older male members, or fictive "uncles," in the community to the experiences of the first generation of Filipinos who had immigrated to the United States. At the same time, the term resonated with the entire elder generation.

Filipino American youth became activists in progressive community politics because those politics manifested themselves at the grassroots. The more radical element developed into what we called "conscious revolutionaries" involved in all aspects of the class struggle, but in our political program, we worked for the extension of democracy principally in the Filipino community. In the first years of the I-Hotel movement, a process began between the youth and the manongs of exchange, synergy, and bonding. For the manongs, there was no previous generation of Filipinos on whom to rely, and there were few at the professional level who could contribute to their causes economically or give them credibility outside their class.[89] Without a natural base within the Filipino community, the manong generation relied on themselves or depended on support from those outside the Filipino community. Unions and leftist organizations such as the Communist Party and its affiliated organizations were among the few "American" groups to help the manongs fight their economic and political battles.

With the new generation of politically active Filipino students, the manongs found a natural base for their causes within their own communities. At the same time, the students could claim the manongs as their political and cultural ancestors. The students, however, had to create a favorable climate so that their parents would accept the manongs' issues as legitimate. Veneration for older members of the community was a deeply ingrained Filipino cultural trait, so this proved to be the opening they needed to win over their parents and other members of the Filipino community. The elderly not only found progressive youths who were open to their plight as working-class members of an oppressed community; they also found a sense of family and community that crossed the generations. In many ways, the Filipino youth had to find their own "fictive" familial relationships, which often were no farther away than their own back doors, or were even part of the family. Almost every youth in the community had an uncle (in the broad, extended Filipino sense of the word, which includes non-blood relations) he or she knew personally. It was only a matter of "consciousness" to give signification to that relationship.

Soon the Filipino American youth and students championed issues that affected the first-generation Filipinos: the lack of decent health care, inadequate housing, and the need for workers' rights. It was not enough to learn about our history. We soon realized that we must be involved in the I-Hotel movement and other projects.

As the issues and campaigns to help the first-generation Filipinos evolved, close personal relationships developed between the elderly men and the young activists. The timing of these cross-generational relationships had to do with the confluence of campus and youth activism in the community; city officials' redevelopment plans to raze "blighted communities," particularly minority communities; the need for youth to find their identity; and the elderly generation's search for supporters within their own ethnic community. The bonding between youth and elderly helped to create the core of working-class values of the Filipino youth identity movement. These values melded together traditional Filipino cultural values with an American working-class ethic that included respect for labor. Thus, the term of endearment "manong" that was popularized around this time also designated a Filipino elder generation's political struggle for economic justice through unions and for racial justice in society.

Filipino American youth were proud of what the elder generation contributed to America's economic and political wealth, especially in light of the harshness of racial discrimination and economic exploitation. The forgotten and despised manong became the subject of young artists in dance, art, flyers, poetry, short historical writing, theater, and even music.[90] We memorialized our working-class elders, highlighted the racism they encountered, and honored the poor and dispossessed immigrants who had come before us as "pioneers" in the struggle. They were the agricultural workers in labor camps, the downtrodden service and domestic worker in the cities, the unmarried "bachelors" living in rundown areas of cities.

The poet Al Robles immortalized the manongs in his many poems and in his children's book *Looking for Ifugao Mountain.*[91] Robles grew up in San Francisco's Fillmore District in the 1940s, where he became involved in the jazz scene. When he was a boy, his father took him to Manilatown for haircuts and gossip, and he was familiar with the aging men and their ways. When Robles became a poet and began to explore his cultural roots, he returned to the manongs.[92]

Robles's poem "The Wandering Manong" begins with a critique of those in the Filipino community who were ashamed of the manongs:

> I am not ashamed of the manong, nor do I feel sad by their tragic story in America. The manongs have been on a long journey and I have been one of those wanderers who they have met along the way. What right does anyone have to judge these manongs who have come to America seeking for a new life? They have lived through so many wars and have scars in their hearts to prove it. They were the brown gypsies, the low-down niggers, the brown apache savages, the uncivilized nomads who wandered from place to place in search of their dreams. They left the water buffalo at home. . . . They lived, as it were, in two worlds—in a world they left behind, and in a dream before their eyes.[93]

These "two worlds"—the world left behind and the dream before their eyes—also spoke to the revolutionary sensibilities of the young, their need to recover what had been "left behind" to make a new dream real.

CHAPTER TWO

A Home or a Parking Lot?

Human Rights versus Property Rights, 1968–69

Resistance and Leadership

"We Want to Stay in Our Neighborhood," read a placard carried by a demonstrator as elderly members of the little-known Filipino community on Kearny Street marched in front of the International Hotel on November 17, 1968. A *San Francisco Chronicle* reporter commented that the march to save the elderly Filipinos' home and the remnants of their once vital community was a "sad, quiet demonstration," the tenants seeming "to plead" rather than to demand.[1] The reporter's perception that the demonstrators were pleading may have been based on their reserved, gentlemanly demeanor. It was a time when raucous student demonstrations were often confrontational; a time when the movements for African Americans' and other minorities' rights were often, quite literally, incendiary.

In reality, the elderly men were asserting what they felt was so altogether self-evident that it required only direct, dignified articulation to receive a sympathetic, common-sense response from the public. These first-generation Filipinos believed they were entitled to stay in the home in which some of them had lived for more than fifty years. The fact that the building, which had become both home and community, would be destroyed to build a parking lot only served to underscore the low regard in which these elderly workers were held: A parking lot simply added insult to what would already be a devastating injury.[2]

The owner of the hotel, Milton Meyer and Company, had applied for permission to demolish the hotel in June 1968. But the tenants only learned of the owner's intent in October. When the first eviction notice was sent to the occupants, panic ensued, and approximately one-third of the tenants quickly left. The elderly were particularly vulnerable and limited in their choices. From November 1968, when the first demonstration was held, to the middle of June 1969, when the first agreement for a lease was signed, the number of tenants age sixty-five and older decreased only slightly, from eighteen to fifteen. In contrast, the number of tenants age forty to sixty-four declined from ninety to twenty-two.[3] The elderly had fewer alternatives for mobility and fewer resources than the middle-aged and young tenants. Though few in number, the elderly tenants would provide the backbone to the resistance in great part because of their lack of choices.

At the beginning of December 1968, 182 people lived in the International Hotel's 184 rooms. The majority of the residents were Filipinos. According to a count taken on April 9, 1969, seventy-three tenants (52.5 percent) were Filipino, twenty-eight (20.2 percent) were Chinese, and thirty-eight (27.3 percent) were from other ethnic groups. By the end of May 1969, after the panic caused by the first notice of intent to demolish the hotel, approximately sixty-five tenants remained; slightly more than fifty of them were Filipinos.[4] The second-largest group was Chinese; the remainder were single, male Latinos and blacks and a few low-income families of a variety of ethnicities.[5] Of the hotel's 120 tenants in the summer of 1971, 60 percent were Filipino; 30 percent, Chinese; and the rest, white, Latino, or black.[6] Thus, from the beginning of the anti-eviction movement, the composition of the tenants, while always diverse and volatile depending on the possibilities of eviction, was overwhelmingly Filipino. And many of the Filipinos were elderly or aging members of the early immigration to the United States.

Mr. Arzadon, as described in the *Chronicle* article, was typical of the I-Hotel's residents. He left Ilocos Norte in the Philippines in 1918 to come to the United States, and he resided at the hotel off and on for about fifty years. Mr. Arzadon received a small pension from his years of working as a merchant seaman, and he expected to live out the rest of his days in familiar surroundings. According to the *Chronicle* reporter, Mr. Arzadon did not "know where he [was] going to live" after the eviction, which was scheduled for January 1, 1969. He had no choice, and, like the other tenants who remained, he had decided to protest out of a sense of desperation mixed with injured pride. Mr. Arzadon and the other pickets may have seemed "sad" to the reporter, but he was not aware that, by simply refusing to flee and then by beginning to organize, the tenants had taken the first, decisive steps in their resistance. This seemingly unremarkable first attempt would ignite a nearly decade-long struggle that would transform the elderly tenants, electrify San Francisco politics, and forge new definitions of Filipino American identity.

The storefront businesses that occupied the hotel's ground-floor storefronts, such as Bataan Lunch, the Manilatown Information Center, Club Mandalay, and Tino's Barber Shop, were also threatened by eviction. Serving as places for inexpensive food, for the company of *kababayan* (countrymen), and for recreation and gambling, the stores constituted an urban "ghetto" known to the residents simply as "the Kearny Street block," and they were essential to the neighborhood's Filipino community.

Tino's Barber Shop was directly to the right of the I-Hotel's front door. Owned by Faustino (Tino) Regino, the shop contained two barber chairs with brass spittoons beside each chair, large round mirrors, photos of friends from Tino's town in the Philippines, and, often, a band composed of washtub bass, scrub board, and mandolin. Tino's was not only a barber shop; it was also an informal information-gathering center for the Filipino community in San Francisco. Those searching for friends, relatives, or town mates often could find them by asking Tino and his Filipino barbers. Fred Basconcillo, who visited Tino's as a young man, recalls Tino and his barbers answering such queries with, "Oh, yeah—he's working in Salinas; he's picking lettuce" or, if it was the fishing season, "He's in Alaska working in a cannery." Tino spoke several dialects. Because of his ability to act as a central, oral switchboard for the community, he became known as the unofficial mayor of the old-timers who lived on the block.[7]

The Lucky M Pool Hall, operated by Manual Muyco and his white wife, Margaret, also served as a gathering place and as a safe hideaway for recreation and small-scale gambling. Although Marguerite was ostracized from the white community for marrying a Filipino man, she was welcomed by the I-Hotel's tenants and other first-generation Filipinos. Known for her kindness and generosity, she often provided meals for the pool hall's patrons. Bataan Lunch, another ground-floor business, offered familiar Filipino dishes along with American food. The Lucky M Pool Hall and Tino's Barber Shop also served as an informal employment center for seasonal workers and casual laborers. Filipino tenants could live, eat, and relax on the 800 block of Kearny Street, the last remnant of the Filipino business district that had once stretched eight to ten blocks to Market Street.[8]

Although these Filipino businesses fully supported the pickets, they were economically fragile and could not withstand the financial strain of an anti-eviction battle. Most left early in the conflict. Of the owners, only Ness Aquino, who had opened Mabuhay Gardens, a handsome restaurant featuring Philippine cuisine, in December 1969, stepped forward to become active in the United Filipino Association (UFA). His idea was to revitalize the area for the Filipino community by re-creating a center for Filipino activity that, at the same time, would have a positive effect on business prospects.[9] Opening the restaurant was his private commitment to revitalizing the Manilatown block. Aquino also understood the need to defend the International Hotel. As he stated, "This is the last of the old ten-block Manilatown. If the hotel goes, it will wipe out a community anchor."[10]

The original Manilatown Information Center, founded in 1966 by Bert Esteva as part of Lyndon Johnson's War on Poverty program, provided social services to the elderly Filipinos in Manilatown. When the initial protest began, however, it quickly became clear that an organization dedicated to advocating housing issues for the elderly tenants was needed, and the UFA was born. It was composed of local businessmen and professionals serving the immediate area and of I-Hotel tenants, and its purpose was to stop the eviction and negotiate a lease from Milton Meyer and Company. To make sure that social needs were met, the UFA continued to operate a service center providing welfare assistance, social security, and medical care in the hotel. It was still called the Manilatown Information Center and was funded in part by a ten thousand dollar a year grant from the city's Economic Opportunity Council.[11] Through the Manilatown Information Center, social workers such as Pete Marasigan and his wife, Violeta (known as "Bullet"), helped organize new recruits to the cause of rehabilitating the hotel. Others, such as Violet Sanchez, Mrs. Pastoretti, and Joaquin Legaspi, oversaw young interns.[12]

The UFA took up the defense of the I-Hotel's tenants in December 1968, and it remained the main vehicle for the anti-eviction fight until 1972. Members of the UFA's board included Aquino, who served as its president as well as chair of the Economic Opportunity Council; Luisa Castro, publicity coordinator for the UFA and an employee of the Filipino Information Center in Oakland; Joaquin Legaspi, an I-Hotel tenant who was well known in the community as a poet and an intellectual; and Joe Diones, who was also a tenant and a retired longshoreman and union organizer. Three months after the first demonstration and in response to the crisis that followed a mysterious, fatal fire at the hotel, Luisa Castro invited student activists to join. With the consent of its other members, the UFA board expanded to include the UC Berkeley students Frank Celada, Bruce Occena, and Emil de Guzman. Serving as chief negotiator and pro bono attorney for the tenants was Sidney M. Wolinsky of the San Francisco Neighborhood Legal Assistance Foundation. The foundation had just mobilized each of its neighborhood offices to conduct a study that concluded there was a housing crisis in the city. Attorney A. Marquez Bautista, assistant to the chairman of the Filipino American Council of Northern California on Senior Citizen Matters, was also a board member.

The initial UFA board contained a combination of dynamic individuals, ranging from the middle aged to the elderly, rooted among neighborhood merchants and social-service professionals, as well as hotel residents. This alliance of business and professional people with the lower-class tenants was significant. It allowed for greater support from the Filipino community beyond the Kearny Street area because the more privileged members of the broader community generally regarded the lower-class tenants of the hotel in a disdainful, elitist manner. Bill Sorro, one of the early activists, related a story about visiting his father's regional organization, the Iloilo Circle, to seek support for the tenants. Despite the deep kinship-like ties Sorro had to the organization, he was rejected, because the Iloilo Circle did not want to be associated with the likes of the I-Hotel tenants.[13]

As I noted in the previous chapter, only 4 percent of the Filipino community had attained professional status before 1965, although a small and stable Filipino community that regarded itself as "middle class" developed after World War II.[14] Both the tenants and the radical students felt that it was more difficult for Filipinos who thought of themselves as middle class to overcome their embarrassment in associating with the less fortunate bachelors. Their perceived middle-class status undermined a sense of ethnic-community solidarity. Over time, the middle-class sense of shame would be counterbalanced by ethnic pride, particularly when support for the elderly became increasingly voiced by respectable, non-Filipino figures. Eventually, their shame would be mitigated when support came from Glide Memorial Church and other churches, the UFW and other unions, the San Francisco Human Rights Commission and other city agencies, and national organizations such as the Ford Foundation, although they did not overcome much of their shame until after the eviction.

Without an organization like the UFA, which blended the different class and social forces within the community, the anti-eviction struggle most likely would not have gone beyond the hotel tenants or their immediate neighborhood. Most anti-eviction tenant battles in the United States during this period were lost.[15] Only struggles that involved broader alliances proved successful. For example, a similar tenant battle erupted in the summer of 1969 that involved mostly white working-class men in San Francisco's South of Market area. Resisting what would become known as the Yerba Buena Project—a large-scale hotel, arts, and commercial development—tenants organized Tenants and Owners in Opposition to Redevelopment (TOOR) with the support of professionals and other community activists. Their protracted, and ultimately successful, struggle did gain low-income and elderly housing as part of the redevelopment project.[16] Both TOOR and the UFA (and its successor organization, the IHTA) followed similar organizing principles and shared similar social bases.

In both efforts, broad alliances with tenants at the core were crucial to developing the combination of moral urgency and political muscle needed for victory. At the same time, there was a strong base of support to stop the destruction of affordable housing in working-class and minority communities in San Francisco, such as the Western Addition and Fillmore districts, where blacks and Japanese had experienced approximately 10,000 evictions as a result of redevelopment. The decimation of these black and Japanese neighborhoods foreshadowed the Yerba Buena and I-Hotel struggles, as housing stock was increasingly depleted.

Professionals and, later, students conducted much of the UFA's organizing work, such as holding press conferences and attending meetings with city officials. But the tenants remained at the core, and their tenacity and militant stance provided many of the students who became involved with a learning experience in organizing, particularly since the most outspoken tenants at the International

Hotel had been labor-union organizers with experience in political mobilization. While city officials, politicians, and other professionals responded to the role of the middle-class activists in the UFA, the active role of the tenants themselves kept the struggle a grassroots effort and true to their needs.

As a businessman and government employee, Aquino provided the link between the Kearny Street neighborhood and the generally more conservative Filipino American community. Luisa Castro said, "It seemed natural for him to step forward because of his recent appointment as an official working with the EOC."[17] Aquino's business background, along with his appointment to the EOC, projected him as someone with credentials as a Filipino American leader.[18]

Castro was the daughter of a successful Filipino American businessman who had come to the United States in 1919 and married a white woman from Oregon. She had been involved in the farm workers' struggle and had been active in fighting for social services for the Filipino community before she joined the UFA board. She conducted the publicity and was instrumental in rallying support from students and from other professionals who helped with renovation. She began participating in Filipino community efforts at an early age because of her direct experiences with racism. The fact that her father had prospered in the midst of intense racial discrimination was not typical of families of the few mestizas born to first-generation Filipino immigrants. After raising two children by herself and achieving relative prosperity, Castro gave up her house at middle age, went to college, and joined the thousands of youth who were radicalized in the student struggle at San Francisco State and UC Berkeley.[19]

Joe Diones and Joaquin Legaspi represented the tenants. Diones, the manager of the International Hotel, was born in Hawaii among the first generation of children of sugarcane workers imported from the Philippines. Schooled as an organizer in the International Longshoremen's and Warehousemen's Union (ILWU), he applied his union skills to forging the tenants' organization. He had strong ties to Harry Bridges of the ILWU and other labor leaders and to the local San Francisco political scene, such as the well-connected and well-known left-wing Hallinan family. He also had links with the communist Hukbalahap guerrillas in the Philippines, and he knew American communists in the labor movement. A rough and fearless man, Diones was admired for his toughness as a militant trade-union activist, and he employed these qualities in organizing and, later, managing the I-Hotel. Diones did not hesitate to make alliances with anyone, whether they were part of the community, labor, the church, or the political elite. However, he had the mentality of a union boss, a rough-and-tumble character ready to use intimidation and even violence to get his way. This style of work would become increasingly problematic as the struggle evolved.[20]

Legaspi, the other tenant representative, was an intellectual, an artist, a businessman, and a poet who had obtained a good education and had traveled to many parts of the world. Legaspi arrived in the United States in the 1920s. Like many others, he continued to educate himself while working at back-breaking menial tasks. He was one of the few in his generation who finished his college education. Legaspi was among the first tenant leaders to influence Filipino American youth and students. He wrote in the tradition of nationalist poets, criticizing foreign domination and promoting liberation in the Philippines. In a poem published in 1975 in *Liwanag*, an early Filipino American poetry and art publication, he expressed anticolonial outrage:

> *Helmeted crusaders . . . illustrious conquistadors!*
> *Armed with banyan image of God, invade the shores*
> *Of heathen Islander's beckoning tropical floors.*[21]

Legaspi's eloquence and dapper style, along with his education and understanding of the political struggle, appealed to the youth searching for their Filipino identity. He was the epitome of the committed intellectual. His example inspired the young people to write poetry and to sympathize with the poor and elderly tenants more deeply. Legaspi's Third World and nationalist consciousness, as expressed in his poems and in conversation, challenged the students to question their colonized mentality, assert Philippine liberation and freedom, and treasure the values and culture of the Filipino.[22]

Bruce Occena remembered Legaspi as "the natural spokesman for the tenants. He wasn't a haughty intellectual. The tenants deferred to his leadership, and he spoke for them. The students viewed him as the grandfather of the struggle. He provided the youth and students a tie to the past they never had."[23] Legaspi, in fact, is credited with coining the term "Manilatown," giving the Kearny Street neighborhood a sense of belonging and identity. Highly respected by the tenants and sharing their generational experience, Legaspi played a pivotal role, providing the "organic" links to the tenants and serving as a bridge to supporters, particularly the Filipino youth and students. Unfortunately, his influence was cut short when he died at seventy-nine in 1975.

The different individuals of the UFA combined to create a unique leadership core that included business acumen, political energy, street-smart organizing skills, and the ability to be self-reflective and articulate. This confluence of qualities may seem coincidental, but it actually reflected the broad experiences that older Filipinos had gained during the first wave of immigration: the struggle to gain small-business footholds; the active, often decisive involvement of the few women; the participation and education of workers through the trade-union movements of the 1930s and '40s; and the often unacknowledged presence of educated leaders among menial workers. As a result, the initial leadership of the UFA proved highly effective in attracting broad support, all of which created a stable basis for the I-Hotel struggle to reach its next stage.

City Officials and Agencies Support the I-Hotel

Some city officials and politicians were quick to join the pickets and help the tenants fend off the impending eviction. A few politicians were concerned, not only about the tenants, but also about the rapid expansion of downtown interests. Supervisor Jack Morrison, who marched with the pickets that first day in 1968, gave the tenants a tip: They could appeal the demolition plans to the Board of Permit Appeals. Assemblyman John Burton lobbied Walter Shorenstein, president of Milton Meyer and Company, to suspend any action, and he appealed to private developers that "the IH is not an isolated incident of the conflict between low-rent housing and the urge of private enterprise to improve profits. Over the years, the development of modern office buildings has marched down Kearny Street. You can see this concrete monster marching on, and what do you do about the people?"[24] The Human Rights Commission also jumped into the conflict in support of the tenants, strongly opposing the January 1 demolition and requesting a "full discussion of the issue with residents of the community and the hotel owners, Milton Meyer Co." At the December 5 meeting with the Human Rights Commission, Filipino leaders told the commissioners that if the hotel went, so would the surrounding, small Filipino community.[25]

Shorenstein, then the largest owner of real estate in San Francisco, had become a partner in Milton Meyer and Company when he had married Milton Meyer's daughter. When his father-in-law died in 1950, Shorenstein became president and director.[26] Shorenstein was a major force in local and national Democratic politics, and he lent his political support and considerable fund-raising talents to various Democrats, such as Hubert Humphrey in his 1968 presidential race and Joseph Alioto, who ran for mayor of San Francisco in 1967. Shorenstein was appointed to the President's Task Force on U.S. Urban Problems in 1968 and chaired the San Francisco Mayor's Citizen's Housing Task Force.[27]

As a major figure in the Democratic Party, Shorenstein had to balance support from minority communities in urban areas, where much of the party's potential voters were concentrated, and the needs of the pro-growth coalition in San Francisco, a set of forces that involved many of Shorenstein's business associates, who were also potential funding sources of political campaigns. First through New Deal initiatives and, later, through President Johnson's Great Society programs, Democrats had cultivated a significant base of support among minority communities, along with labor unions, in urban coalitions. But by the 1960s, San Francisco's private-property interests, along with the city's need to expand its tax base by enlarging its business sector, conflicted directly with housing and neighborhood preservation. Mainly poor and minority communities were deemed "blighted" and targeted for redevelopment.[28] The tension between the Democratic Party's liberal agenda and its need to accommodate capital expansion through urban renewal explained Shorenstein's vacillations. Pro-growth Democrats had to contend with alienating minority communities that were targeted for urban-renewal projects.[29]

With broad support, and capitalizing on the political vulnerabilities of Shorenstein and his allies, the tenants gained a temporary reprieve. On March 15, 1969, Shorenstein agreed to sign a lease agreement with the UFA as the representative of the tenants.[30] Shorenstein's wife, who was also on the company's board, pressured him to settle in fear of embarrassment, and it seemed that the tenants had won some breathing space.

Fire Galvanizes Tenants and Supporters

Early on Sunday morning, March 16, 1969, a day before the scheduled signing of the lease agreement, a fire swept through the north wing of the International Hotel's second floor. Three tenants died: Robert Knauff, who had stayed there for only a few days; the long-time tenant Pio Rosete; and Marcario Salermo, an unemployed janitor.[31] Tenants and supporters suspected that the blaze was arson. Fires plagued rundown hotels and apartments in the 1970s, and residents often suspected that landlords torched the buildings to collect insurance as well as to get rid of undesirable tenants.[32]

Five months earlier, after the first protest by tenants in November 1968, Shorenstein had declared that the building was "deteriorated and unlivable. We do not want to be slum landlords. If there were ever a fire there, with those people in that building, I would not want to have it on my conscience." After the fire, Shorenstein canceled the lease agreement, saying that, had it not been for the opposition of the tenants and their supporters, such as Supervisor Morrison, "these three unfortunate men might be alive today." Morrison responded, "In accusing others, Mr. Shorenstein is looking for a little salve for his conscience. . . . [T]he fact that I and others wanted help for these people doesn't at all mean that the owners of the building ought to be freed from living up to fire safety regulations."[33]

Whereas landlords had allowed many single-room-occupancy hotels to deteriorate, the I-Hotel was structurally sound. When the city inspected the building after the fire, inspectors found nineteen violations of municipal housing and building codes but no structural damage beyond the areas in which the fire was confined; only fire sprinklers needed to be installed. At a hearing on March 26, Chief Albert Hayes, head of Fire Department's Bureau of Fire Prevention, reported, "I think this building is safe for the people that are living in it."[34]

As a consequence of the fire, a new eviction notice ordered the tenants to vacate the premises by June 1, 1969. The tenants, however, were not intimidated by Shorenstein's attempt to blame them for the deaths of Knauff, Rosete, and Salermo. They insisted on remaining and upholding the new lease agreement. Instead of being scared off, the tenants called for another public meeting to explain their position regarding the fire. They testified to the commissioners, housing experts, structural engineers, and architects at a March 20, 1969 Human Rights Commission meeting that "despite the fire no one wants to move."[35] Still, Shorenstein stood his ground, saying, "I don't want to have to be in an 'I told you so' position again."[36]

The fire strengthened the tenants' resolve, particularly since they suspected intimidation. The eviction of the tenants and the demolition of the Palm Hotel at Kearny and Washington streets, only half a block from the I-Hotel, in January 1969 gave them a concrete illustration of what would occur if they did not fight. The city had not made any plans to relocate the Palm's approximately ninety residents, at least 75 percent of whom were Filipino, and they were left homeless.[37] The Palm Hotel's commercial residents, including a restaurant, a photo store, and a TV and radio repair store owned or operated by Filipinos, were also evicted. The Palm Hotel's tenants had not been organized, and the disaster served as a grim reminder for the I-Hotel tenants that there were no viable alternatives other than adamant resistance.

Few outside Manilatown, whether Filipinos or not, could grasp why anyone would want to live in a cramped room in a hotel. The rooms were dirty and unpainted and filled with roaches. Yet they were home and community to those who had lived in a bachelor society most of their lives. For rent ranging from forty-five to seventy dollars a month, depending on the size of the room, one could live adequately and without government assistance and intrusion. The men lived with dignity, were fiercely independent, and thrived as a kind of family. Their surroundings seemed meager by lower-middle-class standards, even to the primarily working-class Filipino students who came to help them. Most of the students lived in modest working-class single-family homes, away from the noise and dirt of downtown. The tenants' insistence on remaining underscored the degree to which the hotel had become an actual home, and their determination discouraged supporters from accepting compromises that equated removal with an improvement in tenants' living conditions. The tenants had internalized a crucial strategic concept of any anti-eviction or housing struggle: Remaining on the site maintains pressure on the opposition, while acceding to any compromises that involve even temporary removal invites defeat.[38]

"Filipino Hotel Tenants Set to Fight," announced the headline in the *San Francisco Chronicle* on March 27, 1969. Residents of the I-Hotel told S. Myron Tatarian, director of the city's Department of Public Works, that they would not leave the hotel if ordered to do so, and if the hotel were demolished, it would be done "over our bodies." According to the attorney for Milton Meyer and Company, their stubborn resistance stood in the way of progress. The attorney gave voice to what property owners and those who did not sympathize with the tenants believed, saying that these "poor unfortunates did not realize what they were subjecting themselves to. Don't let this single little case stand in the way of progress."[39]

The coroner investigating the fire expressed uneasiness about the testimony of Fire Inspector Ernest Capper, who had interviewed John Davilla, the resident in whose room the fire was thought to have started. Capper reported that Davilla had given him a different name when he was interviewed the night of the fire, and that he could not account for an hour's time immediately before the fire was discovered. Despite these inconsistencies, the city found insufficient evidence to determine that the fire was arson. However, despite the Fire Department's inconclusive report, the student activist Frank Celada recalled that tenants and their supporters continued to insist that the fire was suspicious in origin.[40]

Meanwhile, in an effort at least to prevent a repetition of the Palm Hotel debacle, Sid Wolinsky of the San Francisco Neighborhood Legal Assistance Foundation filed a federal suit alleging that removal of the residents without adequate alternative housing for them would violate their constitutional rights. "We had a meeting, and Sid told the tenants about the situation," recalled Edith Witt, a staff member of the city's Human Rights Commission. "He asked them, 'Are you gonna stay?' And those fifty guys said, 'YES!' Sid was saying, 'It all depends on *YOU*,' and they felt it. They stuck firm. And they went through hell."[41] Wolinsky attempted to negotiate with Shorenstein, meeting the landlord with Ness Aquino of the UFA. Shorenstein would not budge. He asserted that "progress was a train coming down a railroad track. If you don't get out of the way, you'll get run over."[42] On May 8, Federal Judge George B. Harris dismissed the suit, determining that "it is manifest to the court that there is no federal question involved."[43]

Even Mayor Joseph Alioto's advisory committee to the Office of Aging opposed the destruction of the I-Hotel unless adequate relocation housing was found. The committee's action followed a hotel march staged the previous morning at Mayor Alioto's annual Earthquake Party on April 18, commemorating the 1906 disaster. Wolinsky asked student supporters and community organizations to march to the Earthquake Party hiding their placards under their coats. With the mayor before the press, the tenants and their supporters suddenly pulled out their placards in front of the crowd and media. Tenants claimed that the hotel was "a home and cultural center for the older generation of the city's Filipino community. Destruction of the hotel would mean the destruction and displacement of that community." War on Poverty community organizations such as the Mission Coalition and the Western Addition Community Organization joined the protest against the hotel's proposed demolition.[44] The "sneak attack" was a public embarrassment to Mayor Alioto, and he was incensed at being upstaged.[45]

Meanwhile, the tenants called a press conference on April 23 to charge Milton Meyer and Company with harassment. Tenants asserted that the building's management periodically shut off the electricity, ignored routine maintenance, and engaged in constant harassment. Agents for the landlord told residents that they had to move and that all legal avenues for remaining were closed. Tenants recognized such actions as common tactics of landlords trying to pressure tenants to leave: By making life intolerable through constant harassment, the landlord hoped to force the tenants to move out "voluntarily."

Responding to the tenants' allegations, five members of the Human Rights Commission inspected the premises on June 12, 1969. Celeda, then the publicity liaison for the UFA, told *Chronicle* reporters that the tenants lived "in a state of siege."[46] They were being denied toilet paper and clean sheets; toilets were clogged; the community kitchen was never cleaned; and garbage was being removed "very irregularly." One of the commissioners touring the hotel, Curtis McClain, who was also an official with the ILWU, found that the community recreation room was locked and the television set had been out of order for two weeks. Shorenstein and his attorney denied all charges, but McClain told Darald Dickerson, who managed the premises for Milton Meyer and Company, "We'll be stopping by every day or two to see that you're living up to your assurance that adequate services will be maintained as long as there are tenants."[47]

Despite the harassment, opposition to eviction kept growing. At a press conference on April 29, the San Francisco City Family Service Agency urged Mayor Alioto to use his power to halt plans to destroy the I-Hotel. L. Warde Laldman, a member of the agency, offered his opinion of the effects of this destruction:

> When families or groups of individuals who perceive themselves as families are broken into separate segments and torn apart by forces beyond their control, this places the whole concept of American family life in jeopardy. In the IH we have a family of elderly Filipino men who have in the United States found each other and established a home together. Now they are being told to move on. And they have nowhere to go together. An opportunity exists for Mayor Alioto and other civic leaders to use this crisis to exert dynamic, responsible leadership and to exert creative efforts toward solving the hotel crisis and the city wide housing problem.[48]

Mayor Alioto was unmoved. He could only retort that "the Family Service Agency is incredibly wrong in its facts in the past and is wrong again."[49]

The Family Service Agency's invocation of "home" and "American family life" resonated deeply with the tenants. Keeping their homes and community made sense to them not only because there was no other available low-income housing in the city, but also because the I-Hotel was a close-knit community who pooled resources and enjoyed a sense of brotherhood. Tenants at the I-Hotel could enjoy meals cheaply at lunch counters in nearby Chinatown or buy fresh vegetables, fish, fruit, or meat for Filipino meals cooked in the hotel's community kitchen. Since there was no refrigeration, daily shopping was critical to food preparation. Those too old to work, those who were on Social Security or drawing pensions, and veterans of foreign wars could survive well enough in a single-room-occupancy hotel. Fiercely independent, many of them disdained receiving charity, and they feared becoming anonymous residents of nursing homes. Others may have been undocumented immigrants who absolutely would not rely on outside agencies for support or who were suspicious of government officials, which was particularly true among Chinese tenants, some of whom were "paper sons" who had been brought to the United States with false papers.[50]

The tenants identified as a household and depended on one another for support in their everyday activities of survival at the International Hotel—whether relaxing in the community room and the surrounding pool halls and barber shops, eating and cooking meals in the community kitchen, or buying cheap meals from *kababayan* or Chinese restaurants. When asked why he wanted to stay in the hotel, a sixty-five-year-old tenant replied, "Have here a good neighborhood, and good and very kind countrymen, old and new friends. . . . I have stayed here so long that I called this Hotel my HOME." Another man, sixty-two years old, answered, "All the Filipinos are here to help me, I'm helpless. . . . I have a friend to help me cook and buy groceries for me."[51] A few years later, Felix Ayson, one of the most visible leaders of the tenants during the final anti-eviction struggle, expressed the sentiment simply: "During the years I was living at the International Hotel it was a real home to me. . . . The other tenants were so kind to me, and we were all kind to each other." For the tenants, mutual kindness born of simple household interactions connected them to a sense of their rights and the need to take action.[52]

A sense of home was not on Mayor Alioto's agenda. His position regarding the fire and the building's subsequent upkeep aligned with the dominant pro-business sentiment of city officials. According to this view, as most clearly expressed by Shorenstein, the owners should have the right to do whatever they wanted with their property, and if they refused to repair the building as ordered by the Department of Public Works, private-property rights should prevail over access to housing as a human right. If the tenants were unhappy with poor living conditions, they in turn should exercise their own rights as renters by relocating to a more suitable environment. To Alioto and Shorenstein, housing was a commodity to be exchanged just like any other. While values of "home" or community that stood outside the cash nexus might have been worthy, they could not supersede the fundamental dynamics of capital.[53]

As the central business district began to encroach on San Francisco's Chinatown and North Beach districts, parking lots and office towers became more profitable than the low-rent hotels that had dotted the area. In 1968, office buildings under construction or completed included the fifty-two-story Bank of America building, the thirty-four-story Pacific Gas and Electric building, the twenty-six-story First Savings Building, the twenty-seven-story Crocker Building, and the thirty-two-story Mutual Benefit building.[54] Furthermore, the land on which the International Hotel stood was assessed for $101,625 and the building for $102,175, for a total of $203,750. If the hotel was replaced with a parking lot, taxes would be reduced. Through this arrangement, the owners would receive a higher annual rental from an auto parking company than they would from the hotel, making a low-income hotel far less appealing as a business proposition.[55]

Such a polarization of values between those of the tenants and those of the downtown real-estate interests, as represented by Alioto, had consequences beyond a mere conflict between community sentimentalists and business realists. In reality, the notion of profitability generating progress advanced by downtown interests meant nothing short of destruction for the hotel and for the remnants of the Kearny Street block, and for the elderly Filipinos themselves, removal meant death. Thus, the battle lines were drawn. The "Manhattanization" of San Francisco as part of the Pacific Rim Strategy of U.S. finance capital meant that the business district needed to expand at the expense of the International Hotel.

Mayor Alioto's Plans Rejected by Tenants

Joseph Alioto, the son of Sicilian immigrants, ran a successful antitrust law practice but had been a political unknown until he ran for mayor in 1967 after a pro-growth coalition in San Francisco encouraged him to make a bid. In return, Mayor Alioto appointed major players in the redevelopment of San Francisco whose vision was to transform the downtown area into a world financial center and headquarters for capital expansion throughout what was just becoming known as the Pacific Rim. At the same time, Alioto offered deals to labor unions such as the ILWU, Local 10, and Laborer's International, Local 261, both of which had large minority memberships. He also courted with political favors minority leaders whose communities might be affected by the redevelopment plans for San Francisco. The labor vote was instrumental in electing Alioto.[56]

With such a divided, potentially volatile electoral base, Alioto had to respond to community pressure in some fashion. To avoid potential bad publicity, he agreed to hold a meeting on May 5, 1969, with the I-Hotel tenants and civic leaders of the Filipino community, including Chairman Ariston P. Armada of the Filipino American Council of Northern California and the Philippine consul-general in San Francisco. Alioto also invited key heads of city departments and their assistants to be on hand to give recommendations. They included M. Justin Herman, executive director of the San Francisco Redevelopment Agency, and his assistant, Gerry Flamm; Eaneas Kane, executive director of the Housing Authority; and John H. Tolan, the mayor's staff deputy for development.[57] Herman and his assistants were major figures in planning the expansion of the city's financial district. Their proposals included removing 4,000 working poor from the Yerba Buena District.[58] The tenants and organizers viewed the meeting as a publicity stunt designed to allay public fears.

At the meeting, Mayor Alioto proposed a three-step solution to the I-Hotel controversy. His first step was to move the residents into nearby hotels. If the rents were higher than the thirty-five dollars a month the I-Hotel charged, the City Rent Supplement Program would make up the difference for a period of up to eighteen months. Then the tenants would be relocated as a group to a new, 110-unit housing center built by the city's Housing Authority at 550 Ellis Street, a site already approved for construction of senior-citizen housing. Finally, Mayor Alioto would ask Shorenstein to give him assurances that the property would be sold or leased only to people who were interested in developing a Filipino cultural center on the site.[59]

At first glance, Alioto's plan seemed reasonable to outsiders who did not live at the I-Hotel—especially to Filipino community members who might be lured by the proposal to develop the cultural center. The tenants, however, rejected it after further investigation. They objected to the proposed Ellis Street site because it was located in the well-known, high-crime Tenderloin District and because it was far away from Chinatown, where they bought their Asian food. They also objected to the temporary relocation to the Padre and Hyland hotels because it would scatter them and shatter their informal personal networks.[60] As a reporter for the *Philippine News,* a leading San Francisco Filipino newspaper, observed, "The tenants ha[ve] become so emotionally attached to the hotel that the threat of eviction strikes [them] as inhuman and unfair. They want to stick together where they are."[61] Moreover, according to Emil de Guzman and Frank Celada, the tenants did not trust the city officials' promises to keep them together as a group. They knew, intuitively, that staying in control of the building was the key strategy for tenants in any dispute with a landlord.

At a meeting with Mayor Alioto held in the UFA's basement office on Kearny Street, the tenants presented a petition, signed by sixty-eight of them, rejecting the three-step plan. They demanded instead that they be allowed to lease the hotel from its owners. The mayor, irritated by their obstinacy, retorted that the tenants had to "face the realities of the world and realize that getting a lease on this property might be a difficult thing because of the economics. Without being emotional about it, let's be humanitarian and then practical about it." Assemblyman John Burton fired back that he would be "emotional," because the basic issue was "between a parking lot or a dwelling place for people." Mayor Alioto conceded, "I'm going to explore fully the possibilities of staying here. But consider my plan and yours. I'm quite convinced mine is better." He also asked Filipino community leaders "not to give false hopes to the tenants." Ness Aquino, however, believed that Alioto's plan did not meet the tenants' needs, and at the meeting he shouted, "The Mayor has not answered our problem. He has made no commitment."[62]

Meanwhile, support for the tenants grew. On May 23, 1969, the Center for Community Change of Washington, D.C., a social-action foundation financed by the Ford Foundation with close ties to the United Auto Workers, pledged fifty thousand dollars to renovate and restore the I-Hotel to save the building from demolition and its residents from displacement. The money would be useless unless the UFA could lease the hotel from its present owners and managers, and, at least initially, this proposal did not meet with an encouraging response. According to the *San Francisco Chronicle*, when he heard about the foundation money, Shorenstein told Marquez Bautista, the UFA's attorney, by phone that he "wasn't leasing the hotel to any do gooders."[63]

Half of the 196 tenants who had been living in the hotel at the time of the fire left because they feared eviction or more arson. Those who remained steadfastly resisted eviction and relocation. To defy eviction, the UFA held an "Eviction Day Party" at the hotel's Manilatown Information Center, only to find out that the date of the eviction had been extended for another month, to July 1. At the time, sixty-nine-year-old Aniano (Antonio) Runiviar, a thirty-year U.S. Army veteran and pensioner, told a *Chronicle* reporter, "I only hope Mayor Joseph Alioto will do his utmost to help us." Other tenants declared that they "intend to stay since there is nowhere we can go and remain together as a community."[64]

Professional architects came forward to work with the UFA on developing plans and analyzing costs for renovating the hotel. Among them was John Bailey, director of the University of California Extension Community Design Center. At a meeting sponsored by the San Francisco Planning and Urban Renewal Association (SPUR), the official citizens' action committee created to fulfill the citizen-participation requirement for all of the city's renewal projects, Bailey posed the question succinctly and forcefully: "Is displacing these people at the hotel into this current housing market not ultimately more detrimental to their physical and mental safety than their living in a so-called fire trap?"[65] Few understood the housing crisis in San Francisco as Bailey did. The federal government had set standards for minimum vacancy rates to ensure mobility of 3 percent; by 1969, the residency vacancy rate in San Francisco had fallen to 1.1 percent, indicating just how threatened by displacement the tenants were.[66]

Although SPUR generally advanced redevelopment interests, it was by nature a citizen's committee, which meant that it had to provide a forum in which alternative views such as Bailey's could be voiced. SPUR passed a resolution to retain the hotel as a "community and living quarters" for its Filipino residents. In other words, Bailey's statement, linked to the mobilization of the I-Hotel supporters, forced SPUR to contradict—at least, temporarily—its intention to "gentrify" San Francisco, as expressed in its 1966 "Prologue for Action":

> If San Francisco decides to compete effectively with other cities for new "clean" industries and new corporate power, its population will move closer to standard White Anglo-Saxon Protestant characteristics. As automation increases, the need for unskilled labor will decrease. Economically and socially, the population will tend to range from lower mid-

> dle class through lower upper-class. . . . Selection of a population's composition might be undemocratic. Influence on it, however, is legal and desirable for the health of the city. A workable though changing balance of economic levels, social types, age levels, and other factors must be maintained. Influence on these factors should be exerted in many ways—for example, changing the quality of housing, schools, and job opportunities.[67]

Such plans to give San Francisco the ability to "compete" with other cities were in line with those of the Bay Area Council (BAC). Founded in 1944 as the Bay Regional Council, the BAC had a board of directors that included high officials from Bechtel Corporation, Pacific Gas and Electric, and other major corporations. BAC articulated a vision of San Francisco as part of a regional division of labor that facilitated the area's ability to exploit the so-called Pacific Rim:

> Under [the BAC's] plan, each part of the Bay Area would assume a specialization and thus eliminate inefficient replications of industries and/or tasks. San Francisco would become the administrative, financial, business, cultural, and entertainment center. The Greater East Bay would maintain the heavy industries and serve as the transportation center. The Northern East Bay would concentrate on oil refining, and the Peninsula would headquarter light manufacturing and electronics. A system of high-speed freeways would link these areas together while a mass transit system [Bay Area Rapid Transit] would shuttle workers back and forth from their working places to their homes. BART specifically was designed to transport suburban white collar workers to the financial district.[68]

Thus, the notion of "home versus parking lot," no matter how imperfect the "home," conjured up competing visions of the city's future. Given the tight housing market, real questions arose about whether a future San Francisco would have any low-income and, specifically, non-white communities. Certainly, "a population closer to standard White Anglo-Saxon Protestant characteristics," as SPUR's "Prologue for Action" called for, did not include elderly Filipino bachelors. Yet the city's overwhelmingly Democratic leadership faced the difficult task of appealing to its natural base to support progress that ultimately would undermine that constituency's own self-interest.

In that light, Mayor Alioto met with Filipino American members of the Richmond Optimist Club of San Francisco in early June to explain the history of the controversy and the issues involved. He hoped to appease the audience, most of whom were prominent local professionals and leaders in Filipino American organizations, as well as Democratic Party voters. At the meeting, Deputy John Tolan explained:

> There is a limit to what the Mayor's Office can do. We are trying our best to mediate so that the controversy will be resolved to the satisfaction of all concerned, but we have to realize that the duty of the Mayor is to protect the rights of all citizens. In the event of conflict of interest between human rights and property rights, the sympathy of the Mayor is for the former. However, in such a case, the Mayor's Office does not possess the power to suppress private property in favor of human rights.[69]

At the same time, Tolan informed the Filipino leaders that the Mayor's Office still stood by the recommended solutions outlined earlier. Tenants and Supporters wondered whether Mayor Alioto understood that relocation of the tenants to housing comparable to the I-Hotel was next to impossible. The fact that the two hotels Alioto had proposed as temporary relocation sites had been both condemned in 1966 did nothing to reassure the I-Hotel tenants. Edith Witt, a member of the Human Rights Commission staff, was invited to view a third site, the Reno Hotel in the South of Market area. She described that inspection:

> The hotel had been vacant for over ten years. It was owned by the Potlatch Corporation, which said it would rehabilitate the building for the tenants. Well, it was vacant because that whole area was sinking—it was built on bay fill. The hallways looked like this—and she made an inverted V with her arms. . . . There stood John Tolan, the mayor's assistant, and the Potlatch representative, saying, "Oh, no, no problem at all." Later they found it would have cost $1 million more to fix up the place than if the building weren't sinking.[70]

Tenants and supporters believed not only that the mayor's plans and promises were flawed but that they were disingenuous. Offering such doubtful sites at the same time that vital services such as electricity, heating, and plumbing at the I-Hotel were being disrupted raised further questions. Were central relocation efforts that were purported to help the tenants genuine, or were they actually designed to harass the tenants into moving out of the I-Hotel, thereby eliminating any basis for contention?[71]

A Lease Is Signed

On June 18, one week after the city's meeting with Filipino American community leaders, the UFA and Milton Meyer and Company reached an agreement that would become effective on July 1, 1969. The lease agreement's terms included a rental fee of about forty thousand dollars per year to be paid to the landlord for three years, until June 30, 1972, a sum that tripled the rent from thirteen thousand dollars. Milton Meyer and Company also had the option to cancel the lease at any time after the first two years, provided that the company gave six months' written notice and reimbursed the UFA for costs incurred in the rehabilitation of the hotel, a sum of nearly thirty thousand dollars. The UFA also guaranteed to buy a 25 million dollar insurance policy to protect Milton Meyer and Company against any potential liability. Finally, tenants would be responsible for paying an additional twenty-three thousand dollars for yearly property taxes.[72]

Student supporters of the I-Hotel considered the terms of the lease exceptionally onerous, particularly the requirement that "the UFA would be held responsible for the repair of the fire damaged wing (a cost of over $80,000)."[73] Still, the UFA hailed the lease as a victory. The association had mobilized support from sympathetic politicians, professionals, and prominent leaders in the Filipino community and obtained a commitment from Bank of America to borrow forty-eight thousand dollars for repairs to the fired-damaged section of the hotel. Mayor Alioto reaffirmed his commitment to help find the residents an acceptable permanent home, and city officials assured them that they would have a reasonable amount of time to meet code requirements. Finally, the Center for Community Change of Washington, D.C., agreed to guarantee the rent under the three-year lease.[74]

Buoyant with the news of a new lease, Aquino, the UFA's president, challenged the community to refurbish the entire building and resurrect community life. Some radical students and others complained that Aquino was "bourgeois" and that his restaurant, Mabuhay Gardens, which he had opened on the ground floor of the I-Hotel in December 1969, profited greatly from the activists who frequented the hotel. Aquino's goal was to create a bustling area for the Filipino community at large, just as Kearny Street had been from the 1930s to the 1950s. His own economic vitality was always part of that vision, and he never disguised that fact.[75]

Still, Aquino's ambivalent class position was reflected in many of his views. Perhaps his business sense told him that private-property rights ultimately would trump low-income housing. After the agreement was signed, he announced that the UFA had assured Shorenstein that it would not oppose demolition of the I-Hotel after the new lease expired. He even thanked Shorenstein and called him a "tough negotiator."[76] Nevertheless, the signing of the three-year lease seemed to end the battle—or, at least, offer time to build support against future threats of eviction and to allow Filipino American students to rebuild the International Hotel.

CHAPTER THREE

"Peace with a Lease"

Renovation and Revolution, 1969–74

Claiming a Space

The signing of the three-year lease in 1969 ushered in a new period of renewal that the tenants and their supporters called "Peace with a Lease." The tenants and students felt proud to have defended their community. The Asian American students believed that they had combined militancy and service in ways similar to the Black Panthers' free breakfast programs for children and other activities to aid the African American community. At that moment, an assertion of community consciousness could be rooted in an actual place.

During this period, intra-ethnic ties within the Asian American movement strengthened, and cross-generational bonds within the Filipino community matured. However, the various ethnic groups within the Asian American movement began to be pulled in apparently contradictory directions. At the same time that the pan–Asian American movement consolidated, developing class-based analyses of oppression that linked all Asians as a single racial or national minority, individual ethnic groups increasingly focused on organizing their own communities. The more radical elements joined the "multinational" and "multiracial" New Left parties that had begun to emerge after the demise of Students for a Democratic Society in 1969. These parties often promoted a strong Third World nationalist consciousness, reflected in ongoing debates on whether to characterize ethnic groups as "racial" or "national" minorities.[1]

Despite jubilation at the signing of the lease, the number of tenants at the I-Hotel did not return to the level it had reached before the first eviction notice was served. The reduced number of tenants, coupled with the visibility of Asian youth in the renovation, persuaded some of the public and politicians that the struggle had been overrun by radicals, displacing the elderly from its center. At least fifty of the original tenants remained—they had nowhere else to go;

resistance was their last stand. But as new elderly tenants arrived after being evicted from nearby hotels, the base of the struggle among the elderly eventually expanded.

The uncertainty and stress of the conflict weakened the hotel's economic base. The fire partially ruined a floor, preventing those rooms from being rented. Only 65 of the hotel's 184 rooms were occupied, and the ground-floor, commercial storefronts had long been vacant. The I-Hotel's manager, Joe Diones, decided to look for commercial renters, hoping to net thirty thousand dollars a year in rent for the next three years. He sought businesses whose political character would lend support to the tenants. Diones was politically and economically pragmatic: He rented spaces not only to small, Asian-owned businesses, such as a key shop and a sundry shop, but also to new Asian American organizations that wanted to open offices and community centers. Diones also recruited Charles Smith, a tenant, to help him manage and coordinate support for the I-Hotel.

Among the groups that moved in was Leways (Legitimate Ways), a self-help group of street kids founded to combat juvenile delinquency. Inspired by the Black Panthers, they named themselves the "Red Guards" and opposed the traditional Chinatown leadership. Other Asian American groups established community centers, an art center, a bookstore, and headquarters for Asian American revolutionary organizations. The Asian Community Center (ACC), the Chinese Progressive Association (CPA), Everybody's Bookstore, the Kearny Street Workshop, and the newspaper *Kalayaan* were among the community groups that set up storefronts during this period. For the youth-oriented Asian American organizations, the space became available at the right time. When they moved into the storefronts on Kearny Street, the core of support for the I-Hotel expanded. Because they were commercial tenants of the I-Hotel, the public and politicians would perceive their involvement in the fight against eviction as legitimate. All of the groups gathered on Kearny Street created a concentrated space that provided easy access and exchange between Asian American students and the community. "Kearny Street" now came to mean not only the social scene of the manongs but also the site of Asian American mobilization.

The Kearny Street block may have been the only place that these "upstarts" could have rented space. Traditional Chinese organizations were wary of the new youth groups because they openly questioned the status quo in Chinatown. Traditional Chinese leaders believed that youth activism upset the image they had carefully cultivated during the postwar years as an obedient, law-abiding citizenry whose only desire was to advance their material success—that is, a "model minority." The young activists exposed the deplorable and cramped housing conditions, delinquency, unemployment, and, especially, police harassment in the area. Young professionals conducted housing studies to investigate living conditions, revealing that Chinatown had the highest population density and the worst housing conditions in San Francisco.[2]

Although the model-minority image may have been an improvement over the old "Yellow Peril" stereotype, the youth felt it was time to address pressing community issues openly. Traditional leaders had acted as gatekeepers for the community in dealing with the so-called outside world and publicly opposed voicing internal community problems. For example, they were particularly worried that drawing attention to police harassment would also highlight the gang problems in Chinatown. The Chinese Chamber of Commerce regarded gangs as an embarrassment; it also worried that tourists would be scared away. When youth groups wanted federal government funds to set up their own centers to deal with gangs, traditional leaders were opposed. Young activists proposed more recreational facilities and employment. The Chinese Chamber of Commerce blocked these efforts, as well. When Leways moved into the I-Hotel, it brought in pool tables and made the space a youth hangout.[3]

The conservative politics that dominated Chinatown had a base in the politics of China itself: Chinatown's traditional leaders continued to support the nationalist Kuomintang even after it was defeated by the Chinese Communist Party in 1949. Traditional Chinese organizations led by the Chinese Six Companies—the alliance of kinship-based mutual-aid societies that effectively had ruled Chinatown since the Gold Rush—opposed the communist regime of Mao Tse-tung. The Kearny Street groups, by contrast, supported the Chinese revolution and admired Chairman Mao and his Cultural Revolution (although reliable information about the actual course of the leftist upheaval in the People's Republic of China was very limited). Traditional leaders attempted to isolate the young activists by labeling them communists, a label that was usually enough to scare landlords from renting them space. Many of the groups found refuge on Kearny Street, where they opened both public and social spaces to conduct their own organizing.

Filipinos, who were not so affected by Chinatown's politics, established two organizations in the I-Hotel's commercial spaces: *Kalayaan*, a newspaper for the left wing of the Filipino community, and the Manilatown Information Center. Manilatown–Chinatown was considered an underserved community under the criteria of President Johnson's War on Poverty. Led by Bert Esteva, the Manilatown Information Center received funds that allowed young community activists and budding professionals to provide needed social services to the community.[4]

At first, the elderly were suspicious of government help. Some of the old militants were used to demanding their fair share from private businesses, but demanding equal rights from the government had not been part of their experience. Further, their pride prevented them from accepting anything that smacked of the dole.[5] Despite the manongs' wariness of the government, the Manilatown Information Center's young activists told them that they deserved assistance as contributing members of society; that they paid taxes and helped build the wealth of society and thus were entitled to a payback from the government. Many of the manongs were veterans who had fought battles side by side with Americans, and they began to feel that they were entitled to receive aid because of their military service. With the help of the young activists, the tenants began to make necessary links between government accountability and the anti-eviction battle. As one elderly manong said, "We just want our fair share—no more, no less."[6]

Students from all over the Bay Area came to help with the renovation of the I-Hotel and to join in the various community activities on Kearny Street. The period of "Peace with a Lease" allowed time for pan-ethnic Asian American unity, as well as individual Chinese and Filipino ethnic identities, to develop. For the Filipino American community, this was a period of intergenerational bonding between elders and youth and of the development of a distinct Filipino American left wing rooted in community politics. While activists grasped the need for Asian American political unity to support the I-Hotel, the Chinese and Filipinos understood that they would have to target their own communities to gain support for the cause.

Renovation and Renewal

Ness Aquino, UFA's president, put out the call to renovate the hotel right after the fire in the spring of 1969. The number of volunteers was initially low.[7] At first, only a few students from San Francisco State, City College of San Francisco, and UC Berkeley responded. But news of the lease spread, and during the summer, students of all races and religious affiliations joined in renovating and refurbishing the hotel. By the end of 1969, the UFA's appeal to the community had attracted an even wider range of volunteer groups than Asian Americans students. Students from Lowell High School devoted several weekends to cleaning and painting the rooms. Two groups of Quaker college and high-school students from the San Francisco Bay Area volunteered; other Bay Area church groups and the American Jewish Congress joined; and students involved with the Jewish Community Center provided materials, furnishings, and paint. Individuals who had heard about the hotel dropped in to volunteer their energy, while Diones and a volunteer, Richard Barkley, coordinated contributions and work schedules.

The Center for Community Change retained an architect, Alice Barkley, and a licensed building contractor, Jim Holland, to plan and supervise the repairs and reconstruction. Some of these activists represented established, older civil-rights groups. Groups in Chinatown such as Self-Help for the Elderly regarded the threat of eviction as an attack on Chinatown, and the UFA was able to solicit help from them.

The highest priority was given to ensuring the safety of the tenants. Building-code violations that were most critical to the safety of the tenants were addressed first. Fire exit signs went up; fire extinguishers were placed at the end of every hallway; a sprinkler system and firebreak doors were installed; and some rooms were left vacant to be used as fire exits. No longer could detractors claim that the building was a fire trap. In addition, tenants maintained a twenty-four-hour security watch to protect the building against arson, particularly since they suspected arson in the previous fire. All building-code violations in the residential portion of the hotel were repaired. When the day-to-day work centered on the rehabilitation—that is, painting, refurbishing, and reconstruction—the center of gravity shifted from the experts to the students.[8] In addition to repairing the fire damage they cleaned all of the rooms and halls; painted; repaired plumbing and electrical wiring; and replaced broken windows. A wing of one floor had been devastated and needed to be completely rebuilt.

Asian American college students from UC Berkeley , San Francisco State, and City College of San Francisco did the bulk of the volunteer work, with the Berkeley students shouldering most of the day-to-day tasks. Some even decided to live at the hotel so they could stay in touch with the volunteer efforts and the needs of the elderly. "I first got involved in the IH through [the] UFA downstairs, providing social services to the tenants," recalled Jeanette Lazam. "Jovina Navarro got me a job as a work-study student at San Francisco State through Human Resources Development. . . . There were other activists there, such as Wilma and Raddy Cadorna, John Foz, Bullet Marasigan. I had an emotional connection to the IH. On the day-to-day level, I constructed a dry wall but mainly did clean-up with the UC Berkeley students."[9] Ed Ilumin, a student from PACE, the Filipino student group at San Francisco State, initially became involved as part of the off-campus activities funded by the Associated Students Union. He later became the UFA student liaison, a staff position funded by the Center for Community Change.[10]

Bill Sorro, another early activist, had grown up in the Fillmore District, and his father had often taken him to visit Manilatown as a child and teenager. He was not a student. He performed with the Buchanan YMCA dance group and did occasional work on the waterfront. He moved into the I-Hotel, staying there as a tenant until 1974:

> I was just another tenant, I paid my $45 a month in rent, I mean, I had responsibilities there—I painted, cleaned bathrooms, really whatever needed to be done. I wanted to get involved in the Filipino community, so I knew the issues, but I really saw myself as another tenant. . . . I related to the old-timers. I was part of them. They were like the relatives in my family. They were like my uncles, you know.[11]

Sorro became a spokesman for the tenants, and he developed such strong family bonds there that, when he married Giuliana Milanese in 1972, the wedding was held at the hotel.

With the new lease securing the building for at least two years, along with the possibility of a one-year extension, the hotel could become a comfortable home for the elderly and a location for Asian American youth to get involved in their communities. Emil de Guzman, who took an increasingly leading role in the anti-eviction struggle, told of his early experiences of transforming the hotel:

> The Hotel has changed from a flophouse to something better. Now we have a recreation center, we have a social center. We used to have a clinic. We weren't only getting the place to look nice, but we were developing a relationship between the tenants and the supporters. We painted, tore out old rugs, fixed walls, to make the hotel a better place to live and we also won the trust of the tenants. We were so angry—why didn't the owners do this? Why didn't the city do this? We weren't hotel managers.[12]

Despite anger at the owners because of their negligence—or, perhaps, because of it—the work of transforming the hotel became a tremendous organizing tool. For almost the entire period of the lease, UC Berkeley students organized youth from community organizations, churches, and the colleges. Filipino organizations on campuses and the Asian American community were the strongest supporters, particularly in the wake of the Third World campus strikes.

Every Saturday during the lease, contingents of student volunteers went to the International Hotel to work on the repairs. Sympathy for the tenants from the Filipino community reached the entire West Coast as news of their plight spread through the Filipino identity movement. Students came from Stockton and Los Angeles, and from as far away as Seattle and Honolulu. Filipino American students who were reluctant to join in the Third World strikes on campuses were proud to help the elderly Filipino and Chinese men.

I visited the I-Hotel in 1970 as a member of Search to Involve Pilipino Americans (SIPA), a new youth organization based in the Los Angeles area. Our goal was to bring Filipino culture back to young Filipino Americans who had been assimilated into American culture. We performed a skit for the tenants. We also found time to party with Bill Sorro, Emil de Guzman, and other young activists and to catch the sights. We visited Coit Tower and saw a spectacular night view of San Francisco Bay. This was the first time I had left my home community on a field trip, and I was not the only one to explore the wider world and to discover other student activists because of the allure of the I-Hotel.

The renovation of the I-Hotel was an unprecedented moment that energized Filipino youth. The process of fusing generations and outlooks formed by varied class and immigrant experiences generated a new-found excitement, as if long-lost relatives had been brought together for the first time. "A lot of people have struck a nail there and lost some sleep and been affected emotionally by those tenants over the years," said Reverend Antonio Ubalde, the Methodist minister who presided over the UFA. "There's something in Filipino culture that just won't let its people suffer so much. It's something young adult whites haven't had before. We call it the *Kababayan* spirit, that extended family spirit."[13]

The elderly bachelors had found enduring respect and recognition from the children they had been prevented from fathering. The students had found their history, their cultural roots, and their living forebears along with the possibilities of political activism rooted in concrete community concerns in a homelike hotel within a mythic space aptly named "Manilatown." With all the painting, hammering, and sweeping that went into the building's renovation, the construction of a previously undeveloped sense of Filipino American ethnic identity had begun. The relationships became intensely personal and political. The students felt that they had a stake in the struggle. Sorro described some of the activities that brought tenants and young people together:

> As part of our work as budding revolutionaries, we tried to figure out how to change the environment of the community of people in the hotel to see themselves as being part of more than just their locked-in building. We provided social activities; we got a bus from UC Berkeley and took them out for day trips to the beach to have a barbecue and that kind of thing. I think we really succeeded in developing a trust between the young people and the tenants. Now they may not have agreed with all of our revolutionary rhetoric, but they were like your grandparents. They understood your heart and showed a lot of patience with you. It was a special thing.[14]

Because of their own personal experiences with class struggle, part of the "special thing" for the elderly was seeing a new generation of radicals appear in the community. After having been ignored for so long, they felt vindicated. And the young people rediscovered the manongs, the ancestral roots of their own radical impulses, allowing them to recover their own sense of historical connection.

At roughly the same time, other community projects brought together youth and students with similar concerns about the elderly and poor in Manilatowns. In the International District of Seattle and the International District of Honolulu, Filipinos, other Asian Americans, and progressive white people formed alliances to stop evictions that were resulting from urban redevelopment. At Agbayani Village, a UFW project in Delano, California, students mobilized to help construct the retirement home that would house Filipino workers. In Delano, Isleton, and Walnut Grove, in California's Central Valley, youth set up free clinics for farm workers and the poor in which social workers and health-care workers volunteered time to provide free health care.[15]

In each of these projects, the focus was on the manongs. The youth discovered and venerated their elders, and they sought out the various ways to come to their aid as a part of their own effort to build a self-conscious Filipino American movement. In Oakland, the Pilipino Youth Development Council expressed this combination of concern and rediscovery in brochures and flyers to generate support for Project Manong, a housing project for the elderly, in 1972:

> The Manongs, pioneers of the Filipino community, constitute a vast number of poor and retired men who are spread throughout the United States. Their entire adult lives have been hampered by severe social and economic hardships which are now becoming more exposed and uncovered. The Manongs' issues and problems are becoming the concern of the Filipino Community. The struggle is to alter the unchanged course that has deprived them of their humanity and democratic rights. To understand their present circumstances is to unravel their past history and to view their lives in a clear perspective.[16]

The process of building support for the International Hotel tenants was an organic part of the struggle to build a movement of Asian American consciousness as well as an ethnic-based identity within the Filipino community. The I-Hotel struggle became the place where Asian American students could serve their communities. As a result of the Third World Strike, courses were designed to do fieldwork in the community: "Only through our initiative are we able to meet the people we study, learn from them the knowledge they have gained from first-hand experience, know them as people, and together work for solutions."[17] Community involvement was eventually institutionalized as part of the Third World Colleges and, later, ethnic studies programs, and involvement became an enduring component of higher-education pedagogy as "community service learning."[18] As one student broadside explained, "The hotel has brought on a new consciousness among us by encouraging an interaction between the people and our education."[19]

With all the activity by the youth to renovate the building, the International Hotel began to attract new tenants. By 1972, there were about 130 people living at the hotel, about double the number when the lease was signed. A *San Francisco Chronicle* reporter described the room rented by Claudio Domingo as "light, clean, and freshly painted—far different from the dank Tenderloin hotel rooms he faces if the eviction resistance fails. He refuses to even think about losing. No longer a 'fleabag hotel,' an elderly pensioner could not find a cleaner, safer, or more pleasant place to live."[20] Recreational activities such as bingo, movie nights, Sunday morning brunches, and picnics helped to promote a family and community atmosphere.[21]

The bonds created between the tenants and organizers had long-lasting effects. "I credit Emil [de Guzman] and all the rest of his companions," said Carl Regal, an I-Hotel tenant. "If it was not for the student worker, this hotel should have been broken down already, and I credit these girls for cooking the good food for the picnic. Now those picnics—there's food once or twice a week—they are building the morale of the people staying here. That promotes a very good feeling, people's closeness of feeling."[22]

Another tenant, Frankie de los Reyes, told the reporter about the atmosphere at the hotel: "I have no place, no relative or friends except the people here. There is no place I can go except on the sidewalks. I am old. I had a stroke two years ago which makes it difficult for me to move around. I have many friends here. We have a wonderful Filipino community. We take good care of each other."[23]

By the time the agreement approached its end on June 30, 1972, the UFA felt that it had accomplished its task of stopping the eviction and renovating the I-Hotel. Aquino and the other members of the UFA decided to disband. The students and tenants felt that the leadership should come not from a community-led organization but from the tenants themselves. Students helped the tenants to establish their own organization. At the same time, they set up a separate United Committee to Save the International Hotel and for Low-Cost Housing to drum up support in the Chinatown–Manilatown community.[24] Although the United Committee did not truly function as an organization, the coordination of community groups with the tenants continued to grow. Over the course of 1973–74, the International Hotel Tenants Association (IHTA) was established. The IHTA was the prime vehicle for the tenants' political involvement, and it took on the leading role, bringing the tenants together with student activists, represented by Diones, the hotel's manager, and supported by Emil de Guzman, the leader of the young activists.[25]

After June 30 passed, the landlord made no move to evict the tenants. Shorenstein appeared to maintain the status quo by extending the lease another year. Rent was collected from the tenants monthly, with no significant changes, and the hotel continued to develop its own culture during relative calm. This did not mean that there were no internal struggles. Charles Smith, vice-chairman of the IHTA, began to take on a more domineering role. He was ousted by the tenants in 1974. Joe Diones, the chairman, appointed Emil de Guzman to take Smith's place, and the alliance of tenants and supporters was brought into the official core of the IHTA. Finally, it was revealed in March 1974 that a new owner had bought the hotel, and the struggle entered a new stage.[26]

Cross-Generational Bonding and Gender

The fact that the I-Hotel was primarily a male environment and that the elderly were "bachelors"—whether unmarried or married to women in the Philippines they had not seen in a very long time—was not lost on the youthful organizers. Awareness of the cruel history that caused the gender imbalance in the manongs' community helped the youth to understand how class exploitation and racial exclusion can perversely distort and destroy human values. Many of the bachelors relied on prostitutes for female companionship and sexual relations. Until 1971, it was an open secret that prostitutes came to the hotel to service their customers at night. When Joe Diones and Emil de Guzman mobilized volunteers to rebuild the fire-damaged hotel and create a more wholesome environment, they also "cleaned up" this aspect, discouraging prostitutes as well as drug addicts from entering the hotel.[27]

Most of the time, the female volunteers were respected for the help and support they gave to the struggle and were treated like nieces or daughters. Sometimes, however, they were subjected to sexual advances from the elderly men. "There were times when some tenants had romantic thoughts about me, but I didn't entertain any of those thoughts, nor did I encourage it," Jeanette Lazam remembered.[28] When the issue was brought up to the I-Hotel's young male organizers, they did not know how to approach it, particularly because gender dynamics were not seen as central to the struggle. The activists tended to subordinate women's concerns, Jeanette recalled: "Women-of-color activists were considered 'pure revolutionaries.' Women's oppression was secondary, and any thoughts about it were suppressed."[29]

Filipina activists rarely organized separately from men, and they did not address women's issues outside the context of Philippine liberation or the democratic rights of Filipino Americans. On a programmatic level, Filipinas asserted that the experiences of the Filipina could not be separated from broader issues of racism, imperialism, and bourgeois class rule. Also, when the Katipunan ng mga Demokratikong Pilipino (KDP), the main left-wing organization in the struggle, was formed in 1973, it promoted the full equality of women within its ranks—and more broadly—as necessary for the revolutionary transformation of society. Both the advanced qualities and limitations of this stance were expressed in a resolution on combating male supremacy within the ranks of the KDP:

> The complete liberation of women can be accomplished only hand in hand with the revolution and the victory of the working class. . . . Manifestations of male supremacist ideas may consist of their assumption that women comrades are inherently less politically developed and incapable of developing equally like their male comrades; or that women comrades are less capable of leading and making correct political decisions. Being a form of elitism, male supremacist ideas result in shutting off the female comrades from active participation and the fullest development of those comrades' leadership potential.[30]

A great number of women would play leading roles in the KDP, and the need to support that participation was understood early on. When I arrived in San Francisco in 1971, for example, I already had two children, and a third was born a year later. Members of Kalayaan and then the KDP took collective responsibility for organizing a child-care system. Without this help, I would not have been able to play any role—much less one of leadership—in the I-Hotel struggle. However, tensions between men and women within the Filipino movement for the most part were subsumed for the sake of unity and considered "secondary" to the primary struggles against racism and national liberation for the Philippines.

Coping with the romantic inclinations and sexual frustration of elderly men was never discussed in a theoretical fashion within the framework of the activist groups. An advance by an old gentleman posed a practical problem to be tackled within this particular struggle, and most of the young Filipinas from UC Berkeley and San Francisco State simply tried to ward off the manong and avoid any larger issue or complaint. However, young Asian American women who had moved into the I-Hotel to help with the organizing formed a women's caucus to discuss the matter. The caucus, inspired by the newly emerging women's liberation movement, was unusual, although the action it decided to take remained within the bounds of the hotel's traditional social structure. The women told Diones about the sexual approaches, and he chastised the offenders by asking them how they would feel if their own daughters were treated in such a manner.[31] Diones responded in his usual rough, gruff longshoreman style. Although his build was average, he had large, muscular arms, and he looked tough. His years of working with longshoremen and sailors gave him the background to take on adversaries. His mannerisms were up front and confrontational, and the intimidation usually worked. The offensive behavior abruptly ended.

Social activities at the hotel, including brunches, dances, and outings, or just taking walks, sometimes became fertile ground for friendships between the generations. One seventy-nine-year-old manong, Frankie Alarcon, talked about having girlfriends in many lands and showed snapshots of his many romances.[32] Social events on Sundays and sometimes on Saturday evenings at the Manilatown Information Center provided opportunities for Frankie to show off his foxtrot, tango, and two-step, and he loved to dance with the young girls who came to help. No other tenant was as smooth or as eager a dancer as Frankie. One Filipina activist recalled his enthusiasm:

> "Virgie, you just in time to dance!" Frankie greeted me with glee. There was no escape now. "I've been waiting for you!" [H]e took my hand and led me to the small space between the band and the dining area. Scattered applause and shouts of admiration for Frankie's boldness. Frankie led me gracefully into a foxtrot, while I tried not to step on his feet or bump his belly.[33]

I also danced with Frankie every Sunday, and he was always a perfect gentleman.

Frankie was a sailor and often left the I-Hotel, but he felt that the hotel was his home, and he regularly returned. He had lived at the I-Hotel off and on since 1918. He was among the many Filipinos who joined the U.S. Navy when the Philippines was still a colony and the United States occupied bases at Sangley,

Cavite, and Subic Bay, Zambales.[34] Frankie, an enthusiastic, lively, and worldly character, was a familiar figure on Kearny Street. He was always perfectly manicured, with slicked black hair, and dressed in a fine suit; his dedication to the struggle was as strong as his loyalty to his service in the military and his love of life. He fought, undaunted and filled with warmth and humor, until he succumbed to illness.

Gender dynamics erupted in other parts of the movement—such as women's ability to lead or take power—but they did not come up in the context of the I-Hotel struggle because cultural traditions made it seem "natural" for Filipinos to respect the ideas of women, especially those who worked to advance the struggle. Filipino indigenous values have persisted despite the influence of Spanish values that relegated women to a peripheral role or American values that subsumed women within the nuclear family. Filipino culture tends to elevate women's participation and opinions, especially as they relate to issues of family, home, and children. Except for those in the upper classes, the majority of women in the Philippines tend to be productive members of the family, working side by side with their husbands or brothers. Bilateral relations within the family were prevalent in Filipino culture before the Spanish instituted patriarchal relations, and these indigenous patterns of women's roles persist in the lives of Filipino families today.[35] Jeanette Lazam recalled that Filipina activists in the I-Hotel struggle "were revered, held up on a pedestal, such as the mother of the Filipino race and so forth." At the same time, Jeanette, as a young activist, was able to assert herself with ease: "I felt like I was just one of the boys and treated as such by the other manongs."[36] In the struggle for the International Hotel, Filipino women figured prominently because, in terms of cultural memory, they had never hesitated to help in situations in which the family was at stake. The I-Hotel movement was experienced subjectively as the "family" of the Filipino community.

Still, Filipinas did not fully understand how they affected the elderly men throughout the struggle. While young Filipinos found their identity in the struggles of these elderly men, the "bachelors" felt that they were finally getting the attention and respect they should have received throughout their lives. The women cemented these bonds as members of a family, but that did not necessarily relieve the elderly men's sexual frustration.

Although most of the tenants were men, the few women who lived at the I-Hotel played important roles. For example, Luisa de la Cruz, wife of Alfredo de la Cruz, served as a role model for the younger women. When the de la Cruzes arrived in San Francisco from the Philippines in April 1969, Alfredo suggested that they live at the International Hotel so that Luisa could stay active and busy, especially because she had no children. She agreed, and they immediately moved into the hotel.[37]

Mrs. D, as Luisa was affectionately called, was not known to the broader public as a leader because she chose to work in the background. She rarely made speeches, except once in March 1977 during an International Women's

Day Celebration. Even then, she was nervous and insisted that Emil de Guzman write the speech for her. Afterward, she declined all other invitations to speak in public. She had no problem speaking up among the tenants, however. She helped by providing a much needed family atmosphere for the elderly residents. On Sundays, she coordinated brunches that included music and dancing. These family-type gatherings were important for the elderly who had no families. The homelike atmosphere that she created also helped to cement the ties between the youth and elderly. Mrs. D made curtains for the hotel's airshaft windows and brought in plants to cultivate in the airshafts. These touches livened up the place and made it more pleasant for everyone. Also, because Mrs. D spoke Tagalog, she could provide a bridge between the assimilated youth who spoke no Filipino dialects and the elderly, who spoke mainly Tagalog. She encouraged the elderly to come to meetings and public gatherings, although she could not attend the meetings unless they were held at night, because she worked during the day.

Luisa de la Cruz was born on December 8, 1925, in Colocoan, Philippines. She worked all of her life and became quite sophisticated as a result of her various jobs. When she was fifteen, she worked in a rubber factory in the Philippines. During the Japanese occupation of the Philippines in World War II, her father disguised her as a boy so the Japanese soldiers would not sexually abuse her. As a young woman, she became tough and independent. As soon as she arrived in the United States in 1969, she found a job in the garment industry. During her eight-year stay at the I-Hotel, she also worked in a factory that made jewelry boxes and as a seamstress. She held a full-time job during the day, and in the evenings and on the weekends she worked at the I-Hotel preparing Filipino foods for the various outings and celebrations. She even had time to tend her small garden in the airshaft.

Mrs. D was an activist early in her life. She participated in union organizing in the Philippines because, as she explained, "the factory owner was a New York Jew, a liberal who allowed union organizing to take place at his factory." She seemed always to know what she wanted and was very blunt about it. She was not brash, however; in fact, she was quite sweet and charming. But when her leadership was called on, she usually responded affirmatively and forthrightly, especially if she knew what was required.[38] For example, one of the tenants, Claudio Domingo, made her the executor of his estate. After he died, she had to go to the bank to retrieve his belongings from a safe-deposit box. The bank representative rebuffed her and told her to come back later. She refused and patiently waited outside until the representative was forced to deal with her. He relented and opened Claudio's box. It was this kind of determination and sense of responsibility that Mrs. D brought to the I-Hotel struggle.[39]

Part of Mrs. D's commitment to the struggle came out of her sense of duty and responsibility to take care of family members. She had what we called the *bayanihan* spirit—that of helping your people or countrymen—and a sense of caring for the elderly. Both traits are valued in the Filipino culture and were important in the I-Hotel struggle, and her example had a great influence on the young Filipinas.

From Kalayaan to Katipunan

Another sector of Filipinos arrived on Kearny Street during this period: young revolutionaries radicalized in the Philippines who sought out their counterparts among progressive Filipino Americans. In June 1971, a dozen Filipino American activists and recent arrivals from the Philippines founded the anti-imperialist organization and newspaper collective Kalayaan (Freedom) International. The newspaper *Kalayaan International* took its name from the official organ of the revolutionary league founded by Andres Bonifacio, the peasant leader of the 1896 anticolonial struggle against Spain. The paper articulated opposition to racism and imperialism along with community support for the Philippine "national democratic" revolutionary movement, particularly the Communist Party of the Philippines (CPP) and the New People's Army (NPA). In the first issue of *Kalayaan International*, its editors stated:

> The *Kalayaan International* is today's answer to the need of the overseas Filipino to be aware of the multi-faceted problems of his people, both here and back home. Like its predecessors, it hopes to serve as the vanguard of truth and dissent, where truth is shielded by ignorance and dissent intimidated into silent discontent. We see the need for Kalayaan to be an important part of the Second Propaganda Movement to educate the people and to learn from the people. In the United States, this need becomes more acute as we realize the intricate workings of the American system and the Philippine experience.[40]

The First Propaganda Movement, led by Jose Rizal in Spain, preceded the revolutionary movement for independence in the Philippines. Inspired by Rizal, Filipinos launched the revolutionary newspaper *Kalayaan International.* Radicals in the 1970s linked their struggle to the past and, in calling for a Second Propaganda Movement, the new Kalayaan collective shouldered the responsibility for bringing about a renewed national liberation movement. Although exiles also established national democratic groups in Chicago and New York, Kalayaan was the only one to embody the merger of two distinct trends of radicalization within the community: radical student exiles who had recently arrived in the United States and American-born Filipinos, or Fil Ams.

When the United States relaxed its immigration laws in 1965, immigration opened to a new sector of Filipinos for whom the United States was the choice destination. The decision to come to the United States for middle-class professionals, college students, and political elites was determined by several factors, including the legacy of American colonization of the Philippines, the political repression of President Ferdinand Marcos's regime, and the attraction of America's economy. Philippine revolutionaries and student exiles arrived in the United States carrying the radicalized student movements' demands against imperialism and for the decolonization of Filipino national consciousness.

The radicals from the Philippines arrived with experience in the nationalist and student movements that opposed the Marcos dictatorship and, particularly, the reemergence of the communist movement. The Philippines' Maoist-influenced radicals declared the need to "rectify and reestablish" the old, pro-Soviet and moribund party. As a result, the new Communist Party of the Philippines (CPP) was founded in 1968 and launched its armed struggle with the formation of the NPA. Rene Cruz, who later chaired the KDP, described the growing radicalization:

> By 1969, the nationalist and student movement was already becoming more visible. The cry against U.S. domination, feudalism, corruption, and the country's use as an American launching pad for the war in Vietnam was getting louder. . . .
>
> In 1970, the ferment exploded into the First Quarter Storm. Attacks on the presidential palace and the U.S. Embassy echoed the revolutionary call for true independence, an end to landlordism and militarization—and the call for the overthrow of the corrupt order through armed struggle.[41]

The "First Quarter Storm" refers to massive student protests in the Philippines during the first quarter of the academic year. The protests were violently suppressed by the Marcos government.

The recent arrivals thus defined their identity and consciousness in terms of relations with both the Philippines and the United States. According to Linda Basch and colleagues, many immigrants can "forge and sustain multi-stranded social relations that link together their societies of origin and settlement."[42] Although physically dispersed, these immigrants remain socially, politically, culturally, and often economically part of the nation-states of their ancestors. At the same time, however, they face pressure to define themselves as Americans—even if hyphenated Americans. The circulation of people and relationships between home and host countries has come to be known as transnationalism. This is a global process that today is often associated with "globalization," or the flow of international capital, but it also involves colonial dynamics and other economic and social forces that predate the exiles of the 1960s and '70s. The manongs were also linked to their communities back in the Philippines, but the situation had changed in the new, post-independence, neocolonial environment. The class differences between the new immigrants and the manongs were dramatic, and the circulation of identities was more dynamic, faster, and more all-encompassing. At the time, the activists never referred to the idea of "transnationalism" or spoke about "transnational identities." They always referred to themselves within the context of nation-states and national liberation. But the reality was quite evident: The radical student exiles operated simultaneously within both fields, crossing cultural, political, and geographical boundaries. While maintaining political ties with their counterparts in the Philippines they formed new political alliances in the United States.[43]

Within this flow of cross-national and ethnic politics, the exile activists chose issues related to their home societies. The radicalized student exiles brought with them a sense of nationhood and a pride in a nation that was counterpoised to both Spanish and American colonial histories. This identity became a base for them to oppose racial subordination and white domination in the United States. Nationalist ethnic organizing was a response to their integration within the Filipino American community. However, only the revolutionary elements sought out a base among Filipino American youth searching for their identity. Newly formed immigrant groups usually do not organize among the American-born because of the fissures caused by economic, political, and cultural differences. Kalayaan and its successor, the KDP, were unique in this regard. Because of their consciousness about racism, imperialism, and colonialism, these new immigrants could ally easily with American-born Filipinos. Nationalist pride and the painful effects of racism helped to blend the two sectors.

The immigrants' pride in nation translated into many responsibilities. Sending remittances to their families "back home," as other generations of Filipinos had done, was only one aspect. Political relationships remained strong even as they became permanent residents or U.S. citizens. Their nationalist dream was deferred; they regarded themselves as exiles who, when the situation changed, would return to the Philippines. Immigrants of this new wave were acutely aware of the "brain drain" marked by their migration. The formation of U.S. organizations with "home roots" became the format for most ethnic organizations begun at this time. Professionals and semiprofessionals began to form organizations such as the Filipino Nurses Association, Filipino Postal Employees Association, and Filipino Medical Technicians alongside traditional regional or town organizations such as the Bicol Club and Pangasinan Club. Within the context of ethnic organizing, Kalayaan and the KDP were not unique formations but, rather, logical extensions of these broader social dynamics between the Philippines and the United States.

The new immigrants called themselves "Philippine nationals" or "foreign nationals," which emphasized that they would never fully assimilate culturally into their host society. But even the term "exile community" outgrew its usefulness as it became clear that the new arrivals were also settlers in the United States. The term the left used for these expatriate radicals was "revolutionary nationalists," emphasizing their anti-imperialist or anticolonial nationalism. When I asked Leni Marin, a recent exile at the time of KDP's founding, whether she had felt that one organization that combined "revolutionary nationalists" with Fil Ams should be formed in the United States, she gave a straightforward response: "Absolutely."[44]

Kalayaan, and the KDP, combined the Philippine student movement—characterized by advanced political theory, organizational sophistication, radical action, and direct experience of violent repression and resistance—with Filipino American radical politics, which challenged racism and class society in the United States. In the storefronts of the International Hotel, Philippine revolutionary nationalists sought out Filipino American radicals. The profound effect of the Philippine-born radicals on the Fil Am youth added to the radicalization already under way as a result of the anti–Vietnam War mobilizations, the growing awareness of national liberation movements for self-determination in the Third World, the Civil Rights Movement and Black Power Movement, and the struggle to build support for farm workers in the valleys of California.

When revolutionary-minded Filipino American activists radicalized on the campuses and Third World liberation movements arrived on Kearny Street, they came seeking a Filipino identity, which they found among the elderly at the International Hotel. Emil de Guzman recalled his experience of finding his identity on Kearny Street:

> Here was a place where I could see that my experience has put me through the context of the manongs and minority peoples. This was real first attempt to really see things—it was like a second birth. Up until then I always felt like it was something about me that I couldn't quite fully understand in my experience. When you see manongs as living proof of people who have been really subjugated socially, the miscegenation laws, a million stories, and you begin to really understand what it meant to be a minority.[45]

The proletarian history of the manongs inspired them, and they developed a deeper sense of what being an oppressed minority meant.

But the Fil Ams usually had weaker ties to the Philippines than did the transplanted youth from the Philippines, and they knew almost nothing about their history and culture. Although they may have participated in Filipino customs and community events as children, as young adults they did not continue these cultural practices. There were no language classes in the community among the American-born, as in Chinese and Japanese communities, where cultural ties were maintained in after-school programs or cultural courses. Ethnic politics as practiced by their parents no longer seemed relevant, and their parents' political views tended to be conservative and prowar. The generation gap between parents and youth developed into a chasm.

The assimilation strategy their parents had pursued did not work for the young Filipino Americans. Instead, they began to see themselves as "overseas

Filipinos"—as part of the Filipino diaspora—although the notion of return to the homeland did not necessarily mean a literal, physical or a permanent return. Returning to the homeland could be achieved through memory, written and visual texts, visits, monetary contributions, demonstrations, or a combination of all of these.[46] Filipino Americans began to identify themselves as part of the Philippine nation, despite their American birth and citizenship. Their identity had been transformed from American to "Pilipino" as transnational politics permeated the Filipino American community.[47]

As contacts with Philippine activists deepened, Filipino American political and ethnic identity grew away from its pan–Asian American political roots. While maintaining ties with other Asian American groups, Filipino American activists transformed political and ethnic identity from what was a romantic, even quaint and nostalgic, cultural connection into a self-aware political consciousness of anti-imperialism. The revival of precolonial values was part of the effort to liberate themselves from a colonial mentality. Histories of the Philippines produced by Filipino nationalists highlighted resistance to foreign domination and oppression. For example, Philippine revolutionary nationalists educated Fil Ams, and the Asian American movements more broadly, about the derivation of "gook," which was used as a derogatory term for Filipinos in the Philippine–American War of 1899–1902. Philippine activists also drew parallels between Filipino resistance to American annexation of the Philippines and the Vietnam War, between Filipino and Vietnamese opposition to foreign domination, and between the American war atrocities committed against Filipinos and Vietnamese.[48] Likewise, Filipino American history situated the Filipino immigrants' experiences within the context of other immigrant peoples who face exploitation, racism, and national oppression. When they elevated Filipino farm workers of the 1920s and 1930s to heroic status because of their fight against exploitation and their efforts to unionize, Filipino American activists found a way to draw on the Philippines' anticolonial past and its traditions of class resistance in the United States.

Without the early intervention by Philippine radicals, Filipino American activists might have joined the other emerging left-wing Asian American organizations formed around similar politics. Filipino Americans shared a history of oppression and exploitation with the Chinese community, for example. Both Filipino and Chinese I-Hotel tenants were used as cheap labor in agriculture and as low-wage service workers in the cities. Filipino and Chinese men had been subjected to the same anti-miscegenation laws and similar exclusion in bachelor communities. Without the Philippine radicals, the trajectory for progressive and radical Filipino Americans, like that of many Asian American organizations, would have been to merge into the various Marxist–Leninist party formations that had developed within and outside the Asian American groups on Kearny Street.[49] For example, one Chinese activist described her organization, I Wor Kuen, as a "pre-party formation"—a group seeking to forge a new U.S. communist party that could embrace a Chinese wing.[50] Instead, Filipino activists formed their own national Filipino organization, the KDP, and deferred the party question to be resolved outside the revolutionary nationalist formation. The KDP, like the other radical groups, advocated what could be described as Third World Marxism.[51]

In September 1972, Kalayaan called for a conference in San Francisco to set up a nationwide group to oppose repression in the Philippines. I attended the conference, and I remember feeling the jolt of surprise, dread, and excitement that went through everyone when we learned, soon after the conference began, that President Marcos had declared martial law. We were stunned by the serendipity of attending a national conference against repression just as Marcos was grabbing for total dictatorial power. The activists immediately began to plan nationwide demonstrations to protest Marcos's draconian measures, forming a new organization, the National Committee for the Restoration of Civil Liberties in the Philippines (NCRCLP). For the next several years, the NCRCLP became the major left-led coalition in the Filipino community that spearheaded actions to oppose the Marcos dictatorship.[52]

During the weekend of July 27–28, 1973, in the Santa Cruz Mountains of California, about seventy Philippine radical exiles and Filipino Americans formed the Katipunan ng mga Demokratikong Pilipino, or Union of Democratic Filipinos. When I saw so many radicals in the same room taking steps to launch this new organization, I shared the feeling that we were making history. The meeting established the KDP as a nationwide revolutionary mass organization patterned after Kabataang Makabayan (Nationalist Youth) and other youth organizations in the Philippines that had an affinity with the CPP. I really did not understand what a "revolutionary mass organization" was. Cynthia Maglaya, Melinda Paras, and other leaders explained that these organizations had a mass character—that is, anyone could join if he or she united with the principles of the organization. There were no elaborate structures or training. Yet I also learned later that such organizations had a discipline and structure like those composed of a core of highly disciplined cadre organizers. Most of the top leaders were eventually paid a nominal living wage for their full-time services, and the membership paid dues to maintain them. At first, though, everyone worked without organizational support.

The KDP, which initially united about two hundred activists from around the United States, was led by a nine-member National Council. The National Executive Board, the day-to-day leadership, included Bruce Occena, a mestizo Fil Am who had been radicalized during the Third World Strike at Berkeley; Melinda Paras, a mestiza Fil Am active in the antiwar movement in Wisconsin who had joined the Kabataang Makabayan in Manila and had been deported back to the United States after the declaration of martial law; and Cynthia Maglaya, a KM activist "instructed to build a support movement here."[53]

The core organizers lived in the San Francisco Bay Area, and the KDP's first national congress was convened in Berkeley in 1975. The new organization stated clearly that no dual memberships would be allowed with any communist party formation in the United States. This distinction between "mass" and "party" formations was adhered to rigorously and allowed the KDP to remain independent from most of the internecine battles of what was known as the New Communist Movement in the United States. By the late 1970s, a number of KDP leaders had become involved in broader U.S. "party-building" politics, but only after they had resigned their memberships in the KDP.

Soon after the KDP's founding, the *Kalayaan International* newspaper was replaced with a new national newspaper, *Ang Katipunan* (The Union), carrying the same name as the revolutionary group Andres Bonifacio led during the anti-Spanish revolution. The headquarters moved to Oakland. The move in some respects reflected the new, nationwide focus of the organization: The headquarters was no longer rooted on Kearny Street, which had ramifications for the ways in which the struggle to save the I-Hotel would be conducted. Except for one activist, Emil de Guzman, Filipino revolutionaries did not frequent Kearny Street until the KDP decided to treat the International Hotel as a local organizing campaign toward the end of 1975. Although individual activists allied with the KDP were already deeply embedded in the I-Hotel struggle, the KDP as an organization had not been involved. Other priorities became far more important, including launching chapters across the country, establishing regional leadership bodies, setting up the national office with bureaus and departments, and publishing and distributing a national newspaper. For a time, these political priorities had a negative effect on the number of activists actually deployed in the local San Francisco Bay Area and particularly at the I-Hotel.

The KDP's political program also involved a characteristically "dual" quality that would deeply affect the International Hotel. In the words of one longtime member, the "KDP would be a socialist organization with an uncompromising stand against racism and the capitalist system that begets this particular form of oppression."[54] This aspect of its program reflected the analysis that the Filipino community was a permanent component of American society, particularly the broader, multiracial working class, for which the International Hotel struggle was an integral part. At the same time, the organization "would oppose U.S. imperialist domination of poorer nations. In particular, it would organize support for the armed revolutionary fight in the Philippines against the U.S.-backed Marcos dictatorship."[55] This aspect of the KDP's program reflected the community's continuing involvement in the political struggles of the Philippines. Attempting to balance both aspects of this program became an ongoing challenge, particularly because there were social bases that encouraged an emphasis on one side or the other. Fil Ams tended to be more interested in the "domestic" side, while the revolutionary nationalists tended to be more concerned with fighting the U.S.-backed Marcos dictatorship.

Philippine revolutionaries espoused anti-imperialist politics and supported a Philippine national democratic revolution. Jose Sison, chairman of the CPP, whose analysis in *Philippine Society and Revolution* decisively shaped the party's program, followed China's strategy of People's War—that is, surrounding the cities through armed mobilization of peasants in the countryside—linked to an analysis of the uniquely archipelagic nature of the Philippines. He argued that the national democratic stage of the revolution, which included the democratic demands of land reform for peasants and rights for workers, as well as the development of a genuine, "national" capitalist sector, would eventually move on to the second, socialist stage.[56] Within a few years of organizing through Kalayaan on Kearny Street, Philippine revolutionaries won over new recruits to the communist-led national democratic cause among Filipino Americans, and a core of Filipino activists was forged.

Fil Am activists were not as clear about a political program for the United States. They understood that Filipinos were a minority and far too small numerically to launch their own revolution. (Asian Americans in total made up less than 1 percent of the total U.S. population in the 1970s.[57]) Filipinos would have to unite with others in a working-class front—a very complex, difficult task that could mean subsuming "Filipino" issues within a far broader range of concerns.

This uncertainty in the political program tended to give the Philippine revolutionaries more influence in the KDP in terms of deploying human and economic resources. Their political relationships back home also gave the Philippine revolutionaries fresh insights into the political situation in the Philippines. Their analysis and campaigns occupied Filipino American activists' main political and organizational work for at least a decade and a half.

As a result of its nationwide publicity and multiple organizing campaigns, the KDP became publicly known primarily as an anti-Marcos organization. Yet the KDP was more than a solidarity network for Philippine revolutionaries: It incorporated community-based issues in the Filipino American community that were essential to unity within the U.S. working class. Thus, being involved in a working-class struggle such as the I-Hotel was a logical trajectory for the KDP. It not only provided another venue for liberation politics; it was also an experiment in how the U.S. working class would unite. We anticipated that, at some future time, the Filipino American sector would merge with a newly revitalized American communist party, not a Philippine-based party, as a national and racial minority.

The KDP was the conduit through which the exiles conducted campaigns in the United States indirectly led by the Philippine left, while some leading Fil Ams gained their political training by traveling to the Philippines. In a short time, the KDP became the voice of the Philippine left in the United States and the official, militant opposition to the U.S.–Marcos dictatorship. It grew in prestige within the solidarity networks; developed alliances and sophisticated working relationships (along with conflicts) with the ruling class (or "elite") opposition forces; and ultimately gained the authority to speak for Filipinos on the left.

This legitimization, despite constant struggles with non-leftist forces within the community, marked the KDP as different from the other Asian American organizations that would flourish in the I-Hotel's storefronts.

When radicalized intellectual leftists from the Philippines arrived on Kearny Street in the early 1970s (as well as in other U.S. cities, such as New York, Chicago, and Los Angeles), the Filipino American community was already polarized between the youth generation and their parents' generation. In the 1950s and 1960s, the parents had involved themselves in ethnic-enclave activities that tended to close them off from the broader society, and they adopted conservative stances. As Rene Cruz explained, "To cope with racial slights, a simple set of reflex behavior was good enough: prove you don't like Blacks also; prove to the whites you are a deserving citizen; the kids' accents should not be thickened by the use of Tagalog, Visayan, or Ilocano at home. Suffer everything in silence and steer clear of trouble."[58]

In this political climate, Philippine nationalist groups that allied with the CPP were to be avoided like the plague. However, the radicalized Filipino American youth, already in motion because of the student movements, were receptive to radical politics. As in the Chinese community, a sizable number of American-born Filipino youths had become educated and actively engaged in the issues of the community for the first time, and accommodation to racist subordination was rejected along with anticommunism.

As the KDP began to mature and gain a reputation for effective organizing among the traditional and established groups, opposition to its politics became more vocal among conservatives in the Filipino community. This made it increasingly difficult for the activists on Kearny Street to gain new supporters for the I-Hotel struggle. Known adherence to leftist politics became an open invitation for attacks within the community. For example, the *Philippine News*, a leading San Francisco-based Filipino newspaper, launched an attack on the NCRCLP. While the leftists considered the NCRCLP a genuine left–liberal alliance, the conservative nationalists, as represented by the *Philippine News*, viewed it as nothing more than a communist front. The NCRCLP's ties with the Kalayaan organization "had been taken . . . as an infiltration of NCRCLP by Maoist Communists. Kalayaan is reported to be in the blacklist of the Federal Bureau of Investigation as a Maoist front," the *Philippine News* declared in its attempt to frighten the community away from working with the radicals.[59] This was the same tactic President Marcos employed: By using the threat of communism, he justified his own hold on, and further abuse of, power.[60]

With these conflicting political priorities, as well as the anticommunist reactions in the Filipino community, the KDP played a decisive role in the International Hotel struggle. It exercised leadership even though its social base and its programmatic agenda pulled in two directions. At the same, the KDP's disciplined, serious, bold, and broad initiatives gained the organization credibility, even though it faced anticommunist attacks. Despite all the contradictions inherent in these dynamics, KDP activists managed to help the elderly tenants to lead the struggle, while the manongs—wary, determined, and militant—kept the young activists from losing their bearings.

Storefront "Vanguards"

The Kearny Street block also became a hub of activity for progressives and the left wing of the Asian American movement. With so many Asian American groups moving into the storefronts on the ground floor and in the basement of the I-Hotel, in close proximity to one another, relationships developed between them. These organizations included the Manilatown Information Center; the Asian Community Center (ACC), organized by Wei Min She, which allied with the Revolutionary Union (RU), which in turn became the Revolutionary Communist Party (RCP) in 1975; the Chinese Progressive Association (CPA), organized by I Wor Kuen, which would merge with other Chicano and African American–based groups to form the League for Revolutionary Struggle (LRS) in 1978; Everybody's Bookstore, an initiative of the RU/RCP; and the Kearny Street Workshop (KSW), composed of independent activists and cultural workers.[61] For a short while, there was even a cooperative garment factory operating in the basement.[62] A hardware store and key shop owned by a Chinese immigrant settled in the storefront corner and remained a successful business until a few months before the eviction.

Both the ACC and the CPA were volunteer community organizations dedicated to "serving the people," the slogan and practice inspired by the Chinese Cultural Revolution and the programs of the Black Panther Party. They provided services to the I-Hotel tenants and to the surrounding community, particularly to the Chinese tenants. The services included musical programs, meeting places for community groups, recreation rooms for the elderly, food-distribution programs, youth programs, English- and Chinese-language classes, and other social, cultural, and educational activities. All were offered free of charge.

The KSW provided community-based art programs to anyone in San Francisco. Community people and tenants, particularly residents of the Chinatown area, were given opportunities for artistic development and expression. The KSW offered classes in photography, silkscreen, pottery, graphics, poetry, and prose writing, again free of charge. Murals produced by the KSW adorned the building, and posters, T-shirts, and other artwork either created or inspired by the KSW became important parts of the struggle. For example, the logo of a tiger lunging through a circle designed by Jack Loo of the KSW became the universally recognized icon of the struggle. The KSW was more open to differing political views than the other organizations on the block. It did not get involved in "party politics," as did other Asian American leftists on the Kearny Street.[63]

These organizations played a prominent role in galvanizing resistance to the eviction, and the I-Hotel struggle eventually came to be identified with the left-wing Asian American movement. Kearny Street also became the site of organizing for New Left parties that allied themselves with Marxist–Leninist–Mao Tse-tung thought. Because of its pro-Soviet and anti-Chinese sympathies, the much older and larger Communist Party of the USA (CPUSA) had little influence within the I-Hotel storefront organizations, although the CPUSA became more influential through its labor and community ties as the anti-eviction struggle approached its climax and gained broader community support. An advantage of the involvement of these New Left organizations was that scores of political activists helped to build support for the I-Hotel tenants. Grassroots organizers among different sectors of the working-class population were drawn in as supporters during demonstrations and eviction threats, and the left-wing activists trained themselves under conditions of constant political turmoil. A disadvantage was that old-time and more mainstream supporters distanced themselves from the I-Hotel as the Asian American organizations began to evolve toward ultra-left and vanguardist politics. Tendencies to adopt positions of dogmatic militancy; to misjudge the revolutionary possibilities of a reform struggle; to address the public in stilted jargon; and, perhaps most problematic of all, to put the interests of their own organization-building projects ahead of the mass movement tended to isolate the revolutionaries farther from their "mass base," as potential supporters were called.

As support from the progressive and leftist movements broadened, the "mass base" in the Chinese and Filipino communities grew deeper, though narrower. The Chinese organized immigrant workers, such as the garment workers in Chinatown, while the Filipinos organized immigrants and students against the Marcos dictatorship and around other local community issues in the South of Market neighborhood of San Francisco, as well as in Daly City, Oakland, and other areas of Filipino concentration. The "masses" closest to the struggle, the tenants, did not mind the left-wing politics because the leftists were the backbone of their help and support. However, some liberal and unaffiliated potential supporters distanced themselves, while anticommunism grew in relation to the degree that "left-wing communism" took root.

The emerging Maoist parties in the Asian American communities in many ways further complicated the I-Hotel struggle because of conflicts between them. Each ethnic Chinese group and the KDP had to deal with how to organize citywide coalitions with politicians and other progressive and housing groups while being narrowly defined within their nationalist politics. By the end of the period, the extreme segmentation between the ethnic groups and the competition between the revolutionary leftist organizations caused political rifts, rivalries, and distrust. This separation hampered the organizing efforts needed to defeat the landlord as well as to pressure the city to solve the housing problems of the poor and elderly. As the revolutionary leftist groups grew more ideological, differing analyses of the overall political situation in the United States often undermined practical day-to-day politics at the I-Hotel.

Wei Men She, which had close ties to the RCP, saw itself as playing a vanguard role, which meant that other communists that did not join or ally with the group were "opportunists." I Wor Kuen, which aligned itself with the LRS after the eviction, shared a similar attitude toward its rivals. The KDP, which did not view itself as playing the role of a party, nonetheless cultivated its own sectarian tendencies in relation to those who did, attempting to win over "independents" to its side as the legitimate voice of the Filipino tenants. (Independents who recoiled at the dogmatic Maoism of the other groups would call KDP "the good Maoists" because the organization non-dogmatically supported pro-Soviet Cuba and would unite with other radicals and noncommunists more readily.[64]) In the midst of this cauldron of Asian American revolutionary politics, each group would compete for cadre, leadership, and a chance to champion the "advanced worker" (usually a politically conscious and outspoken tenant) as a supporter of its organization.

Throughout the anti-eviction struggle, the grassroots organizing power and commitment of these groups made a tremendous contribution to the tenants at the I-Hotel. Young revolutionaries from all of the different groups stood out for their dedication and hard work and the personal sacrifices they made for the I-Hotel battle. Yet because almost all of the activists were young and relatively inexperienced, their commendable commitment was not matched by political maturity and broad-mindedness. Instead, impatience, dogmatism, and ultra-militancy created an environment that was often fractious and self-destructive. The leftist parties that formed around each ethnic organization made it even more difficult to establish unity when the struggle needed it the most. Most of these developments took place behind the scenes at the I-Hotel, and they were rarely noticed by outsiders.[65] When ethnic-based organizing erupted into communist-party building, the differences over the assessment of the political situation, the role of parties and mass organizations, and—perhaps even more important—the role of alliances with liberals, politicians, and other forces became so fraught that the sectarian in-fighting threatened to destroy the movement from within, particularly in the final period. Despite these problems, the KDP and the tenants held the core together.

CHAPTER FOUR

The Tiger Leaps

Fighting the Four Seas Investment Corporation, 1974–77

Enter Supasit Mahaguna

On September 24, 1974, the tenants of the International Hotel received an eviction notice from the new landlord, the Four Seas Investment Corporation. After five years of relative calm, the tenants had to fight for their survival again. This time, however, information regarding the tenants' new nemesis was not immediately known. Mounting an anti-eviction campaign against the new landlord, who seemed elusive and phantomlike, proved more difficult than the previous battle.

The Four Seas Investment Corporation bought the property from Milton Meyer and Company on October 31, 1973, although the transfer of property was not made public until March 1974. Ownership was first transferred to the Transamerica Title Insurance Company, acting as middleman, on December 31, 1973. Four Seas paid Milton Meyer and Company the asking price of eight hundred fifty thousand dollars for the property. The deal was arranged so that Milton Meyer and Company would pay no taxes on the sale. Court records also showed that Shorenstein would bear the burden of eviction expenses.[1]

The eight hundred fifty thousand dollar asking price seemed like a paltry sum for such a potentially valuable piece of real estate in the financial district. Supporters of the I-Hotel speculated that the low price reflected the fact that Shorenstein was anxious to get the building off his hands. It also signified that it might take years of expensive litigation before Four Seas would be free to do whatever it wanted with the property. Selling to a foreign corporation also seemed logical because American businessmen who knew about the I-Hotel probably would not want the trouble or expense related to the property.

Shorenstein did not make it known to the tenants that he had sold the building. The first public mention of the sale came from Herb Caen, the celebrated

San Francisco Chronicle columnist, who wrote, "The residents of the International Hotel are in for a surprise because the hotel's been sold to a Hong Kong firm."[2] In fact, years passed before there was a public exposé of Mahaguna's background and motivations for buying the I-Hotel.[3] Shorenstein, by contrast, was a well-known public figure in San Francisco politics. In addition to the role he played in Democratic Party politics, locally and nationally, he had also served as technical adviser to the United Nations in Bangkok in 1967. Perhaps he had made the contacts to sell his property to Mahaguna at that time. Shorenstein's real-estate portfolio was worth 500 million dollars, so unloading the I-Hotel at such a low price would not be a significant loss.[4]

The IHTA would learn far more about Supasit Mahaguna in the next three years through the work of investigative reporters. Mahaguna's nickname, Cheng Wang-Tuk, which in Thailand's Taechew dialect translates as "Godfather," suggested how far his political power reached and what he could do to maintain it. The members of the board of Mahaguna's monopoly liquor franchise included top-ranking police and army generals who had been overthrown in October 1973. They had killed students and others to suppress violent demonstrations. Though he and his cronies would not have the same political power to oppose local opposition in the United States, Mahaguna remained ruthless; he was not daunted by anti-eviction activism. He used his money to hire the best lawyers to defend his property rights, and they employed the courts and other forms of state power to intimidate, harass, and finally to evict the tenants. This "Godfather" stayed in the background, never participating directly in the court proceedings. Only one photograph of him was available during the entire anti-eviction conflict. It showed him dressed in a white suit and wearing sunglasses, with a big cigar in his mouth. It was not difficult to imagine him as a real-life Asian mafia figure.[5]

Mahaguna's motives, along with this one picture, fully surfaced in 1977 in an exposé published by the progressive newsweekly *San Francisco Bay Guardian*. Mahaguna wanted to get money out of Thailand by investing in U.S. ventures because the October 1973 revolution that overthrew Thailand's right-wing military dictatorship jeopardized his riches. The new, democratically elected government that came to power threatened to increase taxes substantially on his Mahakun whiskey operation, the biggest liquor monopoly in Thailand. His ties to the military dictatorship were cut; his political power was severely weakened; and the new government was making moves against his liquor business. Mahaguna had to get his whiskey profits out—fast.

Soon after Four Seas purchased the I-Hotel, lawyers for the tenants began to learn that Four Seas had more holdings in California: The company had purchased the Cambiaso Vineyard and winery near Healdsburg, California, in September, 1973, and over the course of the next three years, it would buy additional properties, almost all of which were on the same block as the I-Hotel.

Based on this configuration, it was probable that Mahaguna was planning a major development on the Kearny Street block.[6]

Because the relationship between Shorenstein and Mahaguna did not end after Four Seas bought the hotel, tenants soon suspected that they were colluding on bigger schemes. Milton Meyer and Company continued to act as the hotel's property manager, collecting the rent from the tenants for months after the sale was completed. Also, Four Seas served as a holding company for Milton Meyer and Company in several other land deals. All of this led the tenants and their supporters to speculate that Four Seas was acting as a front group for Shorenstein and Milton Meyer, and that it planned to build a high-rise development on the I-Hotel block.[7]

Four Seas consistently denied that it had development plans. However, if such plans had been revealed, Four Seas would have had to file an Environmental Impact Report with the city when it applied for a demolition permit, which meant additional hearings. Four Seas knew about the tenants' war with Shorenstein and that publicly acknowledging intentions to develop the property would only be inviting trouble. Four Seas never did make its intentions public, and the tenants and their supporters were always kept guessing.[8]

In the years to come, Mahaguna proved to be a formidable foe. Part of his strength arose from his local ties to Chinese businessmen and lawyers in Chinatown. The Four Seas board of directors included Arthur Chan, treasurer; Jack Wong, secretary and legal consultant; and G. Alfred Roensch, legal consultant. Chan, who served on the board in 1973–75, handled the money that Mahaguna sent to the United States; he also owned two stores in Chinatown that specialized in trade goods from Asia. Chan's wife was a long-time personal friend of Mahaguna. Wong was an attorney with the law firm Gintjee Chinn, Wong, Shortall and Roensch and a member of the Chinese Six Companies, the powerful and conservative business organization in Chinatown. G. Alfred Roensch was also a partner in Gintjee Chinn, Wong, Shortall and Roensch.[9]

The Chinatown connection was complicated, and the tenants and supporters were never able to tackle the internal dynamics of these business alliances effectively. The political significance of Mahaguna's development plans, as elusive as they were, could not be fully analyzed. Did they contribute primarily to the city's redevelopment of the financial district or to tourism in Chinatown? What personal advantage did Chinatown businessmen anticipate from the plans?

Mahaguna's secrecy only contributed to the difficulties that the tenants and their supporters faced in fashioning strategies to oppose his legal and political maneuvers. We discussed repeatedly how we could counter Four Seas' goals and interests, even though we could never fully ascertain what they were. How could we identify and criticize those plans in a public campaign if we did not know what they were? For instance, Calvin Trillin reported in a *New Yorker* magazine article that, according to Shorenstein, what "Four Seas has in mind is not in fact a high-rise office building but a flashy Chinese commercial development with underground parking and slick shops—in a sort of Ghirardelli Square, but Chinese."[10] If this was in fact his plan, it contradicted the progressive movement's analysis that big business's motivation was to destroy the Chinatown and Manilatown communities. Historically, white San Francisco businessmen coveted the prime piece of property on which Chinatown stands, and Chinese businessmen had always resisted their advances.[11]

If what Trillin reported was true, and Mahaguna planned to develop and expand Chinatown instead of the downtown financial center, the project would appear to sustain Chinese business interests. And if that was the case, we asked, how could the Chinese Six Companies and other Chinese businessmen be brought into the political front against eviction? Organizers knew that such "flashy Chinese commercial development" plans—which were similar to other schemes, such as a proposed mall of Latino boutiques from the new 16th Street BART station to Mission Dolores—would threaten small businesses in favor of tourist-oriented enterprises owned by outside interests. Such development would serve only the wealthiest and could be the means whereby the entire community would be undermined.[12]

The Filipino community and its businesses were located on the eastern edge of Chinatown. Historically, Manilatown served as a buffer between Chinatown and the financial district, and the eastern edge of Kearny was all that was left. The Filipino community had been unable to stop the encroachment of financial business interests in the Manilatown section since the late 1940s. As a new and politically weak community, Filipinos had been invisible to the rest of the Chinese and broader communities. The removal of that part of the community was not a liability for Chinese businessmen and politicians. Their main objective was to bring in tourist dollars. Wealthy Chinese businessmen did not seem to care about the destruction of low-income housing or housing stock. Middle-class and upper-class Chinese had moved outside Chinatown to the Richmond and Sunset districts and to the outlying suburbs of San Francisco. Only recent Chinese immigrants and the elderly chose to live in Chinatown because of the availability of affordable housing and their familiarity with the culture. Chinatown functioned as a way station and a place of choice for new immigrants.[13]

Generally, concerns about housing and welfare for the immigrant community were ignored. Only civil-rights activists and leftist and progressive forces in the Chinatown community, such as Self-Help for the Elderly and, later, Chinese for Affirmative Action, were willing to raise the issues of poverty, the housing crises, and the health and welfare of immigrants in Chinatown. In 1970, the population density in Chinatown was at least seven times San Francisco's average density.[14] Such density was second only to Manhattan.[15] Seventy-seven percent of Chinatown's housing was substandard by city codes.[16]

The Chinese businessmen's class interests superseded any desire to relieve the housing crises or defend the International Hotel. An Asian operator like

Mahaguna could effectively hide behind Chinatown business development interests. At the same time, the youthful Chinese revolutionary activists seemed too weak to repel a local capitalist offensive. As noted earlier, Chinatown's business leaders were politically nationalist and anticommunist, in alliance with the Kuomintang, or Nationalist Party, and its government in Taiwan and opposed to the People's Republic of China (PRC). They were the traditional power brokers of the community and were certainly strong enough to thwart the politics of the young revolutionary nationalists who supported the PRC. In short, the Chinese community was not able to display a united front against any big-business claims against Chinatown, and Chinese supporters of the hotel had to contend with handling the class struggle against the business elite while waging a battle for a multi-class ethnic community's survival.

Four Seas Attempts to Evict

All of this made for a very complicated situation as the I-Hotel tenants and their allies geared up to fight again on legal, political, and mass-mobilization fronts. The legal battle against eviction resumed on January 29, 1974, when the City Attorney's Office ordered Milton Meyer and Company to bring the I-Hotel up to city and state housing codes. The order listed a variety of building-code violations at the International Hotel and required the owners to repair the building to meet city standards or demolish it. Milton Meyer and Company forwarded the notice to the Four Seas Investment Corporation. Robert Thompson, one of the attorneys for the IHTA, found out about the abatement order soon after it was issued.

Thompson was not able to contact Four Seas immediately because the business had no listed address or telephone number. In May 1974, Thompson finally made contact with Jack Wong, attorney and treasurer of Four Seas. Thompson made an offer on behalf of the IHTA that the tenants would repair the building-code violations in the hotel in exchange for a long-term lease. Wong was not receptive to the idea. Four Seas' response was not to contest the city's abatement order. When Superior Court Judge Albert C. Axelrod ruled on July 2, 1974, that the building should either be repaired or demolished, no representative of Four Seas was present. On August 28, 1974, Wong recommended to the Four Seas board that the tenants be evicted and the building be demolished.

These maneuvers ended in an eviction notice served to the tenants on September 24, 1974.[17] It did not take long for the tenants and their representatives to respond, legally and politically. Their immediate goal was to prevent eviction and make sure the building-code violations were cleared up. Their long-term goal was to obtain a long-term lease or to buy the building. In early October 1974, Gil Graham, an attorney for the I-Hotel tenants, and Joe Diones, chairman of the IHTA—along with co-chairman Charles Smith and Bill Lee, a supporter from the Asian Community Center—met with Wong and Roensch in an effort to persuade Four Seas to accept their offer to repair the building and reconsider the eviction or to sell the building to the tenants. Wong refused the proposal and told them that the tenants had to comply with the eviction order.[18]

The tenants and their supporters immediately launched a multifaceted public campaign to resist the eviction. On October 9, they began their first action: The IHTA stopped paying rent to Four Seas and put the rent money in an escrow account. On October 24, tenants and about 350 supporters held a press conference and rally in front of the hotel.[19] They distributed flyers presenting their demands: Four Seas should lift the eviction notice, repair the building-code violations, and sign a long-term lease with the IHTA with an option to buy the building. The IHTA launched a petition campaign to stop eviction, and the tenants began to seek support for their cause from politicians and various community organizations.

Leaders of the IHTA realized that keeping the I-Hotel for low-income housing would require long-term strategies to organize grassroots support. Because San Francisco's housing supply was dwindling due to city-sponsored redevelopment and private speculative development, other poor and working-class communities were receptive. An IHTA flyer appealed to people outside the Manilatown and Chinatown communities:

> The IH tenants are people of many nationalities, primarily elderly Pilipino and Chinese who need low income housing in our Manilatown/Chinatown community. We organized ourselves into the IHTA to change and improve our poor and inadequate living conditions. The hotel serves as one of the main centers that houses community organizations which provide food supplement, educational, language, art and cultural programs and supports community issues.
>
> What can you do? Our success comes from the active support of the people themselves. This particular threat to our home and our community is part of a citywide housing crisis.[20]

The citywide housing crisis would bring together a coalition that would be the precursor of a large citywide movement for affordable housing. The tenants and their supporters anticipated that those most affected by the housing crisis, such as the I-Hotel residents, would be at the core of such a coalition.

The IHTA's call received an immediate response. On October 26, 1974, the association formed a coalition with fourteen other organizations concerned with tenants' rights and the maintenance of low-income housing. Three thousand demonstrators marched through Chinatown, ending in front of the penthouse offices of Four Seas, dramatizing the strength of the new coalition. The term "low-cost" housing was changed to "low-income" housing to clarify that people on the bottom rungs of the economic ladder should obtain housing they could afford, and that cheap, low-cost material for housing was not the goal. The coalition called itself the People's Action Coalition, and it embraced organizations that had similar concerns about the effects of redevelopment; the destruction of available housing stock; and the dispersal of the poor, working-class, and minority communities. These organizations included the Committee against Nihonmachi Eviction, or CANE, an organization that opposed redevelopment in Japantown; Tenants and Owners in Opposition to Redevelopment (TOOR), which consisted mostly of elderly residents contesting the Yerba Buena project in the South of Market area; and the Goodman Group, an artists' colony in the Goodman Building at Geary and Van Ness streets that was also fighting eviction.[21]

The IHTA set up a legal strategy designed to show that the eviction threat was causing undue harm to the elderly tenants—a threat that could easily be alleviated by making the repairs. Lawyers claimed that Four Seas was attempting to evict the tenants in retaliation for their actions. Tenants were being targeted, they said, because they had organized a tenants' association and exercised their constitutional right to free speech to protest Four Seas' refusal to repair the building's numerous code violations.[22] The San Francisco Lawyers Committee for Urban Affairs filed a suit on behalf of the I-Hotel tenants seeking damages and an injunction against their eviction. The tenants asked the court to order Four Seas to pay: (1) fifty dollars per day until the notice was withdrawn; (2) five hundred thousand dollars in punitive damages; and (3) two hundred thousand dollars in damages for "mental suffering" caused by the eviction notice issued the previous month by the owner. The suit charged Four Seas with "willful failure" to correct code violations in the hotel, breaking an implied covenant to keep the hotel in habitable condition in an attempt to evict the tenants without good cause, and inflicting severe emotional and mental distress.[23]

Four Seas responded two weeks later. On November 8, 1974, it filed a complaint of unlawful detainer (illegal habitation of the building) against the IHTA, claiming the legal right to evict the tenants. The Four Seas suit dragged on for nearly two years, with preliminary litigation and other delays. The actual eviction trials did not begin until April 1976.[24]

When the Four Seas suit finally did come to trial, it lasted for almost a month, even though the corporation's attorneys predicted it would be over in a day. IHTA attorneys had estimated that the trial would take seven days; its surprising length indicated the increasing political "traction" of the issue. The IHTA lawyers argued, as they had in the original IHTA suit, that the eviction was retaliatory, while Four Seas' lawyers claimed that they were only following the abatement order with no retaliatory intention. Because Shorenstein and Four Seas had kept the new ownership of the hotel from the tenants for so long, the relationship between the tenants and the corporation was minimal. Consequently, Four Seas argued that it had had little contact with the tenants, and thus it could not have been acting in a retaliatory manner. The judge did not allow the tenants to enter the history of the anti-eviction conflict with Shorenstein, forbidding IHTA lawyers to argue that the collusion between Shorenstein and Four

Seas was part of the retaliatory conduct. The jurors, who deliberated for four days, cast more than twelve ballots and found themselves hopelessly deadlocked. The presiding judge, Ira A. Brown, took over the matter and directed a verdict in favor of Four Seas.[25]

The tenants understood that their human rights to decent housing were on trial. Judge Brown's attitude was evident in court when he remarked to the tenants that they should not have been in the hotel in the first place. Brown, who was six feet, four inches tall and had a razor-sharp tongue, was quite imposing. However, Felix Ayson, an elderly tenant leader, refused to be intimidated and responded to supporters: "Why should he talk like that? What did he mean by that? We are citizens. Mahaguna doesn't even live in this country. Why didn't he tell Four Seas that they shouldn't be here in the first place?"[26]

After the jury left the courtroom, Judge Brown told the lawyers that, even if the jury had ruled in favor of the tenants, he would have been strongly tempted to reverse their decision on the basis of insufficient evidence that the eviction was retaliatory. He ordered the jury to decide on a monetary award from the IHTA to Four Seas. Of the seventy-two thousand dollars claimed by Four Seas in back rent, the jury awarded the corporation only a token four thousand dollars in damages. After the trial was over, one juror told a reporter that some of the jurors had not understood that individual members of the board of directors who testified actually represented Four Seas. Many jurors felt that one Four Seas board member had perjured himself, he told the reporter; he also commented that, had the jurors been clear that the board members represented the corporation, they might have voted in favor of the tenants.[27]

Gil Graham took the case to the State Court of Appeals, but on July 27, 1976, that court sustained the lower court's eviction order. The case was then appealed to the State Supreme Court. Meanwhile, Undersheriff James Denman stated that he would not enforce eviction while tenants were appealing it in court. On September 4, 1976, the State Supreme Court rejected the appeal and lifted the stay of eviction. On December 3, Judge Brown issued a new order to evict the tenants and stipulated that the order be carried out by December 15. On December 14, Judge Brown denied a stay request brought by the sheriff and the IHTA. Judge Brown brushed off claims that the Sheriff's Department did not have the manpower to carry out the eviction. On December 20, Sheriff Richard Hongisto and Undersheriff Denman were charged with contempt of court for refusing to carry out the eviction. They filed a motion with Superior Court Judge John E. Benson for a mistrial, with Hongisto testifying that his failure to evict the tenants was not "willful" and he was not in violation of the court order. On December 30, Judge Benson denied their motion.[28]

On January 7, 1977, Undersheriff Denman attempted to serve eviction notices. The Workers Committee, one of the support groups, had somehow gotten wind of the attempt and mobilized about three hundred activists early in the morning without letting the other groups know. I watched in surprise as

Workers Committee members massed before the I-Hotel's front doors. The demonstration was very well disciplined: It even included a six-piece band of musicians. At 9:45 A.M., a convoy of sheriff's cars arrived, and Undersheriff Denman tried to push through the crowd. He was repulsed, but it turned out that he was creating a diversion so that another burly deputy could push his way to the entrance to tape eviction notices to the door. Denman refused to enter the building, fearing for his safety, but he deemed that the evictions had been officially served by posting the notices on the front door. The demonstrators tore down the notices and dramatically set fire to them.[29]

On January 10, Hongisto and Denman were both convicted of contempt of court and fined five hundred dollars each for failing to carry out the eviction.[30] Judge Brown ordered that the tenants must be evicted by 5:00 P.M. on January 19, 1977. This was the fourth eviction order by Judge Brown. Again, Sheriff Hongisto contended that his office had neither the money nor the manpower to conduct such a large-scale eviction, and he was concerned about injuries. Judge Brown was unpersuaded.

The next evening—Tuesday, January 11—at 7:45 P.M., I looked out a second-floor window of the I-Hotel and saw Sheriff Hongisto drive up and jump out of his car. We were caught by surprise and had not mobilized our supporters for this sneak attack. We also did not know that Undersheriff Denman's attempt to post the eviction notices a few days earlier was deemed only partially successful, because it applied only to the storefront businesses and not the tenants, and that another posting was required. Sheriff Hongisto ran to the front of the hotel and nailed a two-inch wad of papers to the door. He turned then scooted back into the waiting car. The papers were five-day eviction notices to vacate the premises, which were required by law prior to eviction. Thus, any time after January 12, 1977, the tenants could be subjected to immediate eviction.[31]

We had already planned to hold a demonstration at the hotel on January 12, but that action took on even greater urgency. Supporters were told to be on constant stand-by, ready to come to the defense of the hotel at a moment's notice once they were alerted by the IHTA's telephone tree. On that day, the IHTA was able to mass 2,500 to 3,000 demonstrators in front of the building. The size of the demonstration was impressive, reflecting the extent and breadth of the coalition, and the response increased dramatically in the next week.[32]

Resisting court-ordered eviction became the first political line of defense for the tenants. They understood that, to prevent the eviction, a movement would have to be built that would gain the sympathy of the majority of people in San Francisco. The courts would tend to side with private property, and housing and human rights would not enter the equation—as in Judge Brown's and other judges' rulings. The key problem was whether mass support would be enough to pressure the judges and, after that, to push city officials to the side of the tenants. That is, if public opinion could not influence the courts, then the tenants and their supporters would have to pressure city government to take care of the needs of its citizens by devising policies and plans to protect the poor, the elderly, and the vulnerable.

During the fall of 1976, as the legal battle proceeded, a growing number of city officials came to support the tenants and the anti-eviction movement. Between July 15, 1976, and January 1977, the tenants were not evicted, despite the court order, because the liberal sheriff, under pressure, refused to carry out the court's eviction order. According to David Prowler, a Human Rights Commission staff member, "The sheriff was in no hurry to evict the tenants because he knew that if he did, he would lose the liberal constituency that had supported his election."[33] Undersheriff Denman, Hongisto's deputy, articulated liberal opposition:

> I get a real sense of being on the wrong side of the fence. . . . I see elements of a class struggle here. Here I am, a middle class person, evicting poor people for the benefit of Four Seas, a wealthy corporation. It's a property rights versus human rights issue, and poor people don't have any property, it's the upper classes, the corporations, that do. . . . We are evicting a community and destroying a symbol. It's a profane thing to do. It's sacrilegious.[34]

Sheriff Hongisto seemed to be expressing sympathy with the tenants when he said, "Laws in our society are written to protect people with property and money."[35] The resistance by Hongisto and Denman, who repeatedly stated throughout 1976 that they would not carry out the eviction while court appeals were in progress, demonstrated the degree to which the I-Hotel had fractured the private-property consensus of the political elite.

Building Support for the Anti-Eviction Movement

The tenants had time to organize the IHTA and to build support for the cause in the two years leading up to the April 1976 trial before Judge Brown. However, time was not on the side of the tenants, given their age and health. Illness and infirmity took its toll on some, and fear of eviction forced others to leave. Their numbers were dwindling. But for the most part, the most vulnerable tenants—that is, the oldest and those with the fewest resources—tended to stay for the fight. More than fifty tenants stayed throughout this very tense period.

Critics of the I-Hotel anti-eviction movement charged that not enough tenants had chosen to remain to make saving the hotel worth the fight. And some skeptics who were close to the struggle thought that young people had taken over and, suspicious of our radical politics, questioned our sincerity and whether the IHTA truly represented the elderly tenants. There were observers in the Filipino and in the broader communities who did not grasp that what was actually motivating broad support was the dire need for low-income housing and the fear of being forced to leave San Francisco. These critics also did not understand that preventing eviction was the first line of defense—and, perhaps, the most important battle. They also did not realize that the anti-eviction movement would have implications far beyond the I-Hotel itself. The media and liberal politicians did not fully grasp the deeply emotional reasons that these tenants fought so hard to maintain their home. All of these critics—the media, conservatives in the Filipino community, and liberal politicians—underestimated the elderly tenants' fierce determination. None of them realized that it was the tenants who kept the young students from losing their nerve.[36] In an interview, Joe Regadio, who had lived at the hotel since 1956, said: "For me, I will never leave this building, and I'm willing to go to jail for it."[37]

The period between 1974 and 1976 was especially difficult because disagreements among tenants and their close supporters heightened at the same time that public support grew. The IHTA's supporters built a massive anti-eviction movement, and the image of a tiger leaping head first—the symbol for the I-Hotel movement created by Jack Loo of the Kearny Street Workshop—appeared on leaflets, posters, and T-shirts throughout the city.[38] By 1976–77, the coalition to defend the hotel would grow to hundreds of organizations and thousands of individuals.[39] But such wide support was nonetheless fraught with competing coalitions and disagreements over strategies within the IHTA itself. Within the anti-eviction movement, there were three well-organized groups that took different approaches to conducting the battle: the IHTA and its ad hoc supporters; the Worker's Committee to Defend the International Hotel and Victory Building; and the Support Committee of the International Hotel. I will discuss these groups more fully later.

The IHTA necessarily paid a lot of attention to organizing and pressuring city officials. Although the city officials held power, they proved to be the most problematic sector in which to find support, and even when they agreed to back the IHTA, ensuring that they stuck to their commitments required constant vigilance. At the urging of the IHTA, Democratic Supervisor John Molinari proposed an ordinance to the San Francisco Board of Supervisors in March 1975 that was designed

> to protect tenants in San Francisco from the wanton demolition of housing that has been going on unchecked for the past twenty years. This ordinance prohibits the demolition of residential housing if the vacancy rate in San Francisco is under 3% for comparable housing. The owner can still demolish if he provides replacement housing which is functionally comparable and which has comparable rental prices for the residents who would be displaced by the demolition. If a demolition permit is denied under this ordinance and the building is substandard, the city then has the obligation to repair and rehabilitate the building by using the building fund, and thereafter charging the owner for the cost of repairs. In my opinion, this ordinance will help correct the present

> situation in San Francisco whereby the available housing supply is being eliminated, which is forcing residents to move out of the city or into substandard dwellings.[40]

Supervisor Molinari's ordinance was reviewed by the city's Human Rights Commission and other community organizations and government agencies, and a revised version subsequently was submitted. The new proposed ordinance sought to govern the issuance of demolition and alteration permits throughout the city and would apply to all multifamily buildings in the San Francisco occupied by three or more families.

The ordinance stipulated that four findings be submitted to the Bureau of Building Inspections before a permit could be issued: (1) that the proposed demolition or alteration would not have any adverse environmental effects; (2) that the proposed demolition or alteration be consistent with the city's General Plan (especially the plan's Housing Element); (3) that the proposed demolition or alteration be accomplished in a safe and non-disruptive manner; and (4) that the owner of the building to be altered or demolished find replacement housing for all of the affected tenants. The ordinance provided for ninety days' written notice to the affected tenants. If the permit was denied and the bureau found the building to be substandard, the Department of Public Works would be responsible for arranging the repair and rehabilitation of the structure, and the owner of the substandard building would be liable for costs up to three thousand dollars per repaired unit.[41]

Business interests were uniformly opposed to the proposed ordinance. City administrators who shared economic interests with large investors were also opposed. For example, the chief of the city's Bureau of Building Inspections, Alfred Goldberg, strongly opposed the measure on the grounds that it would cost his agency too much money to enforce. Arthur Evans, head of the Redevelopment Agency, admitted that "it was not a simple matter to find decent housing." However, he concluded, "This [is not] sufficient reason to burden private developers in their quest for profits."[42] During a stormy meeting, Peter Bourdoures, a member of the Board of Permit Appeals, stated that owners of the building had the right "to get a better return . . . and put on a new building that will mean a lot of jobs and business."[43] A local newspaper columnist, by contrast, took the position that owners of hotels and apartment buildings, rather than taxpayers, should foot the bill for replacement housing for displaced tenants.[44] The ordinance was defeated when it finally came to a vote in January 1976.

The Moscone Plan

In 1975, the overall political situation in City Hall seemed to improve for the I-Hotel tenants when Mayor Alioto's second term as mayor came to a close and State Senator George Moscone was elected mayor. Moscone's constituencies—

the leftist, liberal, labor, minority, and gay communities—elected him as part of a left–liberal insurgency that hinged on support for a new system of district elections. City supervisors would no longer be elected on a citywide basis but according to district—that is, they would be elected by voters in the neighborhoods in which they lived. This amounted to a revolution in city politics because it attempted to break the stranglehold of downtown interests and gave power to neighborhoods. As part of the organizing for district elections, conferences were held in all of the proposed districts to articulate a people's agenda on a wide range of issues, including housing. The proposition for district elections won in November 1976 by a margin of 52 percent to 48 percent, and the first district elections were held in November 1977.[45]

Consequently, Moscone's election in 1975 represented a move toward progressive and liberal politics that paralleled the radical call for new city politics. However, he was still a politician who wanted to be reelected, and his promises to his liberal constituents inevitably were tempered by opposition from forces on the right, particularly the supervisors against district elections who remained in office throughout the anti-eviction struggle. Pro-growth forces, especially within the Democratic Party, as well as property owners exerted strong pressure on Mayor Moscone to abandon support for the I-Hotel, affordable housing, and the Manilatown community. While he was still a state senator, Moscone had expressed strong support for the I-Hotel tenants. On January 2, 1975, he had visited the hotel and met with the tenants. At that meeting, he wrote a letter by hand to the IHTA that reaffirmed his commitment to the cause: "I am unalterably opposed to the eviction of tenants at the International Hotel. This is basic housing essential to the well being of the tenants within. Before any tenancies are terminated there must *first* be provided safe, decent and suitable housing within the community and at a comparable rental."[46] Under his signature, he added: "The proposed eviction is a breach of commitment made to the tenants of the International Hotel in 1969 in the presence of John Burton, Jack Morrison and myself."

Soon after he was elected mayor, Moscone revealed his own plan to save the hotel. About a week before his announcement, the State Court of Appeals had turned down an appeal of a lower court ruling ordering the evictions on July 23, 1976. Undersheriff Denman told reporters that he would soon serve notice that the tenants must be out by five days, but that he would not enforce it while the tenants were still fighting the eviction in court. By the summer it appeared that city officials—and even the courts—might be swayed by public opinion in support of the tenants. Meanwhile, lawyers for the I-Hotel appealed the case to the State Supreme Court.[47]

Moscone's proposal, unveiled before the Housing Authority on July 29, 1976, essentially called for nonprofit ownership of the old Manilatown building by its elderly tenants. The mayor's initiative came at the same time as a decision by the State Supreme Court to stay the Superior Court's eviction order so that the higher court could review the dispute. It appeared that political support from the Mayor's Office had stopped the courts from ordering the eviction. The plan had been worked out by the mayor and a few leaders of the IHTA—namely Joe Diones, Charles Smith, and Gil Graham. According to the plan, the city would lend 1.3 million dollars of community-development money to the Housing Authority, which would then purchase the hotel from Four Seas. After the city repaired building-code violations, the tenants would form a nonprofit association, borrow from a lending institution, and use funds from charities and tenants' savings to buy the hotel from the Housing Authority. The Board of Supervisors had to approve the plan before city funds could be used for the initial purchase, but the Housing Authority immediately agreed to spend six thousand dollars for two independent appraisals of the building to determine how much would need to be authorized. Moscone said that the Housing Authority might use its powers of eminent domain to acquire the hotel if an agreement on a sale price could not be reached with Four Seas. The independent appraisals returned with almost identical amounts: approximately 1.25 million dollars.[48]

Mayor Moscone's plan seemed radical, especially as it related to the use of eminent domain—the taking of private land for public use, with compensation paid to the property owner at fair market value, regardless of whether the owner wants to sell. The idea of using eminent domain as a legal tactic in an anti-eviction fight was a new one for the people's movement. City governments liberally used eminent domain to remove poor people from areas that were designated by city agencies as blighted; such areas could be appropriated for what these agencies determined were "higher" and "better" uses—that is, development projects that yielded higher profit returns. The federal Housing Act of 1949 allowed government bodies such as the San Francisco Redevelopment Agency to employ eminent domain, which the agency did use as part of its Yerba Buena development, removing 4,000 poor people from the South of Market neighborhood and replacing them with high-end hotels and other projects. As in South of Market, the Western Addition, and other areas targeted for urban renewal, the courts had no problem in giving power to redevelopment agencies to forcibly take away properties from minorities and low-income working people in the name of "public use." Private financial institutions and corporations ended up benefiting from the transfer of monies and properties.[49]

Although it was unusual, the use of eminent domain to acquire property for a public use such as low-income housing did have precedents in California. Public interest and necessity involve all aspects of the public good, including, but not limited to, social, economic, environmental, and aesthetic considerations. In California courts, the definition of public use had been interpreted broadly to include "public utility or advantage." In this case, Moscone argued, the Housing Authority could legally acquire the International Hotel through the use of eminent domain with the intent of turning the property over to a private entity for the purpose of operating it as a low-income-housing project.

The Housing Authority would be fulfilling its public purpose of providing low-income housing by selling the building to a private corporation, the IHTA. According to legal precedents, the fact that private individuals might receive benefits was not sufficient to take away from the enterprise the characteristics of a public purpose.[50]

Moscone insisted that the plan was not only legal but also practical: It would not alienate private businesses or use up taxpayers' money, because the city funds eventually would be paid back. The plan had to go through a process of hearings and approvals by city bodies, and it eventually faced court challenges. All of these maneuvers took place against a background of simultaneous, nerve-wracking court actions to evict the tenants that were opposed by the IHTA's lawyers.

On October 21, Moscone's plan was brought to a hearing of the Housing Authority, which designated the hotel as a site suitable for low-income housing—the first step for approval.[51] However, the Housing Authority also had to conduct a public hearing on the public necessity of the eminent-domain action, which was scheduled, after a mandatory waiting period, for December 23. The Housing Authority's commissioners were appointees of the mayor, and the tenants had no difficulty in getting a unanimous decision in their favor. The hearing was attended by the elderly tenants and their enthusiastic supporters, but opposition came from unexpected quarters: tenants of other Housing Authority public-housing projects, who feared that they would be denied scarce resources so that the city could buy the I-Hotel.

Further, the Board of Supervisors had to approve the use of Community Development Funds for the city to buy the building. This proved difficult because Moscone did not have unanimous support for his plan. Complicating the issue was that the Board of Supervisors' Finance Committee had recommended in early October to funnel 1.3 million dollars into police and fire protection; the money was to come from the 2.6 million dollars that had already been allocated to buy the I-Hotel. The board supported the measure to spend the money on police and fire protection until Moscone vetoed its decision. In an emotional plea, Supervisor Dianne Feinstein asked other board members to sustain Moscone's veto because the hotel's residents faced eviction the next Monday. On November 15, the Board of Supervisors upheld the mayor's veto in a close 6–5 vote.[52]

On November 30, the Board of Supervisors was scheduled to vote on Moscone's plan. About three hundred tenants and supporters gathered in front of City Hall before the meeting to pressure the board to support the plan and witness the vote. The vote was 6–4 in favor of Moscone's plan, with Supervisors Feinstein, Robert E. Gonzales, Bob Mendelsohn, John L. Molinari, Alfred J. Nelder, and Ronald Pelosi in the majority. The politically conservative Supervisors John J. Barbagelata, Quentin L. Kopp, Peter Tamaras, and Dorothy von Beroldingen opposed. Supervisor Terry Francois was absent.[53] Thus, the tenants won a key victory, although by a slim margin. After the victory, the Housing Authority formally made a bid to Four Seas to purchase the I-Hotel for 1,262,500 dollars. Four Seas was not willing to sell, even though the offer represented a 50 percent profit over its original investment.[54]

The final phase of Moscone's plan was to establish the public necessity of purchasing the International Hotel at a Housing Authority hearing on December 23, 1976.[55] Five hundred to eight hundred supporters attended the all-day hearing at the school district's Nourse Auditorium. Supporters overflowed the auditorium and crowded onto the street. Three questions had to be decided at the hearing: (1) whether "the public interest and necessity require[s] the proposed project;" (2) whether "the proposed project is planned or located in the manner that will be most compatible with the public good and the least private injury"; and (3) whether "the property sought to be acquired is necessary for the project." Four Seas' attorneys repeatedly tried to show that the building had reached the end of its useful life; that it should be razed and never had been adequately safe for the residents. They argued that it was not necessary for the public interest and that it was impossible for a group of aging, low-income pensioners to handle such a deal.[56]

Two witnesses provided convincing rebuttals to these arguments: William McBride, former chief building inspector in Mill Valley, Marin County, and Hal Dunleavy, who had served as the Housing Authority's information director in 1939 and as a financial consultant on housing since then. According to McBride, the I-Hotel would be excellent for the proposed use of decent low-cost housing:

> I think I could sum it up, unless you want to go into some of the more technical aspects of the building. Very simply, I'm a grandfather, and I value my children and grandchildren. And I'm not kidding you and I'm not trying to make a point, but I would feel as safe to stay in this IH overnight as I would in the Mark Hopkins, the Fairmont, and this big square device up on Van Ness and some of the other hotels I've been in here. And I mean that quite sincerely.[57]

Dunleavy, a renowned and respected housing activist, spoke about the feasibility of the Moscone plan, refuting objections about the amount of money it required. He further stated that the incoming presidential administration of Jimmy Carter would pour money into the cities, some of which would find its way into the I-Hotel.[58]

The five commissioners voted unanimously that obtaining the hotel was a public necessity. However, one commissioner, Cleo Wallace, was disturbed by outbursts among the hotel's supporters in the auditorium. She declared that she had been poor all her life and for eight years lived in public housing, and she may have thought that the tenants were being manipulated. "I don't like anybody using us," she said. "I think a lot of games are going on, and I don't like to be used as a tool." Referring to the outbursts, she offered advice to the tenants:

> I think the IH tenants ought to stop and think about who's with them, how long, and what is their motive. I have grave concerns when people make clear statements as "I am with you" and "We pledge." With all that pledging, no dollars are in the bank. . . . My vote is on some conditions, very clear. Not one dollar coming from the tenants presently in public housing, basically because [public-housing tenants] put a resolution and that body stated very clearly that they do not want that to happen. So with this in mind I vote that you may have the International Hotel.[59]

Her comments reflected some of the fears of the poor in public housing first expressed at the October 21 hearing that money might be taken from them in favor of others.

Reverend Jim Jones of People's Temple, who was also a Housing Authority commissioner, tried to allay Wallace's fears and bring unity to the room by stating to the crowd: "I hope we heard, loud and clear, the message of Mrs. Wallace, that we should be equally concerned with all minorities and all poor people when they are facing eviction." At the same, time, Jones urged the city to take financial responsibility for the I-Hotel because he thought that the Moscone plan was not adequately thought out. "To this day," he said, "[it] remain[s] unresolved in my mind, such as the financing for the operation and maintenance of the project."[60]

After the victory at the Housing Authority, the tenants were guarded in their joy. They knew that the struggle in many ways had just begun. Many details had to be worked out between the IHTA and the Housing Authority, such as the terms of a lease agreement, the formal incorporation of the IHTA as a nonprofit corporation, and the securing of insurance coverage for the building. All of this was to be completed by January 10, 1977. The day after the hearing, the petition for immediate possession of the I-Hotel by the Housing Authority was to be filed. If all went well, the eviction order would be voided.

This was not to be.[61] When Tom Vizzard, the attorney representing the Housing Authority, went to the Superior Court the next afternoon, he got a nasty surprise. Four Seas' attorneys had been there earlier in the morning and had filed a "Writ of Mandamus and Review" on the Housing Authority. A writ can legally demand that a public body either carry out an obligated action or stop some prohibited activity. This writ was designed to block the Housing Authority from exercising eminent domain. Four Seas contended that the public-necessity hearing was illegal, and the Housing Authority could not take property on behalf of a third party. In this case, the third party was regarded as commercial interests, such as the bookstore and the community centers in the International Hotel.[62]

The hearing on Four Seas' challenge to the eminent-domain action was to be held in the courtroom of Judge Byron Arnold. This was bad news for the tenants. Arnold had earlier overruled the Board of Permit Appeals's finding that Four Seas' demolition permit had expired. Further, he was a major real-estate operator himself. The *San Francisco Bay Guardian* exposed Judge Arnold as a big landlord who had been involved in twenty-two real-estate transactions within the previous four years. Perhaps even more disturbing was his family relationship to Judge Donald B. Constine, the brother-in-law of Nancy Jane Constine, one of the previous owners of the I-Hotel. Lawyers for the IHTA petitioned for Judge Arnold to disqualify himself, but he refused, stating that this was an eminent-domain issue, and his real-estate holdings were not relevant. After the local newspaper's exposé, he did step down from the case, however, offering the excuse that he was too busy with his responsibilities as Port Commissioner.[63]

There were other complications, as well as disheartening news. Hal Dunleavy, the consultant in charge of financing the I-Hotel, entered the hospital, very sick, and the tenants lost a major figure in local housing politics. The Housing Authority's chief counsel, John Sullivan, thought that Moscone's plan was too risky and insisted on indemnification terms that froze the IHTA's assets. Judge Brown continued to press Sheriff Hongisto to evict. By May 1977, the IHTA was to present evidence of financing, and commitments that proved monies would be reimbursed to the Housing Authority. The IHTA had a one hundred thousand dollar grant from the Catholic Bishop's Campaign for Human Development, approximately fifty thousand dollars in back rent, and an application for an additional one hundred thousand dollars from the Catholic church. The possibility of getting the rest of the 1.3 million dollars seemed dim at that moment. Leaders in the Mayor's Office, on the Board of Supervisors, and at the Housing Authority were growing impatient. Moreover, disagreements about the Moscone plan within the IHTA surfaced publicly as more tenants voiced criticisms.[64]

Opposition to Moscone's Plan and Joe Diones

From the start, Mayor Moscone's plan had opponents among the tenants and their supporters, making it difficult to generate support. The most vocal opponents among the tenants were Felix Ayson, Frankie de los Reyes, and So Chung, who called it the "buy-back plan." They maintained that it was not financially feasible for the tenants to obtain such a large amount of money and essentially agreed with Four Seas' argument that, overall, the plan was financially unrealistic. They contended that even if they could buy the property, they would not be able to pay the property taxes and would end up being evicted just the same. These critics insisted that the city use eminent domain in a different way: The city should take the building over by eminent domain and hand it over to the IHTA to administer as a city-owned low-income housing project. That way, no third party, such as the IHTA, would be required to buy the building back from the city. Moscone repeatedly rejected the idea.

On the surface, the alternative plan seemed to free the tenants of the burden of raising the money to buy back the hotel. However, it also had serious drawbacks. If the I-Hotel were operated as a city-owned housing project, the Housing Authority would have to give those on the public-housing waiting list the first chance to live there. At the time, the waiting list had more than 5,500 people—over half of them elderly—and they would be placed ahead of the I-Hotel tenants. Thus, the building would be saved, but the tenants would be made homeless, and Manilatown as a community would be destroyed. When black women from San Francisco's Hunters Point area criticized the Moscone plan at the October hearing out of fear that their demands for housing would be undercut, the IHTA's attorneys responded that the Moscone plan would not affect public housing policies and priorities.[65] The rights of current applicants for public housing posed a very difficult complication for the alternative plan.

As disagreements began to unfold, tenants looked at their own leadership and began to seek changes. Felix Ayson, who had considerable rapport with many of the young supporters, frequently voiced his opposition to the Moscone plan. He said:

> We are asking the city to buy this hotel as its responsibility to provide us with low-rent housing. The city planned to buy the building using eminent domain and sell it to us. We were never consulted. They expected us to pay back the loan in one year. We were opposed to that plan because we could not raise enough money to pay it back. . . . We believe that the city should use eminent domain. They can get federal housing money to buy the hotel. But instead of trying to sell it to us, they should make it into public housing run by the Tenants Association.[66]

Many within the coalition of supporters also strongly opposed the buy-back plan because they believed the small shops and progressive community organizations—that is, the commercial tenants—would end up paying higher rent or subsidizing the residential tenants for the cost of maintenance, repairs, and taxes.

As criticism of the so-called buy-back plan increased among the tenants, so did their opposition to the leadership of Joe Diones. Diones had worked closely with the Mayor's Office, the IHTA's lawyers, and the Housing Authority to formulate the plan and facilitate its execution. As he became more isolated, he defended the plan even more vociferously. In addition, his health was deteriorating, and his illness caused him to act irrationally. I watched as he signed documents he did not comprehend, instigated violence at meetings, and even unwittingly welcomed the deputies when they came to post eviction notices on the door in January 1977.

As differences within the IHTA ripened, Diones's leadership both as manager of the I-Hotel and as chairman of the IHTA was increasingly challenged. His style was to run the IHTA like a top-down bureaucratic union organization, with him as the boss at the top. The organizing skills he had learned in the longshoreman's union gave Diones the confidence to make alliances with forces beyond the tenants at the I-Hotel, a task that other tenants were not prepared to undertake at the time. At the start of the anti-eviction conflict, tenants deferred to his leadership. For the most part, they went along with his decisions, thinking that they were fortunate enough to have someone take charge. The respect with which the tenants regarded him came from his forcefulness and—in the initial battles—his effectiveness.

As the struggle became more complicated, however, more tenants had to take on leading roles, and they (particularly the Filipino tenants) no longer appreciated his "dictatorial methods" and bullying style. Unfortunately, Diones met disagreements with the other tenants with threats and verbal and sometimes physical abuse. At times, he would even convince others to do his dirty work. Eventually, these methods backfired. Tenants grew more confident about their own abilities; they felt strength in their unity; and they were supported by the young KDP activists. Their doubts about the buy-back plan grew, alongside their doubts about Diones's abilities to negotiate a plan or even deal effectively with city officials.

Leading tenants questioned the buy-back plan because they viewed it as self-defeating. They thought it would be impossible to pay the 1.5 million dollars back to the city. Many also felt that if they had been brought into the discussion earlier, they could have fully understood its repercussions. The deal had been struck without their knowledge, and their sense of having been mistreated was directed at Diones.

Felix Ayson, a vocal opponent of the Moscone plan, stood out as one of the most articulate and politically astute of the tenants. He was a former union leader who was frequently called on to speak at rallies. Although he had a thick accent, he could summarize in plain language what action was needed. He was charming and sociable to his supporters. Disabled after suffering a heart attack and stroke in 1972, he walked slowly with a cane. He was also almost totally deaf—it was a familiar sight at the hotel to see young people holding conversations with him by yelling into his ear—but this did not stop him from vehemently debating positions with supporters and making speeches on behalf of the I-Hotel. Manong Felix had a great deal of influence over the other tenants and supporters, and his opposition to the Moscone plan gained support.

Manong Felix was born on November 20, 1897, in the Ilocos region in the Philippines and completed high school there. His completion of high school was an achievement in itself, especially among that generation of Filipinos, who rarely completed the primary grades. During World War I, he joined the U.S. Armed Forces. After the war, he became a schoolteacher. American tourists and missionaries told him glowing tales about the freedom and opportunity to be found in America, so he decided to come. He saved his money and sold part of the property he had inherited from his parents and paid his own way, arriving in San Francisco in 1926. Felix told his life story more than fifty years later:

> I was a schoolteacher teaching third grade, and tourists and missionaries came over here and visited in my school, and then during recess we had conversations outside the school. They been telling me the United States is a democratic government, land of opportunity, land of equality. When I came here, [it was the] opposite. I was lost. I feel like I was lost. The only thing that saved me, the first Filipinos who came before me in the International Hotel who helped me find a job. So I feel oppressed, discrimination, race prejudice, and everything—and insulted on the street by young people. When I pass by [they say], "Hey, goo goo!"[67]

When he arrived in the United States, he immediately moved to the I-Hotel. He wanted to continue his education and practice a profession in the United States. But those dreams were dashed when he had to make ends meet, and Filipinos could find only menial jobs—dishwasher, busboy, houseboy. Felix joined the other Filipinos living an itinerant lifestyle, going from the rural areas to work in the fields to the Alaskan canneries, then back to the I-Hotel. During the Depression, Manong Felix was involved in organizing Filipino farm workers, and he even led a successful strike in the fields. During World War II, he became a soldier in the First Filipino Infantry of the U.S. Army and became an American citizen in 1943 at Camp Beale, California. That same year, Felix married a Creole woman from New Orleans. After the war, under the GI bill, he pursued an education in electrical engineering. However, he found that he could not make a living and instead went to work as an elevator operator. His wife died in an automobile accident in 1964. He retired in 1968 and moved permanently to the I-Hotel in 1969. The hotel had been his home intermittently since 1926.

Manong Felix, who was eighty years old at the time of the eviction, had a life history typical of the tenants who lived at the I-Hotel and he was regarded with great respect. Because of his experience, his eloquence, and his true warmth of feeling, his opposition to the Moscone plan had to be taken seriously. Felix was a formidable opponent, and the other leftist groups who also opposed the Moscone plan enjoyed his support, exacerbating the discord and confusion.[68]

The KDP initially supported the Moscone plan, along with Diones's leadership. Emil, Jeanette, and I began to see his inflexibility and authoritarian leadership style as counterproductive, although we regarded the Moscone plan, in one form or another, as a tactic still worth supporting. At the very least, the plan, along with the complicated court appeals, would stall the eviction until a more satisfactory solution could be devised.

The Filipino tenants, in conjunction with the three of us on the KDP's internal team, made plans to neutralize Diones's influence. If need be, we would seek his ouster, but we KDP activists saw this as a difficult and dangerous last resort. First, Charles Smith was ousted as vice-chairman, and Emil de Guzman took his place. Diones respected Emil: They had years of experience working together. Unfortunately, Diones would not accept second billing, nor would he share power. His prestige and credibility were on the line, and he fought hard to remain in complete control. The tenants, particularly the Filipino tenants, understood that if Diones was an obstacle to progress, he eventually would have to be voted out of office and removed. Ousting him would not be easy. He had supporters inside and outside the IHTA, and he recruited them to intimidate the tenants and their supporters. Diones grew more and more isolated. For months, Emil, as vice-chairman, kept the IHTA together as he tried to contain the threats of violence by the increasingly unstable chairman.

Mural on the Jackson Street side of the International Hotel created by the Kearny Street Workshop, 1975. *(Photo courtesy of Tom Drescher)*

Kearny Street facade of the International Hotel, 1975. *(Photo courtesy of Jerry Jew)*

Manongs spending time at the Lucky M Pool Hall in the I-Hotel, early to mid-1970s. *(Photo courtesy of Chris Fujimoto)*

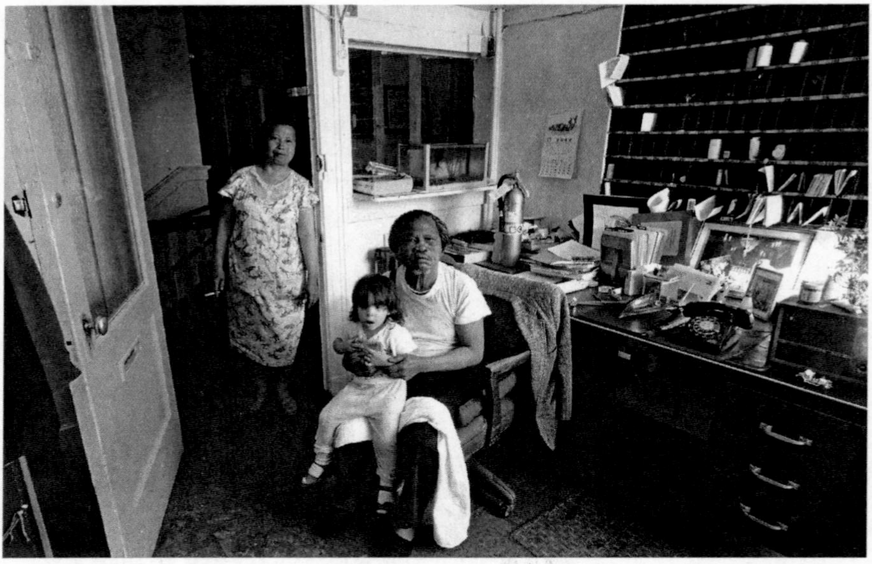

Joe Diones, manager of the I-Hotel, with child in his office in the mid-1970s. *(Photo courtesy of Chris Huie)*

Faustino (Tino) Regino and his wife with friends in front of Tino's Barber Shop. *(Photo courtesy of Calvin "Robbie" Roberts)*

Claudio Domingo, Anacleto Moniz (in window), and Luisa de la Cruz tend the tiny garden in the I-Hotel's light well. *(Photo courtesy of Chris Huie)*

Felix Ayson, one of the most outspoken tenant leaders, in his room. *(Photo courtesy of Calvin "Robbie" Roberts)*

Tenants and young activists on a field trip to the San Diego Zoo: *from left to right,* Wahat Tompao, Luisa de la Cruz, Estella Habal, Felipe Daguro, and Jeanette Lazam. *(Photo property of Estella Habal)*

Wahat Tompao speaking at a rally in front of the I-Hotel. Behind him is the IHTA's Vice-Chairman Calvin Roberts. *(Photo courtesy of Calvin "Robbie" Roberts)*

Demonstration to support the I-Hotel. Holding the banner on the right is the tenant leader Wahat Tompao; on the left is the Latino community activist Juan Cruz. *(Photo courtesy of Kearny Street Workshop)*

Mass demonstration in front of the I-Hotel blocking Kearny Street. *(Photo courtesy of Kearny Street Workshop)*

Sheriff Richard Hongisto swings a sledgehammer to open tenants' doors during the eviction. This photo haunted Hongisto through the rest of his political career. *(Photo courtesy of Calvin "Robbie" Roberts)*

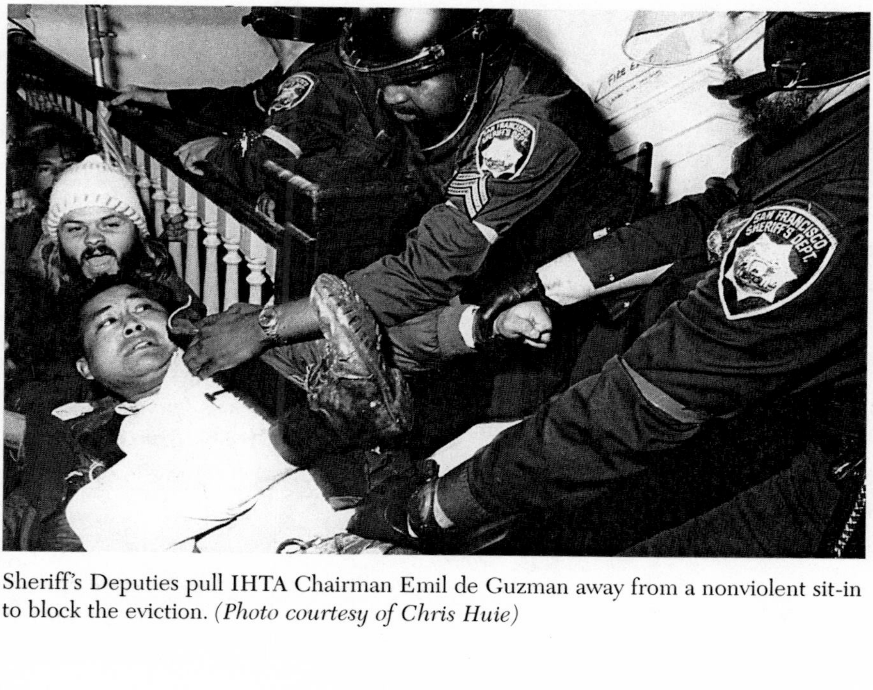

Sheriff's Deputies pull IHTA Chairman Emil de Guzman away from a nonviolent sit-in to block the eviction. *(Photo courtesy of Chris Huie)*

Night of the eviction, August 3-4, 1977: Mounted police charge the human barricade in front of the I-Hotel. *(Photo courtesy of Bob Hsiang)*

Police move against the human barricade defending the I-Hotel during the eviction night. *(Photo courtesy of Chris Huie)*

CHAPTER FIVE

"*Makibaka!* Dare to Struggle!"

The IHTA and the KDP, 1977

Tenants Lead the Mass Movement

STOP THE EVICTION! WE WON'T MOVE!
STOP THE EVICTION! WE WON'T MOVE!

Seven thousand people chanted as they circled the block of the International Hotel on Sunday, January 16, 1977, a day before the expected eviction. Swaying in unison like a giant snake, the crowd shouted in staccato bursts: "Stop the eviction! We won't move! Stop the eviction! We won't move!" A large portion of the demonstration was composed of African American families from San Francisco's Fillmore district who had been brought by Reverend Jim Jones's People's Temple church in several school buses.[1] Dancing the rumba with hands on the hips of the demonstrator in front, the contingent from People's Temple church infected the crowd with a carnival excitement. Jones, a rising star in San Francisco politics, had recently been appointed to the Housing Commission, and the two thousand people he brought from the Fillmore District—the largest single group ever to turn out for an I-Hotel demonstration—added considerable clout to the rally. Because it had such a large and active base, People's Temple's support was sought by politicians and movements throughout the city. No one anticipated the descent into megalomaniacal madness and mass suicide on which Jones would take himself and his followers in Guyana on November 18, 1978.

Adding even more drama, Sheriff Richard Hongisto and Undersheriff James Denman had received contempt-of-court convictions six days earlier. California Superior Court Judge John E. Benson stayed the sentence for ten days to allow Hongisto and Denman to appeal to the California State Court of Appeal.[2] Meanwhile, Judge Ira Brown's order for eviction no later than 5:00 P.M. on January 19 was still in effect. Hongisto's refusal to carry out the eviction and his sentence had alarmed the power structure, and negative editorials had begun to appear in the press. To appease critics, Sheriff Hongisto and Undersheriff Denman nailed a two-inch thick wad of eviction notices on the front door of the I-Hotel at 7:45 P.M. on January 11, timed within the January 19 deadline.[3] This brought 2,500–3,000 supporters out to demonstrate in front of the hotel on January 12.

The sheriff was still fighting his contempt citation, and he faced the prospect of jail time. As a politician who had been elected by the same coalition of progressive forces as Mayor Moscone, Hongisto knew that evicting poor, helpless tenants could tarnish his future career, but he also faced considerable threats from the political and financial elite and Democratic Party establishment. Hongisto had ambitions for higher office. Though the sheriff ultimately would capitulate, at this stage, the tenants and their supporters were astonished at his resistance to court orders, and he had become a hero in their eyes. They hoped that he would continue to defy the law, and he did eventually spend five days in the San Francisco County jail in San Bruno, starting on April 29, 1977.[4] In addition to appealing to Hongisto personally at meetings, tenants and supporters calculated that the growing public sentiment opposed to the eviction would continue to sway him.

Sympathetic local news media reported how the saga had tugged at the hearts of most San Franciscans:

> The International Hotel is the year's cause célèbre. . . . The elderly Asian tenants who face eviction from their $50 a month rooms have gripped the sympathies of some Bay Area liberals and activists like nothing since the Vietnam War. Their battle—drawn as the fight between the "little guy" and a faceless, multinational corporation—has protest crowds as high as 5,000, the largest demonstrations since the anti-war movement of the late 1960s. . . . In San Francisco, where entire blocks of redevelopment area land stand vacant in the Fillmore and [S]outh of Market, the International Hotel is a symbol. A symbol of demolished low-rent housing: rising rents and neglected old people. And possibly, the symbol of a victory. If the hotel survives as a home for the poor, some supporters hope the city will begin to confront the urban ills they believe the International Hotel symbolizes.[5]

As public support for the tenants touched every corner of the city, tenant leaders became bold, and other tenants, such as Wahat Tompao, Nita Rader, Pete Yamamoto, and Mrs. D, emerged as leaders in the midst of the battle. As supporters and politicians alike witnessed their fierce determination to remain in their chosen home, asserting that the young activists were egging the tenants on became increasingly untenable.

On January 16, tenants, organizers, and supporters drew tremendous strength from the seven-thousand-strong demonstration. The tenant speaker that day was

Wahat Tompao, one of the Filipino elders who had come forward publicly to save the I-Hotel and stop the eviction. Although many were active in defending their home and in attending IHTA meetings, very few of the tenants stepped forward as public figures, for a variety of reasons. Some were infirm, and others felt embarrassed by their accents and broken English, and they feared being misunderstood. For Manong Wahat, the struggle was too important to worry about any perceived personal handicap.

Wahat Tompao became one of the most active and outspoken of the tenant leaders in the year before the eviction and eventually was elected treasurer of the IHTA. He spoke English with a thick accent, yet that did not stop him from bravely making many public speeches throughout the city. Manong Wahat's transformation was remarkable as he organized and campaigned for himself and for all the poor and elderly. His courage was in the tradition of his tribal people, the Benguet Igorot, to fight against foreign invaders. History-conscious Filipinos knew that the Benguet people in the Philippines, one of the Igorot tribes, had never been fully subjugated by Spanish colonizers.[6] Manong Wahat's own peers at times derided him for his Benguet ways and traditional beliefs. For example, he believed that being unfaithful to his wife back home would cause sickness or an accident to strike a member of his family. He would proudly don tribal attire during Filipino events, even though other Filipinos expressed concern that Americans might view all Filipinos as "primitives." Their fears had some justification, since Filipinos had insultingly been called "headhunters" and "primitive" from the time the first American soldiers landed on the islands in 1898. But Manong Wahat reveled in the fact that his people did indeed eat dog as a delicacy and laughed at the intended slur that all Filipinos were "dog-eaters."

I spent every day with Wahat Tompao in the last year before eviction, attending meetings with him, driving him to political functions, and simply hanging out, and I grew to appreciate the many sources of his resolve. I remember when the I-Hotel tenants got a glimpse of his heritage when he donned the Benguet costume of feathers and G-string during the Philippine National Day celebration on June 12, 1977, at Dolores Park in San Francisco.[7] He did not seem to pay attention to other Filipinos snickering behind his back when he danced an ancient warrior dance. He refused to be made to feel inferior by the lowland, Christianized Filipinos who thought of themselves as modern and civilized. Despite the taunts by those who observed him, Manong Wahat stood his ground. As support for the tenants grew to a crescendo, he grew bolder, stronger, and more unashamed, and when he spoke at an event of the American Indian Movement honoring activists from the Pine Ridge Reservation, he was delighted to find common "indigenous" bonds. It was at that event that he discovered that some Plains Indians also ate dog, and he laughed at the slurs. He found others who cherished traditional, tribal values and attachment to land and who were willing to fight for their rights.[8]

Wahat Tompao was born on February 14, 1910, in Pico La Trinidad, Mountain Province, Philippines, and served in the U.S Navy from 1928 to 1949. He first came to the International Hotel in 1929 when he was a mess attendant in the U.S. Navy. Like other sailors and merchant seaman, he stayed at the I-Hotel whenever he was in San Francisco, and he made it his permanent home in 1963. His wife and five children stayed in the Philippines, and he sent most of his money home to them. Two of his daughters immigrated to Seattle. Manong Wahat's history as a veteran of the U.S. Armed Forces and a husband sending money to the Philippines was typical of the conditions that many of the tenants faced. They had to live cheaply so they could support their families in the Philippines, and residing at the hotel gave them this opportunity.

Wahat Tompao made his most rousing speech to date in front of the seven-thousand-strong demonstration on that evening of January 16. He was heartened and encouraged by the massive crowd, and the speech was among his greatest personal and political triumphs. But it was also indicative of his political readiness to fight the eviction. On that January evening, Manong Wahat, leaning out a second-floor window, spoke lovingly to his supporters in his strong and loud voice:

> Dr. Martin Luther King said he had a dream. I dream that this building will be for poor people, for the senior people. I dream that this building will never move. I dream you people will never move. I dream you are here tonight. I hope this will be always in the bottom of my heart.[9]

Manong Wahat used the metaphor of dreams to invoke the rights of poor people and minorities, adapting Martin Luther King's words. He identified with King because he saw the I-Hotel struggle as an attack on minority people seeking their civil rights. Although he was in his mid-sixties, he radiated a robust quality that underscored his quiet dignity and elegance, and he stood with the bearing of a warrior.

But would the next day, January 17, be the day of the eviction—even though it was the day the city observed Martin Luther King's birthday? Although King's birthday was not yet a federal holiday, organizers were suspicious, because prior eviction threats coincided with holidays. Rumors of eviction had come during the Thanksgiving and Christmas holiday periods, both times leaving tenants and sympathizers scrambling. The tenants and their supporters saw this as a ruthless tactic on the part of Four Seas, which took advantage of holidays and rest days to launch vicious attacks meant to exhaust and demoralize the resistance. Tenants and supporters had no choice but to prepare for the worst. But on each occasion the end did not come.

On January 17, the tenants once again had a reprieve, although on grounds they suspected were meant to undermine their credibility. Judge Brown stayed his latest order of eviction for five weeks because Police Chief Charles Gain had telephoned him the previous afternoon claiming that automatic weapons had been spotted on the roof of the hotel and that quantities of gasoline had been purchased.[10] Judge Brown, conceding that some danger was involved, said: "I have real concern regarding the probability of violence and death of innocent parties who have no involvement." The "innocent parties" he meant were "mainly police officers of the city and county" rather than the frail, elderly tenants.[11]

The tenants did not know about the reports of the gasoline and automatic weapons until reporters told them the next day. The situation grew even more tense because the groups within the coalition were suspicious of the Federal Bureau of Investigation's Counterintelligence Program (COINTELPRO) and other covert police maneuvers. Most supporters were well aware of the COINTELPRO activities launched against the Black Panther Party in the Bay Area, and we were nervous that the latest stay of eviction might be part of similar covert actions to give the authorities a pretext for a violent attack.[12] During this time, I was regularly followed by unidentified agents in unmarked cars as I drove between my home in the Mission District and the I-Hotel, and others felt they were also under surveillance.

Still, we scoffed at what we knew to be fabrications. Raymond Burciaga, one of the younger hotel tenants, retorted, "The closest thing to a weapon you'll find here is a toothpick." When a local reporter asked Claudio Domingo, a seventy-six-year-old tenant, about weapons and gasoline, he said, "I don't believe it. . . . I am a tenant. I go in every room. Every corner. Every alley. I have not seen it. We have fought this since 1969. It is the last part now. We win or lose."[13] While Domingo understood that this was the hotel's last stand, he also knew that the organizers stressed nonviolent tactics to achieve our political goals.

While the tenants got stronger and support for them expanded, the situation seemed to get bleaker and more desperate. Right-wing antagonists, property-rights forces, and pro-growth city liberals began to launch counterattacks in editorials opposing Sheriff Richard Hongisto's reluctance to evict and trying to discredit the anti-eviction movement as a radical fringe. Judge Brown, who had ruled Hongisto in contempt of court, made an inflammatory statement to the news media: "If this sheriff had been sheriff a few years ago . . . [demonstrators would] still be sitting in on Auto Row, at the Sheraton Palace [Hotel] and, probably, San Francisco State as well."[14] Many in the city were outraged by his references to major civil-rights demonstrations for integration in the 1960s and the student strike in 1968 at San Francisco State. The I-Hotel supporters felt maligned by such overtly racist remarks, particularly because many of them had been student activists and civil-rights advocates who had participated in those struggles, which, by the mid 1970s, were considered key moments in San Francisco's history.

The tenants were ready for the impending confrontation—politically. But with the many false alarms and twists and turns, the struggle took a heavy toll on them. Although they were morally and politically strong, most of the tenants were old, and some were in poor health. Several who had been vocal spokesmen for the struggle died during this critical period. First among these deaths was Frankie de los Reyes, who suffered a heart attack. Born in 1901, Manong Frankie came to the United States in the 1920s, worked all his life as a farmworker and seaman, and moved to the International Hotel for his retirement.[15]

Claudio Domingo passed away on March 26, 1977. For years, Manong Claudio had struggled with complex abdominal pain and a weak heart, and he finally succumbed to heart failure. When he took seriously ill two months before he died, soon after the January 16 demonstration, he was still attending the tenants' association board meetings and mass support meetings, despite doctors' advice to rest.[16] Claudio Domingo, like many others of his generation, had chosen to live at the I-Hotel because it was affordable and comfortable. He had arrived in America from the Philippines in the 1950s and had settled soon after in San Francisco's Manilatown, renting a permanent room at the International Hotel. Like Wahat Tompao, he had left his wife and children behind and immigrated to the United States to send money home to his impoverished family. A veteran, he had guarded the Panama Canal during World War I and served in the cavalry division of the Philippine Scouts during World War II. Manong Claudio was determined to fight this last battle.

Manong Claudio's death was a heavy blow. It drove home to both the tenants and the young activists the great cost of their resistance. A wake was held at the International Hotel in his honor, and as he lay in his open coffin, hundreds of supporters came to pay their respects. Emil de Guzman wrote a tribute to him in the KDP newspaper, *Ang Katipunan*:

> The severe strain and pressures in the last six months have hospitalized four elderly tenants. Manong Domingo was the last to go to a hospital—and the first to fall. In his death, one sees the ruthless character of the Four Seas and the Courts on one side and the courageous tenants fighting for their rights on the other. If there is a trait that Manong Domingo displayed until the end of his life, it was the "will to fight and determination to win.[17]

Claudio Domingo demonstrated his will to fight early in his life, while he was in the military. One day, as he was taking care of horses in the cavalry's stable, a tall, white U.S. soldier derisively called him a "monkey." Domingo grabbed a stick and clobbered the man until he was unconscious. When asked later, during his court-martial, for his reasons, Domingo remarked, "The real monkey got mad and hit him, but not me. We Filipinos are peaceful people and we are equal to everybody." The verdict was not guilty.[18]

Other tenants suffered from mounting health and emotional problems due to the severe stress. In particular, tenants were shocked that the courts had turned against their demands for decent housing. They felt that city government should do more to implement policies that benefited poor people and minorities. They personally felt hurt and shame that the city officials did not care for the poor and elderly, and the soon-to-be-homeless tenants. After working all their lives and contributing to the wealth of U.S. society, they felt that the city should at least find a solution to their housing crisis and prevent their eviction. Frank Alarcon, another veteran of both world wars, told a young reporter:

> Once you love your home, you're going to fight to protect your home. We made this city of San Francisco a rich city on account of all of us working here in this state. We pay taxes. We've paid all kinds of taxes, on things we buy and on our income. Why should we be thrown out from this hotel right on the street there, after they have made their profits? Is that right?[19]

The tenants felt that it was the city's obligation to help those in need, especially those who had risked their lives to help America win its wars.

As a consequence, the political consciousness of the Filipino tenants, particularly those who were veterans, reached a new level. As I worked with the tenants, I could detect a dramatic change. As Filipino veterans who had served in the U.S. military, they felt that they had earned respect, that they were entitled to equal treatment. Their militancy—their willingness to fight City Hall as underdogs—was matched by their growing political consciousness. What had previously been a relationship with their American rulers as loyal servants became an adversarial one as equals. The tenants realized that they deserved the same rights as any other citizen, and they became militant activists. While they felt that the rights and dignity accorded to American citizens should be extended to the Filipino minority, the Filipino veterans' consciousness broadened to other minority and poor people, as well.

During this time, the tenants developed the idea that the city had an obligation to provide low-income housing for all people: workers, the poor, the vulnerable, and the elderly. They developed a sense that they were not just tenants of a threatened building, or even of the remnants of Manilatown as an ethnic community—that is, they were not struggling only for themselves. The tenants engaged in an active relationship with city government throughout the anti-eviction movement as advocates for broader social sectors, and the I-Hotel served as a particular point of conflict to address those needs. In other words, the tenants to a great extent became class-conscious militants—"advanced workers," in the parlance of the revolutionary organizations—aware that their struggle carried profound implications for other poor and working-class communities. In their eyes, housing had become a right for poor people and minority communities, and the tenants no longer asked for their rights. They demanded them.[20]

What I found so exciting at the time was the way the thinking of the tenants began to parallel the way we young radicals thought. The consciousness of the Filipino tenants merged with that of the Filipino youth: All of us called for the democratic rights of all minorities, working people, and the poor. Although age and infirmity tempered the tenants' militancy, their vision extended to the entire world. "I have felt the oppression of the people," Felix Ayson explained in an interview. "Our fight is a human rights fight. By saving the Hotel we are saving the respect for human dignity. We want to restore that. By saving the respect for human dignity, we are helping to save the human race."[21]

Manong Wahat had also gone through that political transformation. He earnestly put all his effort into making the "dream" he spoke about in his speech during the demonstration a reality. He went to City Hall with a delegation to ask Mayor Moscone to stop the eviction; the mayor refused to see them, explaining, "There was no need."[22] Manong Wahat attempted to shame the mayor by saying, "Because I'm brown, because I'm old, because I'm ugly, because I'm Asian, is this why you do these things?" As he went on to explain to a reporter, Mayor Moscone "does this because we're poor. He doesn't care about poor people. What kind of father is he, this father of the city?" He went on to tell the mayor what he could do for them: "You'd better think it over. You and Hongisto can go to jail together. Then the people will love you. They won't care if you went to jail—they'll love you because you stand for poor people."[23]

Wahat Tompao was tireless as well as humble. After he spoke at a rally, a reporter asked him what kind of response he was getting from the public. "Everywhere I go now, people I don't know say, 'I know you, you're Wahat, I saw you on the television.' In public I shout like hell. But I want people to know, I want help. You are well-educated. I have only a fourth grade education. But I am learning. Someday, you will be old, too. Don't end up in trouble like I am."[24] On the morning before the eviction, at 6 o'clock, I took him in my beat-up, yellow 1963 Volkswagen to talk on a show at KPOO, a local radio station on Natoma Street in the South of Market area. When an interviewer asked Wahat what he would do if he was evicted, he answered, "I'll chain myself to the bed." This kind of fierce courage electrified supporters and demonstrated the depth of the tenants' passion.

The Fall of Joe Diones

Meanwhile, Joe Diones continued to defend his position as chairman and advocate for the Moscone plan, increasingly using threats of violence to intimidate tenants who opposed him. With the other KDP activists, I had taken the position that the Moscone plan should be supported—but as a stop-gap measure, a way to postpone eviction to give us time to devise other, more favorable eminent-domain plans. We also thought it was necessary to work with the politicians and other liberals, to keep the front as broad as possible, to win time to gain more support. Diones played a crucial role in keeping that support. Many of the other radicals disdained working with politicians.

When the KDP adopted the strategy that low-income housing was a right and that the principal goal was to elevate human rights over property rights, the tenants championed that position without hesitation. In the KDP's view, the destruction of Manilatown was a result of the city leadership's plans to expand the financial district. If minority communities and poor people stood in the way of these plans, then private-property interests would weigh in heavily to make sure the impediment would be removed. Thus, the battle against eviction was the first line of defense. Housing activists knew from experience that once tenants were out of the building, their legal and political power would be severely circumscribed. According to our analysis, the battle to prevent eviction was paramount; staying in the building was the most important immediate goal—as long as the safety of the tenants could be reasonably assured. Consequently, the KDP had supported the Moscone plan because it was a means to stop the eviction, even if it was flawed and might not have worked. At the very least, it halted eviction plans, and it allowed us time to gather support and develop alternatives.

Those tenants and supporters who opposed the Moscone plan considered it irreparably flawed, and even foolish, because it stipulated that the tenants would be responsible for paying the funds back to the city. Would the tenants be able to repay the money? Could they keep up with property taxes as real-estate values went up? These were serious concerns, and to many what seemed a potential solution was only a trap—"a covert eviction plan . . . since it would justify eviction when its terms could not be met" and a way to evict the tenants through their own bankruptcy.[25] On the positive side, funds had already been secured from private sources, and there was no reason to believe that other sources would not be available or forthcoming, especially with the liberal administration of Jimmy Carter newly installed in the White House.

The KDP also supported Diones's remaining as the leader of the IHTA, a position the other leftist organizations disagreed with vehemently. Diones had a personal relationship with Mayor Moscone. Cultivating such a relationship was indispensable for the political support of affordable housing for the poor and the legal strategy of obtaining eminent domain. However, Diones refused to share leadership with tenants as they stepped forward, and his condescension toward them became more and more of an obstacle to building an effective collective resistance. For a long time before the breaking point was reached, the active tenants and the KDP activists were forced to maneuver around Diones.

During this period, a larger number of KDP activists began to work on the support committees than the three activists who were "internal" to the IHTA—that is, Emil de Guzman, Jeanette Lazam, and me. The additional KDP activists were brought to bolster Diones's position. Our analysis was that, if the opposition to Diones's leadership and the Moscone plan had succeeded, it would have hastened the eviction. We calculated that the Moscone plan—and all of the legal wrangling it involved—could hold off eviction for months. The KDP activists made a tactical alliance with Diones, even though we had sharp disagreements with his violent tactics. Tenants who opposed what they called the buy-back eviction plan were disappointed in us, while the young radicals who supported them denounced the KDP activists as reformist opportunists.

Diones regarded the KDP's support for his position as a green light to expand his influence, a program he took on in characteristic fashion. During the winter of 1976, he brought in three goons to back up his authority. The thugs were used to taking orders from a boss in gangster fashion, and they were willing to bully the young radicals and look menacingly at the elderly tenants. They spent time hanging out in the hotel, acting as if they owned the place. Dealing with them was made even more complicated by the fact that one of the goons was the brother of a KDP activist who was active in the I-Hotel movement. In this instance, family feeling went only so far. This was a very intimate confrontation, on all sides, complicated by the fact that the KDP continued to support Diones while criticizing his leadership. From Diones's point of view, the thugs were there to protect us, too, although he also used them to intimidate us and to make sure we kept in line. The thug who was the brother of a KDP activist once leveled his gun at me in a hallway of the hotel. I had been criticizing Diones to some of the tenants, and the gun sent the clear message to shut up or else.

I was terrified, of course. For a long time, the KDP members were conflicted, and we would discuss the various options with the tenants. We had to argue against Diones's use of threats while still analyzing the political situation as sophisticatedly as possible. If the tenants wanted to oust Diones, was the time right? Would Mayor Moscone withdraw his support? Could we afford a major upheaval when we faced so many threats of eviction? Would a change of leadership in the midst of conflict weaken our base of support? Who would take Diones's place? For a long time, we argued against ousting Diones because we felt that we could not adequately answer such questions in our favor.

The tenants' response to Diones's threats percolated for months, moving from fear to anger and then to calculated opposition. Diones's behavior became more and more erratic. He kept blurting out unsettling revelations and bragging about behavior that we considered shameful. For example, months after the incident, Diones boasted that he had known three days in advance that Hongisto would be posting eviction notices in January, but he had kept it a secret. Supporting the Moscone plan was one thing; now the tenants regarded Diones as a traitor. Some tenants even thought that he had embezzled money from the IHTA during his long reign, although this allegation was never proved.

When asked why he was removed from office, Nita Rader, a middle-aged Filipina tenant who later became secretary of the IHTA, said, "There's no way the tenants can pay the one million point three. It was an old plan, which the tenants had nothing to do with it. It was planned by Moscone, and Gil Graham, attorney, and the manager Diones, the former manager, which we evict him ourselves. Not because of the plan, but because he refused to show us the books."[26]

The KDP activists did actively help the tenants to get rid of Diones when he became unbalanced and violent. But we moved against him only after the tenants had become fed up with his undemocratic methods and unanimously wanted him removed. With the tenants at a boiling point, the KDP activists felt there was no choice but to join them. A vote was held at one of the IHTA meetings in June, and Diones was unanimously ousted as chairman of the IHTA and manager of the I-Hotel. But with armed thugs in the room, the vote had to be followed quickly by decisive action by the elderly tenants. After the vote, Diones was swiftly and forcefully escorted out of the building and banned from returning.

The KDP was harshly criticized by other Asian American leftists who argued that we had not used our influence with the tenants to depose Diones even sooner. Because of our leading position within the IHTA, the KDP was the only organization among the anti-eviction support groups that could have helped the tenants remove Diones. Many activists working closely with the tenants were suspicious that de Guzman, Lazam, and I had curried favor with Diones and had waited so long to oust him so we could exercise control through him. Meanwhile, liberal forces who witnessed these developments from afar criticized the KDP for having removed Diones at all. In hindsight, KDP activists speculate that it might have been possible to retain Diones as a player, in a diminished role, with the increasingly militant tenants overriding his influence. But at that time, we were young and raw novices compared with Diones in terms of exercising and holding on to power—particularly because Diones had no qualms about using violence to maintain control.

The chairmanship of the IHTA fell to Emil, one of the original student leaders from UC Berkeley. He had gained the respect of the tenants because he had volunteered his time at the hotel since the fire in 1969, and he had chosen to live in the hotel as a tenant off and on for more than five years. Although de Guzman had the stocky build of the wrestler he had been at UC Berkeley, he was soft-spoken and polite, and he always deferred to the tenants' opinions and initiatives, providing a dramatic change in style from the pugnacious Diones.[27] Wahat became the IHTA's treasurer; Nita Rader became the secretary; and Calvin (Robbie) Roberts, a young African American photographer who lived in the hotel, became the vice-chairman.

From the outside, Diones's ouster aroused suspicions that rebellious youth—particularly the KDP—had taken over. This was far from the truth. But the idea was fanned by Mayor Moscone, who considered Diones a friend and ally. De Guzman, young and soft-spoken as he was, could not carry the same weight with politicians. Yet despite his earlier contributions, Diones was no longer a respected leader for many in Manilatown. He had been too mean-spirited, talking behind tenants' backs when he disagreed with them and acting like a corrupt union boss.[28]

Diones's ouster and the opposition among some tenants to the buy-back plan caused Moscone to grow increasingly alienated from the I-Hotel. With this key politician less inclined to intervene on their behalf, the tenants had to rely even more on broad public support to influence city government and the courts. Emil was left in an untenable position: He represented the tenants as a legitimate leader at the same time that he was negotiating with city leaders about the Moscone plan, despite sharp disagreements among the tenants and supporters about the viability—and even justice—of that plan.

Some supporters in the Filipino community who had moved on and left the day-to-day International Hotel struggle for careers or families remembered Diones as a shrewd, uncompromising leader who had successfully dealt with community leaders and city officials. Others felt that his removal was untimely or that something must have gone awry. After all, Diones had stuck in there since the first eviction attempt in 1968, and now he was deposed. There was no way that a young leader like de Guzman could take his place, especially since Diones was the one who had worked out the plan with Mayor Moscone.

As KDP members such as Emil became closely tied to the elderly Filipino tenants leaders, some members of the Filipino community close to the struggle, and others on the Asian American left, wondered whether the KDP had simply taken over the IHTA. Other Filipino supporters thought that replacing Diones might hurt the struggle. At worst, they thought, the tenants might be inordinately influenced by the KDP's radical politics. "The community activists who had been involved in the I-Hotel in the past left it as soon as the left came in," Jeanette recalled:

> Even earlier, around 1975, there had been confrontations with community activists who had rejected the KDP's Marxist orientation: They removed themselves from the IH and started working with the Pilipino Organizing Committee (POC), a local organization which centered its activities in the South of Market area, and the operative thinking was that the KDP "wrote them off." Their response was, "You can have the IH. See what you can do with it. Let's see if you can do better. You'll be coming back to us." Yes, they did watch on the sidelines, supported the I-Hotel, but were unwilling to fight the battle alongside leftists. Their ferocious anti-communism prevented them from working with us at the IH.[29]

Another group, Bayanihan, which sought to organize youth in the South of Market area, was set up by Peter Almazol, a leading activist who left the I-Hotel.

Active support from the Filipino community did not go much beyond the left and progressive wing. As noted earlier, strong anticommunist prejudices complicated support within the Filipino community, especially as the KDP began to operate as a key organization in opposition to the Marcos dictatorship and in support of the New People's Army (NPA), the military arm of the CPP.

Of course, the assumption that young radicals had shoved the tenants aside was a problem of perception and preconceived notions and was easily disproved by even brief contact with the tenants themselves. As David Prowler writes in his personal account, Felix Ayson "had an answer for those who claimed that he had been unduly influenced by members of the Asian Community Center in the matter of his opposition to the 'buy-back' plan: 'That's bull——,' he said. 'They weren't influencing me. I was influencing them!'"[30]

The KDP and the IHTA

While there was no "takeover," we in the KDP did find ourselves playing contradictory roles and advancing difficult positions within the different coalitions of the anti-eviction movement. While the KDP united with the other leftists on the issue of liberation of the Third World countries from colonial or neocolonial rule, and even supported socialist and communist governments around the world, the KDP never called for revolution or socialism in the practical political world of the housing struggle. Rather, the organization maintained a keen and realistic sense that, as militant as the anti-eviction movement might be, it did not in itself form the basis for a revolutionary upsurge.

In addition, the KDP's political analysis emphasized that the Filipino community by itself did not have the basis to call for socialist revolution in the United States. The I-Hotel struggle was considered a "broader working-class struggle," as opposed to an issue with particular interest only, or even mainly, to the Filipino community. Even within the Filipino community, the KDP's general guideline meant that organizing for an issue "must be in the interests of the whole working class and not narrowly only the interest of the Filipino participants. . . . Our struggle for influence within the Filipino community should not be seen as an end in itself."[31] This meant that the International Hotel as an ethnic and cultural issue, and the need to preserve the last remnant of Manilatown for the Filipino community, was less important than the effect the anti-eviction struggle would have on the housing issue within the city as a whole. The anti-eviction movement was a fight between human rights and housing rights versus private-property rights and capitalist advantage within the system. With this orientation, meant to prevent any narrow nationalist sectarianism, we sought out alliances with all those who also highlighted the I-Hotel movement as a housing struggle.

Other organizations on the Kearny Street block that considered themselves "to the left" of the KDP perceived the KDP as "soft" leftists who had hopelessly crossed over into reformist politics. The KDP was seen as having lost its revolutionary character in the I-Hotel movement, particularly in the way it deferred to the wishes of the tenants without educating them to take what others felt was the proper militant revolutionary stance.

By 1975, the Chinese Maoist group Wei Min She had merged with a New Left Marxist–Leninist organization, the Revolutionary Communist Party (RCP). Another Chinese-based organization, I Wor Kuen (IWK), was calling for the formation of a new communist party and, in 1978, would join other groups to establish the League of Revolutionary Struggle (LRS).[32] The Wei Min She/RCP and the IWK were both vying to be (or become) the vanguard communist party in the United States, and this rivalry injected itself into the anti-eviction movement. Despite their conflicts, both organizations considered the KDP too willing to work with liberals and sympathetic city officials. Charges had been leveled that the KDP had sold out because it was willing to support the Moscone plan until that option was exhausted with the mayor. For these organizations—and for many of the independent leftists—any negotiation with the city was tantamount to betrayal and fostering illusions among the masses. As one flyer put it, "[Misleaders] tell us to not expose these tricks to the people, that liberals like Moscone and Sheriff Hongisto are our our allies. No! The city, sheriffs, and courts are working *hand-in-hand*! . . . The liberals and conservatives are paid and supported by the same finance capitalists using the tactics of reform and repression to oppose and exploit us."[33]

A large part of their disagreements with the KDP, however, had nothing to do with the immediate situation. Rather, these disagreements flowed from the KDP's unwillingness to follow every position taken by the Chinese Communist Party. The orthodox Maoists of Wei Min She/RCP and the IWK denounced the KDP for being too sympathetic to the revolution in Cuba (which the Chinese party regarded as having degenerated into a mere Soviet puppet) and for not making opposition to the Soviet Union the cornerstone of its outlook on international affairs. These ideological differences manifested themselves in hostility toward the KDP within the anti-eviction front and at times interfered with the political unity of the anti-eviction coalition.

The KDP walked a fine line between its revolutionary vision and its pragmatic, everyday politics, which focused on concrete results. As opposed to the RCP, for example, the KDP understood that revolution would not come anytime soon. Rather than anticipating imminent revolutionary upsurge, the KDP regarded the mass movements of the 1960s and '70s as beginning to ebb rather than expand. The KDP anticipated that the 1980s would be a period of retrenchment and observed that a right-wing backlash was already beginning to gain initiative in state and national politics.

Support from gay-rights activists in the coalition, particularly Bay Area Gay Liberation (BAGL), a rising force in the San Francisco Bay Area, was another point of contention. The RCP considered homosexuals bourgeois deviants and attacked the BAGL openly in the coalition. In response, one BAGL member wrote a paper denouncing the anti-gay attitudes:

> As people of principle and science it is our task to embrace with eagerness a deepening understanding of the shit we all take from male supremacist attitudes, institutions and behavior. . . . Some Marxist/Leninist individuals and organizations have an incorrect position on gayness. It is said that gayness is a part of petit-bourgeois decadence, a deformation resulting from capitalism. . . . This view reveals a lack of scientific investigation necessary for correct analysis regarding human sexuality.[34]

The KDP was sympathetic to gay rights, and gays and lesbians were members and leaders of the organization, so working with the BAGL and other such groups posed no conflict.

Liberals within the Filipino community sought to work with the city administration to get social services and such community needs as housing and health services. When it came to the anti-eviction movement, liberal Filipinos had more unity with the KDP than with the other Asian American revolutionaries. But because of the KDP's revolutionary vision, they were suspicious and tended to stay away.

With difficulty, the KDP tried to keep the organization's various interests separate. For example, we did not conduct a campaign to support the NPA within the anti-eviction front—and we certainly did not advocate support for the NPA as part of the IHTA's agenda. But KDP activists did approach individuals within the local front who we thought were open to these politics. The KDP felt that left-wing politics should be reserved for activities separate from the I-Hotel—what the activists considered propaganda and educational purposes—and the organization was careful about when to present the KDP's position on the Philippines and when to keep it out of the immediate work. However, liberal Filipinos did not care about such principled distinctions, and many could not overcome their anticommunist feelings toward the KDP within the anti-eviction battle. These liberals abandoned active support while criticizing Filipino revolutionaries from the sidelines.[35] Tenants, of course, were willing to accept any support from the KDP. The manongs' experience in the labor movement made them unafraid of radicals, and they grew to admire and trust the young activists.

At the same time, quite a few liberals and progressives in the Filipino community gave begrudging political support to the KDP because they admired our tenacity and ability to organize. We were the only Filipino organization prepared to fight the anti-eviction battle, even though individual KDP members felt ill prepared to undertake the challenge. Despite the disagreements, many within the Filipino community who did support the struggle were thankful that the KDP, with its cadre-style activists, had stepped forward. Because of their families or careers, most supporters could not engage in the twenty-four-hour-a-day battle that was required to keep up the fight to save the I-Hotel.

The battle to stop the eviction was incredibly complicated and required working out strategies and tactics on many different levels. It required engaging city officials and legal professionals as well as organizing tenants and community supporters day to day, at any hour of the day. Not many were ready to make that sacrifice. And working within the environment of increasing sectarianism between different Asian American and leftist forces was an unappetizing prospect for many independent-minded and nonideological individuals. Members of organizations such as the KDP had a level of unity, and the cadre prepared to take on such a formidable assignment. KDP activists accepted the most laborious tasks in the face of difficult conditions. Unfortunately, sectarianism and competition within the Asian American left could consume individuals, even KDP members, and only the hardiest or those who had an organization to buffer them could survive intact. All of these reservations led to the narrowing of the activist base of Filipinos beyond the KDP and our closest allies.

The KDP and the "Invisible" Filipinos

Although the Filipino community in general was sympathetic to the anti-eviction battle and the plight of the Filipino elderly, it stayed largely on the sidelines. Even within the KDP, many members were reluctant to throw themselves into the fray because it meant subjecting themselves to bitter denunciations and constant confrontations with other leftist groups. Thus, the support work for the I-Hotel was led entirely by a small team of KDP members with little of the kind of backing that other campaigns within the organization normally enjoyed. Such support would have meant regular meetings between the team and the leadership to formulate political positions and tactics. It would have also meant that our team could have mobilized a considerable number of other members to assist on logistics or to participate in large-scale events. Consequently, with little organization and support, the KDP team operated without real political muscle; the team was visible, but the KDP was not always so, and we made only limited inroads into the Filipino community about the I-Hotel as an issue. As a result, the overall Filipino character of the I-Hotel movement was diminished. The KDP activists were well aware of the Filipino community's longstanding history of invisibility—for example, the fact that the broader population had generally been unaware that Manilatown even existed—yet the KDP as an organization ironically ended up contributing to that invisibility.

Emil requested that the KDP enter as an organization in early 1976 to assist in the anti-eviction battle, although individuals had already been deeply involved in the IH even before they had become KDP members. The KDP's National Executive Board (NEB), composed of Bruce Occena, Melinda Paras, and Cynthia Maglaya, assigned Jeanette and me, both local San Francisco members, to assist de Guzman. The three of us would be the "internal team," working closely with the tenants and the IHTA.

Jeanette was familiar with the issues of the elderly and had lived at the hotel for a time before she was assigned as a KDP team member. Her father was a self-supporting student who had come to the United States in 1927 to study at Fordham University in New York; when he could no longer pay the tuition, he worked as a bartender. After fighting in World War II, he married a war bride in the Philippines and brought his family to New York. Jeanette grew up in a city housing project on Manhattan's Lower East Side at a time that few Filipinos lived on the East Coast. When her family moved to San Francisco, she lived in the Mission District and graduated from Mission High School. Her father was a regular on Kearny Street, getting his hair cut at Tino's and playing Pai Gow, a Chinese card game, in the back of the barbershop. She first became active in the I-Hotel struggle as a student at San Francisco State College. When she went to Tino's, the old-timers asked her for her family name. "I told the manongs and their reply was 'Are you Francisco Lazam's daughter?'" she said. "Right then and there, I knew I was in the right place, with the right people." Jeanette was street-wise, a tough fighter fueled by tremendous determination.[36]

I had already worked part-time as bookkeeper for Joe Diones between 1975 and 1976. I had also become familiar with the International Hotel as a youth activist in the Los Angeles area a few years before. When I first arrived in San Francisco in 1971, I immediately went to the hotel. It was the headquarters for Filipino activists, and I quickly became involved and developed into a radical. I was the daughter of a U.S. Army veteran who had escaped the Bataan Death March and spent the rest of the war as a guerrilla. He went on to survive devastating battles in the Korean War, as well. My mother was a messenger for the anti-Japanese guerrillas in the Philippines; in America, she worked at a cannery and as a seamstress while raising five daughters and a son. I had grown up on or near Army bases and in adjacent neighborhoods that brought together Filipinos, Mexicans, and African Americans, but I had had very little contact with white people. I was involved in the early identity movement in Los Angeles, and I was excited by all the developments in San Francisco. When I was officially assigned to the I-Hotel, I was a twenty-five-year-old single mother with two sons and a daughter, having given birth to my first son at sixteen. In an organization of young people, a mother was unusual. I always had difficulties with child care, but because of my need to address my family's demands, I added a very pragmatic perspective and a quiet persistence to the team.[37]

Occena led all aspects of the I-Hotel work from the KDP's National Executive Board. He had worked at the I-Hotel as a student supporter in its early days of renovation. Occena, like Jeanette, grew up in New York and got involved in antiwar activities as a student on the UC Berkeley campus, where he had been radicalized. He went to Cuba on the Venceremos Brigade and began to develop Marxist–Leninist politics. In addition to guiding the work of the I-Hotel's internal team, Occena provided the leadership for the "external team," which included Annatess Araneta, Virginia (Virgie) Macaalay, David Poland, Sylvia (Syl) Savellano, and Eleanor Yaranon. None of the external-team members had been born or raised in San Francisco, and they were considered outsiders. "They were supposed to bolster us and build the broader support in the community," Lazam explained. At first the team took up these tasks, but as the demands of the national organization pressed on Occena, his time became increasingly limited. As a result, "the work of the team fizzled and leadership was few and far between, although they participated in the daily work at the I-Hotel, just like any other supporters."[38]

Of all the KDP internal-team members, only Emil had personal knowledge of the local history of Manilatown, and he had personal relationships with Filipinos in the San Francisco community that predated the KDP. Although he had grown up in the Richmond District of San Francisco, his father, Emilio de Guzman, had taken him to Manilatown as a child to see his *ninong* (godfather), a photographer, and to meet up with family and acquaintances on Kearny Street. Lazam and I were outsiders and relatively new to the Bay Area (about five years), and our learning curve was slow. This lack of familiarity with the local Filipino community was debilitating, since the struggle required quick assessments and cooperation with community people.

The KDP had accumulated political experience primarily by working with youth, students, and immigrants, and not with the other sectors of the Filipino community. Moreover, the internal I-Hotel team, operating as revolutionaries within a broader working-class struggle, demanded perspectives and tactics with which the KDP had had little experience. Emil, Jeanette, and I were baptized by fire, so to speak, and we had to learn quickly how to operate. We did have some experience in broader struggles outside the Filipino community. For example, Emil had participated in the Third World Strike on his campus and in the anti–Vietnam War movement before the formation of the KDP. I was involved with solidarity movements with liberation struggles in Puerto Rico, Nicaragua, El Salvador, and elsewhere, and I was the KDP representative on the steering committee of the July 4 Coalition to organize a People's Bicentennial in 1976. I had also gotten involved in labor struggles, including supporting a strike at Blue Shield which involved many Filipino workers. Before the strike, I had participated in an anti-discrimination class action suit against Blue Shield, the first Asian American class action suit of this sort. Members of the KDP knew the different Asian left organizations through our common experiences in the student movements on campuses in the Bay Area, particularly at UC Berkeley, and relating to each other in close proximity on Kearny Street.

By the time the KDP, as an organization, started to focus our attention on the I-Hotel, the IHTA had fallen into shambles, and we harbored no illusions that the struggle would be easy to win—if it could be won at all. Disagreements with Diones and his role in the Moscone plan, particularly the way in which he continued to bully the tenants, had left the IHTA an empty shell. The increasing sectarian rivalries of Asian leftist groups within the coalition also took a toll. The situation was complex: The Asian community activists in Wei Min She and the IWK had become part of separate, competing Maoist factions. This had infused them with a revitalized sense of purpose and additional cadres, which brought positive energy, but also costly sectarianism, to the fight. In addition, they had developed small but important bases of mass support: Wei Min She/RCP had cultivated support among garment workers in Chinatown, while the IWK had links with disaffected Chinatown youth and students. As a result of these political rivalries, three competing anti-eviction coalitions arose that sometimes conflicted with one another, complicating the struggle further.[39]

At first, the KDP's analysis of the I-Hotel as a working-class housing struggle and, consequently, its stance on how to guide the anti-eviction movement were not universally understood, even by other KDP members. Although the concept of "broader working-class struggles" was introduced to KDP members, most questioned why the organization was involved in a fight that might not produce immediate results for the organization.[40] Some KDP members viewed issues that required broad working-class participation and leadership as mysterious and perhaps overreaching, particularly if there were no real opportunities to recruit new Filipino members of the community to the KDP.

The KDP's National Executive Board provided general perspectives on the political situation, but it generally fell short in making this overview relevant to the particularities of local conditions. While the leadership strongly identified that the I-Hotel anti-eviction movement was a working-class struggle in which Filipinos played only a certain part, they failed to emphasize the unique role that the Filipino community played and, consequently, did not articulate how the team would mobilize broader support within the Filipino community—that is, who were the I-Hotel's natural Filipino allies? In particular, the KDP never self-consciously targeted the surrounding Manilatown area, where other manongs lived in residential hotels. Although the I-Hotel certainly was a special place for the Filipino community because it was the hub of activity in the remnant of the old neighborhood, the other manongs in the Chinatown–Manilatown area were also threatened with eviction because of the expansion of the financial district. If they had been adequately involved, they might have added considerable influence in attracting other Filipino supporters.

The KDP's strengths were our determination to find a practical way to save the hotel, our influence with the tenants of the IHTA, and our status as the only Filipino organization at the core of the struggle. Individuals who would join the KDP started creating working relationships with the tenants based on trust, camaraderie, and surrogate family relationships in 1969. Our plan was to build up the IHTA as the leader of the anti-eviction battle, which would join city, union, church, and other forces in a broader housing movement. The KDP felt that the center of gravity for organizing should be the IHTA and that the tenant-led organization should be the leading voice. If the tenants were not the true leaders of the I-Hotel, according to our analysis, the anti-eviction battle undoubtedly would fail. The Filipino tenants were the most politically conscious and unified within the anti-eviction struggle, much to the surprise of liberals and even of some revolutionaries. If the Filipino tenants appeared as figureheads or puppets manipulated by young radicals, and if they did not act with obvious self-conscious unity, their credibility could be questioned—not to mention the credibility of the KDP.

In our political vision, the I-Hotel represented a broader working-class struggle for housing in which Filipinos happened to be leaders. This meant that KDP activists should not restrict themselves to organizing Filipinos—at least, in theory. In effect, however, it became increasingly difficult for the KDP's I-Hotel team to organize beyond the tenants in the IHTA and to help navigate their relationship with the different support coalitions.

At the same time, the KDP's efforts to organize the Filipino community beyond the I-Hotel struggle had the unintended effect of undermining the tenants' credibility. The I-Hotel team, caught between organizing the Filipino community, providing leadership to the broader anti-eviction movement, and working closely with the IHTA, became overextended and, often, exhausted. As the threats of eviction mounted, our efforts to make connections naturally fell by the wayside, and relations with the larger Filipino community came to rank last on the list of tasks. The KDP organization beyond the I-Hotel team did not make use of its ties to the various organizations and activists in the Filipino community to galvanize support for the I-Hotel.

Even the regional KDP leadership failed to educate its members about the struggle. When Emil and I attended an important KDP Bay Area regional meeting in May 1977, which reviewed the political campaigns in which the local chapters were engaged, we were shocked that the I-Hotel struggle was not even on the agenda. There was no analysis, not even "agitation" to involve members, even though the I-Hotel struggle was constantly in the local news. *Ang Katipunan,* the KDP newspaper, was an exception: It became a valuable vehicle for information and analysis, but even then, Jeanette was the on-the-scene reporter, entrusted with yet one more task.

By falling short in terms of organizing the Filipino community, the KDP also unintentionally contributed to the "invisibility" of the Filipino community within the "broader working-class struggle." With the I-Hotel team nestled within the leadership of the IHTA and with the elderly Filipino leaders in the forefront, it may seem mysterious how Filipinos could become invisible. The KDP and the Filipino tenants were certainly prominent among the leftist and progressive forces within the anti-eviction front. But the presence of Filipinos was not apparent to many outsiders for several reasons. For one thing, the KDP did not highlight the particular history of the Filipino community. When it raised the I-Hotel as an issue, it always did so within the broader context of the need for housing and of poor people's human rights to housing. It almost never did so as a specific Filipino community's need for housing, human rights, or cultural preservation. For example, *Ang Katipunan* featured only one article that highlighted Filipino tenants as leaders. And when interviewed, Filipino tenant leaders themselves emphasized the working class's need for housing and broad support. "We must organize and continue to organize broad support. Without their support, we cannot win!" Tex Llamera said. It did not come to the mind of Jeanette, who interviewed him, or to that of Llamera himself, to call for support particularly from the Filipino community.[41]

This tendency to downplay the Filipino ethnic or cultural component in favor of the multiracial class nature of the struggle may have been in part a reaction to the efforts of some of the other radicals to prioritize the "nationalist" aspects of the conflict. This meant they placed more emphasis on "national oppression" and, therefore, on the need to preserve Manilatown as an ethnic community than on the class-wide housing issue. Our position was that the Filipino aspect was crucial but secondary to the overall class nature of the struggle. In addition, independent white leftists had pronounced tendencies to idealize and even romanticize the elderly tenants, often revering individual tenants as founts of Third World wisdom. KDP activists recoiled at such distortions, even as we, too, were influenced by the mystique of the manongs.

Like the KDP, the Filipino tenants did not especially highlight the Filipino community or their leadership roles within it. They felt strongly about the Filipino role in the I-Hotel movement, but they always thought of Manilatown itself as a place with international flavor, not just as a Filipino enclave. Manong Wahat emphasized this point to gain the broadest support possible. "In the Hotel," as he told Mayor Moscone, "it's not only yellow skin, but red skin, black skin, and there is white skin too."[42]

The KDP and the I-Hotel Team

Emil, Jeanette, and I worked as a collective mainly to bolster the IHTA. But the KDP I-Hotel team was also supposed to bring the anti-eviction supporters of the IHTA into a cohesive body. The team met every day to make sense of the quickly changing events and the involvement of the tenants. We wrote speeches and leaflets, organized support for the demonstrations, negotiated with politicians, and dealt with the complicated, often thorny dynamics of the support coalitions. Above all, we had to pay attention to the needs of the tenants, especially their health and emotional stability. We had to help guide the IHTA, which involved patiently explaining to the tenants in understandable language the various legal issues and political maneuvers of city officials. The three team members deferred to the wishes of the tenants, and one of our main tasks was to make sure that the tenants' voices were heard and not overpowered by the anti-eviction coalition, no matter how inarticulate or heavily accented the tenants' voices may have been.

Each of the team members focused on different responsibilities, although we each ended up taking on all of the different tasks at one time or other. The struggle to stop the eviction consumed us, and responsibilities blurred into each other. The load became overwhelming, involving critical tasks whose intensity kept increasing. We did our best, but the demands of the work constantly outstripped us. "I never really had time to think about myself or my role in the IH," Jeanette recalled of her own experience. "The IH consumed me. I rarely thought about myself. I was always tired and never thought I lived up to what was needed."[43] I hardly slept, and I worked on nerves only. But I was also wracked with guilt that my three children were being neglected. Although comrades from our child-care system watched them, I was away, sucked into the center of a maelstrom, and I worried that they would be damaged by my absence.

At the same time, the KDP national leadership basically left the I-Hotel team to fend for ourselves, despite the prominence of the struggle within the San Francisco Bay Area. On the night of the eviction, Jeanette reported to the team that the KDP's National Executive Board was overwhelmed with other tasks, and we had to face the eviction alone. "Good luck. You're on your own," was all the board said.[44] This lack of attention from leadership bodies of the national, regional, and even San Francisco chapter of the KDP had negative repercussions not only for the team but also for the Filipino community and the coalition work.

Emil, Jeanette, and I were also overloaded with other KDP assignments outside the I-Hotel because Sorcy Rocamora and others in the organization's regional leadership demanded that I-Hotel team members not be exempt from other local work. We were in no position to refuse the extra assignments for fear of criticism from local KDP chapter leaders. According to them, everyone else was just as busy with other political assignments. Any relief from local work was viewed as elitist and pulling "veteran activist" rank over others. When health or family or job concerns were raised, the activist was liable to be criticized for bourgeois tendencies.

This style of work burdened the I-Hotel team members with multiple tasks, with no thought of the toll it was taking on us. For instance, during this time the local KDP chapter expected the I-Hotel team members to help with national campaigns for equal rights. We were also expected to join the anti-Marcos work for the Philippines. Besides these political campaigns, we were required to sing in cultural shows and events and sell newspapers at workplaces and churches and by going door to door in neighborhoods. It would not be unusual for one of us to stay up until 3:00 A.M. to keep internal security watch at the hotel and then to be required to sell newspapers at the farmer's market at Bernal Heights at 5:00 A.M.

Eventually, the national KDP leadership criticized the Northern California regional leadership's organizational style for being "ultra-leftist." This "ultra-leftist" style of work was reminiscent of some of the excesses of the Chinese Cultural Revolution. Some activists held notions that revolution could be "willed" into existence—an error termed "voluntarism"—and if someone lacked the will, his or her commitment to revolutionary ideals would be questioned. Eventually this work style did change, but only after the eviction; throughout the eviction period, the I-Hotel team had to keep up with a feverish pace of chapter responsibilities, as well as the pressing demands of the I-Hotel struggle. At the same time, the chapter and regional leadership tended to respond to the hotel as if the KDP were part of the general public. KDP members were primarily mobilized for demonstrations, security, and other tactics to stop the eviction mainly through the I-Hotel support coalition's phone tree rather than through any independent mechanism organized by the KDP's regional or local leaders.

In retrospect, it is clear that the organization's lack of support flowed not from callousness or indifference, but from difficulties inherent in the KDP's dual program. The organization's political misjudgments stemmed from youth and inexperience and, above all, from limited human and material resources in the face of immense political challenges. The KDP had been thrust into the role of "tribune" of the Filipino people in the United States. A new organization made up mostly of people in their twenties had been called on to take up a wide range of struggles that were important to the emerging immigrant community and to lead solidarity efforts within the life-and-death battle against martial law in the Philippines. Against the wealth, power, and experience of San Francisco's political and financial elite, this was a David versus Goliath fight indeed.

The KDP was also deeply affected by the changing nature of the Filipino community. The new immigrants arriving on U.S. shores after the liberalization of immigration laws in 1965 were different economically and politically from the previous immigrants. The post–1965 immigrant community came from the professional classes and migrated from urban areas in the Philippines. Those from urban areas tended to be more influenced by American consumerist cultural values that had continued to proliferate in Philippine culture since the end of American colonization. Moreover, many of them had no knowledge of a previous Filipino community, nor did they look for one when they arrived in the United States. They had little to do with Manilatown or any elderly bachelor community living in a rundown area of town. For new immigrants and minorities, residential segregation was no longer so severe. The new immigrants thus were not motivated by the need to find refuge and cultural familiarity. Instead, they moved to the South of Market area or the Mission District with their families and, later, to the outer neighborhoods of San Francisco, where rents were cheaper. These newer arrivals also concentrated in Daly City, Union City, Hercules, and South San Francisco—areas where they could buy houses relatively cheaply as they became more affluent.[45]

The experience of the new immigrants did not center on the I-Hotel or Manilatown, as it had just ten years earlier. Family and kinship relationships were primary over matters of place and work or cultural familiarity. However, many of these new immigrants had to make severe sacrifices when they arrived. Many of them became part of the working class because their professional licenses were not accepted in the United States. Credentialed Filipino doctors, for example, often could not practice in the United States, and many ended up retraining for different occupations, often at much lower pay and status.

The KDP grasped these emerging dynamics in the Filipino immigrant community and directed most of its campaigns toward the new-immigrant sector. For example, every other weekend, KDP teams sold bimonthly newspapers in the new Filipino neighborhoods in San Francisco's South of Market area, Mission District, and Bernal Heights. They took *Ang Katipunan* newspapers to shoppers at farmers' markets; to workplaces with large concentrations of Filipinos, such as Blue Shield Insurance Company in San Francisco; and to Catholic churches in Daly City. The KDP conducted political campaigns in these new immigrant communities, targeting racial and national discrimination, such as the effort to gain licensure for nurses. The KDP was deeply involved in the defense of two nurses, Filipina Narciso and Leonora Perez, who were falsely accused of murdering their patients in Chicago.[46]

What the KDP did not address was the community's historical links to the old manongs and to the literally dying Manilatown community. A gap existed between the manongs and the new immigrants, and the KDP was not able to articulate a political perspective that bridged it. This also meant that KDP activists who were working with the elderly Filipinos in the farm workers' movement were left out. Similar to the I-Hotel movement, the KDP did not prioritize working with Filipinos in the farm workers' movement, despite its previous, close working relationships with veteran farm-worker activists such as Philip Vera Cruz. The KDP had little to do with the middle-aged and elderly Filipino activists at the Agbayani Village retirement home and Forty Acres Clinic, which serviced Filipinos, Mexicans, and Yemenite Arabs in Delano, the starting point and spiritual center of the farm workers' strike. Bay Area labor activists, such as Manong Pablo Valdez and Manong Mario Hermoso, were close to the KDP, but their efforts were never fully mobilized or supported. The KDP leadership assessed that Filipinos were not part of the dynamic growth of the UFW, which had become overwhelmingly Mexican and, in fact, under the leadership of Cesar Chavez was often identified as a Mexican civil-rights movement. Therefore, the relationship with the farm workers, as well as with the other manongs in the neighborhood around the I-Hotel, was never developed politically.[47]

With the emerging immigrant sector in mind, the KDP leadership mobilized numerous important campaigns. The *Ang Aktibista* internal newsletters of the period often contained summaries of the KDP's projects and plans for future work. Under the "Socialist" category of the "United Front in the Filipino Community," such campaigns as organizing June 12 National Day celebrations (to commemorate the Philippines' revolutionary independence from Spain rather than the July 4, 1946, nominal independence from the United States), annual student-community conventions known as the Far West Conventions, local student organizing, campaigns against discriminatory textbooks in California schools, and efforts to protect immigrants' rights. Under "Broader Working Class Struggles," the KDP got involved in such activities as the People's Bicentennial events in 1976 and joint May Day celebrations as important means to develop unity with other political groups. In addition, there were campaigns against repressive legislation and work with trade unions in which Filipinos played a significant role. Still, there were no discussions of the International Hotel.

Despite all these problems, I soldiered on with Jeanette and Emil. We felt alone, embattled, and worn out. It was only afterward that I could articulate all of the different programmatic and personal stresses that made the relationship between KDP and the I-Hotel team so fraught with problems. But we kept going because I knew that, no matter how difficult the situation, the three of us were playing important roles in a deeply historic movement, and I felt both exultation and sadness. I felt sad because the KDP and the broader Filipino community were pulled in so many directions that we were not as mobilized as we should have been. But I also exulted because progressive people throughout San Francisco had a keen sense that a decisive confrontation was taking place. If the city were to be a place where people who were not rich could afford to live, we would have to make our stand at the International Hotel. The old hotel and its elderly tenants represented the fight for housing rights and the need to place human needs above profits in the hearts of thousands of supporters. And at the center of the movement stood the manongs—fighting as they had in the past but getting respect and honor as never before. All of this was satisfying to me, and it sustained me. I knew that the newly emerging Filipino community eventually would reap the benefits.

CHAPTER SIX

People's Power versus Propertied Elites

1977

The Coalition of Anti-Eviction Coalitions

In 1977, a complicated network of supporters worked to give the International Hotel considerable grassroots political power. This network emerged from the various Asian American storefront radical groups early on in the struggle. When many of these radicals joined Maoist communist organizations by mid-1975, organizing public support became far more systematic and consistent. In the last year before eviction, three major groups or coalitions operated within the broader anti-eviction coalition, with significant political, organizational, and ideological disagreements among them.

First, there was the IHTA with the KDP, along with large numbers of independent leftist and anti-imperialist activists. These supporters included Chester Hartman, a housing consultant, and members of the Northern California Alliance (NCA). The NCA consisted of activists whose views ranged from sympathy for the KDP's flexible Marxism to affinity for the democratic-socialist wing of the American left. The NCA published a popular newspaper, *Common Sense,* and offered classes in politics and culture at its Liberation School. As a result, the NCA attracted a wide range of progressive activists, such as Mike Davis, Max Elbaum, Denise Lombard, and Ann Schwartz. The NCA paid particular attention to local electoral politics and played a key role in campaigns in San Francisco, such as winning district elections for the Board of Supervisors. This alliance of forces did not operate as a formal support group within the I-Hotel struggle but, rather, met unofficially in caucuses to follow the leadership of the IHTA and the KDP. Because this first group of supporters did not create a separate organization, many independent activists may not even have been aware of the IHTA–KDP–NCA alliance.

The second group, the Support Committee for the International Hotel, brought together a large number of independent leftists and grassroots activists, with I Wor Kuen (IWK) playing the leading role. A wide range of organizations participated in the Support Committee, including the People's Food System, a cooperative food-distribution network that reached into the many collective households of the counterculture; the San Francisco Printing Cooperative; Bay Area Gay Liberation (BAGL), an important leftist voice in the city's emerging gay politics; and the Maoist IWK's mass organization, the Chinese Progressive Association (CPA). The IWK and the CPA often presented themselves as the Coalition to Support the I-Hotel, although that coalition did not operate as a separate organization outside the Support Committee. The KDP participated in the Support Committee, as well, although not as a leading force. So did NCA members and other KDP allies. The KDP backed the Support Committee as a public vehicle to mobilize supporters despite differences with the committee's leading group, the IWK. Most of the organizations that supported the tenants could be coordinated through the Support Committee, which became the public face of those backing the IHTA.

The third group, the Workers Committee to Fight for the I-Hotel and Victory Building, included members from the Asian Community Center (ACC), Everybody's Bookstore, and Wei Min She, all of which had been affiliated with the Revolutionary Communist Party (RCP) since 1975. The Workers Committee refused to work directly with any of the other coalitions because of their political and ideological disagreements and emphasized doing its own mass organizing and recruiting within the Chinese community. The Workers Committee also did not coordinate any of its activities with the IHTA. Most independent activists did not work with the Workers Committee because of its ultra-Maoist politics and working style.

All three groups were united in fighting the eviction, but differences over long-range revolutionary programs were often confused with consideration of day-to-day tactics. The Workers Committee, for example, refused to participate in common coalition with "reformists" such as the KDP, "revisionists" such as the IWK, or so-called bourgeois degenerates such as BAGL in the Support Committee. From the IHTA's point of view, the Workers Committee acted almost as a rogue organization, mounting demonstrations on its own, disrupting city hearings with its own positions, and joining IHTA-sponsored activities without coordination.

For the most part, outsiders could not tell the difference among the groups unless they made concerted efforts to study the situation. This was true partly because the public face of the anti-eviction movement largely took the form of big rallies and mass demonstrations. Organizing mass actions was a particular skill already mastered by the pan-Asian and other leftist organizations, and for this kind of activity, especially during the eviction itself, all three groups did manage to work together.[1]

In an article for the *New Yorker*, Calvin Trillin observed:

> The forces resisting eviction of the IH tenants include not only the IHTA and its supporters but a separate organization, usually called the Support Committee, and a separate third organization, usually called the Workers Committee. . . . The International Hotel protest movement is divided into three organizations partly for reasons that have nothing to do with the International Hotel. . . . Some theoretical differences among the groups, though, are considered central to the sort of tactics they have favored to defend the hotel, and even to the chants they are willing to chant at demonstrations. The Support Committee emphasizes the Third World aspects of the controversy—Support Committee members tend to see the eviction as another example of what they called "national oppression"—and the Workers Committee follows the [RCP] line of de-emphasizing race differences in favor of working-class unity. . . . All of this has been lost, of course, on most people in San Francisco—even on those who, out of liberal politics or radical politics or simple sympathy for the plight of the elderly poor, supported the resistance to the eviction.[2]

In his description of the groups, Trillin omitted the KDP, an indication of our "backstage" role and a result of the way we downplayed the Filipino component of the conflict. The KDP team was no secret, but the KDP as an organization was not an official part of the IHTA. KDP members outside the team participated as members of the broader coalition. The KDP's strategy on the anti-eviction coalition was to place a small team to reinforce the IHTA, which it believed was enough to carry on the struggle. This arrangement highlighted the leadership of the IHTA rather than the support organizations. We were present, but we saw ourselves as adjuncts of the tenant leadership.

Unfortunately, the dynamics of leftist sectarian politics often clouded decisions on strategy and tactics in the anti-eviction front. As I described earlier, such crucial questions as how to work with city officials such as the mayor or the sheriff arose. Were they potential friends or enemies? Should community groups negotiate with city officials to devise plans, or should they assume that no common ground or compromise was possible? But there were also other questions that flowed from the fact that Asian American leftist organizations were also storefront tenants of the I-Hotel. The IHTA was composed only of the residential tenants; it had no representatives from the storefront organizations and businesses. The IHTA managed the building, and the storefront tenants subleased from the IHTA. If the Moscone plan or any other eminent-domain scheme were adopted, the storefronts would continue to sublease. Still, the ACC and the CPA raised questions about whether the demands against eviction and for low-income housing should also include the defense of the progressive and leftist organizations on the Kearny Street block. From the perspective of Chinatown, the I-Hotel was the only toehold of leftist politics in the community; if the groups were evicted, the anticommunists would win a decisive victory in terms not only of housing politics but also of community politics. Also, "national oppression" took a more prominent role in the IWK's analysis, which meant that dispersal of the community was at least equal to housing rights in importance. As the IWK would put it, "The attack on the I-Hotel is one of the many attacks on Third World communities to destroy and disperse these historic centers of resistance against national oppression."[3]

These questions and dilemmas were not always obvious to those participating in the broader anti-eviction battle. In fact, the differences did not seem to affect anyone outside the core organizers in the support movement: Many supporters did not even know that the divisions existed. One observer, a doctor who joined the medical team that was organized during the height of the I-Hotel struggle, commented, "It seemed to me the struggle was a good local issue—between big money versus the Asian people who wanted affordable housing. They seemed pretty united."[4] On the surface, the anti-eviction movement did seem united. Those on the inside knew otherwise.

The differences among the support groups did have public consequences, however, especially when it came to the complex, sophisticated process of trying to pressure and persuade public officials. For example, during meetings of the Housing Commission and the Board of Supervisors, and with the mayor, some leftists would heckle and jeer at liberals who supported the I-Hotel solely because they were city officials. As a matter of principle, the different factions agreed that city officials should be held accountable through mass pressure and that human needs for housing should be prioritized over the capitalist need for more profitable office buildings and tourist hotels. In the field of practical politics, however, not everyone was willing to sit at the negotiating table with city officials to force them to take responsibility for the housing crisis and the plight of the Asian elderly in San Francisco. As the RCP put it,

> The IHTA and Support Committee leadership . . . held to the "theory" that there are good politicians (the liberals or "progressive") and bad ones and that the role of mass struggle is either to strengthen the hand of the good guys or kick them in the butt so that they can resolve the issue. . . . Rather than misleading people by encouraging reliance on these officials, it was imperative to expose the nature of these politicians and their schemes from the start and to expose the capitalist system and its drive for profit.[5]

These differences over strategy and tactics played themselves out within the IHTA and among the commercial storefront tenants on the block at every twist and turn of the anti-eviction battle, eventually confusing city officials as to which positions represented the tenants. Such incoherence and fragmentation contributed to the city officials' abandoning the I-Hotel struggle.

The KDP criticized as "infantile" the attitude that anyone who held public office needed to be dealt with solely by confrontation and so-called exposure. Such antics the KDP regarded as posturing by leftists who did not really believe that reforms could be won and were instead devoted to "exposing" the bourgeois allegiances of politicians. The KDP felt it was "a fatal error to confuse the vantage point of practical politics with revolutionary objectives."[6] The organization criticized as "ultra-leftist" the refusal "on principle" to work with city officials; with such a stance, we felt, the I-Hotel could not be saved short of an actual revolution—a totally unrealistic prospect.[7] To the KDP, it seemed that much of the critique of the Moscone plan was based more on some leftists' refusal to negotiate with city officials such as Mayor Moscone than on a criticism of the plan itself. Our assessment of the role of politicians was done against the background of an upsurge of left–liberal politics in city government: District elections had been won in November 1976, and Mayor Moscone and Sheriff Hongisto were part of that alliance. If eviction could be held off, the political climate could become more favorable for the housing movement.

All of the groups understood, however, that the battle lines had been drawn between the forces of reaction representing private-property interests and the needs of working-class and minority communities. Standing in opposition were private-property forces inexorably linked to plans to redevelop the city and expand the financial district that had already brought about the wholesale removal of minority communities in areas such as the Fillmore District, South of Market, and the rest of Manilatown. The political left united on this basic level yet could not agree on how the city should be pressured into making various concessions to the people, particularly with the changing political tides that would bring in district elections and the possibility of a new configuration of elected officials who were willing to bend to popular opinion. In addition, anticapitalist leftist forces were unable to deal with a foreign capitalist with interests in Chinatown, particularly when Chinese businessmen themselves had expanded their properties and contributed to the destruction of housing stock in Chinatown.

As these problems persisted, we KDP activists found ourselves seeking the broad support of liberals while having to ward off the infantile rejection of such alliances from other leftists. This was disheartening, to say the least. Toward the end, liberals increasingly withdrew from active support; the possibility that the hotel would survive long enough to take advantage of the new, more progressive Board of Supervisors to be elected by districts became more and more distant. As a result, the three KDP team members became infected with some of the attitudes of the other leftists and developed a siege mentality. As the end approached, we hunkered down to await the military assault with dread.

In this context, the left played a complicated, contradictory role. On the positive side, next to the tenants, the leftist groups were the bulwark, the activist base, of the anti-eviction movement. But the unfortunate negative side saw crucial differences in strategy as leftist activists from all of the groups jockeyed for power. These groups competed fiercely for the loyalty of certain tenants to increase their prestige in the struggle. Being a public leader of the I-Hotel movement became a kind of proud badge to wear. Left-wing and progressive activists took note of who had influence with which tenant and, consequently, which political faction was on the "rise." The result could be that a new "advanced worker" would be recruited into the Marxist–Leninist party or, at least, lend his support to it, and the prestige of that militant elderly tenant would add luster to the chosen group. Such adulation gave a kind of celebrity status to individual tenants, which could cause jealousy and conflicts among the rest of tenants, magnifying personal problems. The competition for loyalty also created different centers of authority among the tenants, undermining the effectiveness of the IHTA.[8]

The participation of the different support coalitions also exacerbated some of the awkward gender dynamics between the elderly bachelors and the young activists. As support for the tenants broadened, more women of all backgrounds began to participate in the struggle or simply came to socialize. White women in particular posed a volatile combination with the elderly men. According to Jeanette Lazam, "The white women seemed 'missionary' in their attitudes and were unconscious of their power and sexuality as white women. They had a tendency to be patronizing."[9] Unaware of their power and sexuality, they sometimes flirted with the men, and such behavior created additional, unwanted problems, particularly when some of the elderly men became intoxicated with their own celebrity. For example, Mrs. D confided in me that her marriage had been jeopardized by the attention her husband received from a white female supporter.

Such personal problems were often disregarded as just that: personal. But they certainly had negative political effects because of the ill will that developed. In the swirl of political events, hardly any additional analysis of gender and other personal dynamics was undertaken—at least, not by the Filipino activists involved. For example, it was no secret that several Filipino activists and many supporters from the community were lesbians and gays, although there were no outward displays of sexuality, and BAGL was very active in support work. The presence of gays and lesbians alone challenged the more traditional attitudes of the tenants about homosexuality. As the tenants increasingly sought support from the broader community, they were thrust farther and farther beyond their narrow, ghettoized experiences to gain a more cosmopolitan worldview. They came face to face with people at all levels of society and all sorts of lifestyles, including one form or other of sexual revolt. For example, in the fall of 1976, I went with Wahat Tompao and another tenant, Nick Napek, to seek support at a well-known San Francisco costume party, the precursor to the "Exotic Erotic Ball." Napek and I were too shy to don costumes, but Wahat wore a blond fright wig. We were shocked, delighted, and embarrassed at the displays of nudity and sexual antics at the party.

Generally, relationships that developed between peers—including interracial and hetero- or homosexual relationships—were considered appropriate. However, the underlying issues of intergenerational and interracial sexual relationships never were adequately addressed. Understandably, the I-Hotel struggle may have been one of the few places where such an issue would have presented itself; nevertheless, I do not believe that anyone gave it proper analytical or theoretical attention, although, as the anti-eviction struggle heated up in the next stage, tensions from these dynamics would grow more pronounced.

Despite all of these contradictions, the three coalitions that supported the I-Hotel movement continued to mobilize throughout the Bay Area. Legal, media, medical, and security committees operated with hundreds of volunteers. Many mobilized to attend City Hall meetings. Sympathizers within the city government freely offered the IHTA vital inside information on the maneuvers of officials. Urban planners, lawyers, consultants, and many other professionals volunteered their expertise. Garment workers and others from Chinatown came to the support of the hotel, while the San Francisco Labor Council mobilized its members among clerical workers and longshoremen. Though the struggle may have been fraught with problems due to its leftist in-fighting, the fact remained that the International Hotel grew into a mass movement that far exceeded anyone's expectations, whether liberal politician or leftist organizer, and it took on a momentum of its own.

Despite the frustration and exhaustion, the breadth of support that the I-Hotel had developed was remarkable, extending throughout the city and the Bay Area. Demonstrations that circled the hotel were filled with activists and supporters of every type, and participating in the movement—by spending the night at the hotel to do a stint of late-night security, for instance, or organizing one's friends to be part of the emergency telephone tree—took on the character of an institution in Bay Area life. Anyone who was politically or socially active on the left had a personal stake in the fate of the I-Hotel. As Douglas Dowd, an economics professor and antiwar activist, observed, the broad support coalition "was 'extraordinary' in that it extended from pacifists to militants, ordinary decent mainstream people to liberals to radicals, vegetarians to revolutionaries, etc., and because it functioned over a period not of weeks or months but of years, not shrinking but growing, in both numbers and determination."[10]

Moscone and the Left–Liberal Alliance

As 1977 unfolded, it became increasingly clear to the tenants and supporters that we faced long odds. The KDP and the IHTA believed that, if there was enough political support and if the city's communities could be mobilized to pressure office holders and leaders who had a measure of clout, the I-Hotel could perhaps prevail. The KDP and other progressives still thought that liberal city officials could be forced to remain as part of the anti-eviction front. The progressive direction in city politics continued to surge: The renters' and housing movements were increasingly vocal; the movement for district elections had won a clear victory in November 1976; and the San Francisco Community Congress was galvanizing energy around neighborhood-based programs for reform with positions on such issues as housing, health, jobs, environment, and the arts. Each new district of the newly created system of district elections was bubbling with anticipated campaigns for the November 1977 elections, when the first slate of district-based supervisors would be elected. Reverend Jim Jones, who had not yet fled to Guyana and madness, was still influential and able to mobilize members of the People's Temple church as a vital grassroots force, and Glide church, led by Reverend Cecil Williams, Janice Mirikitani, and Reverend Lloyd Wake, brought a growing multiracial constituency into the public arena. In this atmosphere, we believed, the liberals and progressives could be part of the solution and the left should not concede them to the enemy camp, as many of the other revolutionaries based on Kearny Street thought.

The I-Hotel tenants and the KDP were cautiously optimistic about Sheriff Richard Hongisto's support, for example. Hongisto had been elected by the same gay-liberal forces that had voted for Moscone, and he was susceptible to pressure from that base. We felt that the sheriff, having stood up to the court once, might again do what was morally correct—and politically smart—if the movement was large enough. Yet Hongisto continually played both sides of the conflict, appealing his contempt citation while posting eviction notices; carrying out court orders, at least minimally, while complaining that eviction would be unjust. Since he had made a promise not to evict until legal matters took their course, his acquiescence to court pressure looked like vacillation to the tenants and supporters. When Hongisto finally moved to implement the eviction after he had served his jail term in May, many tenants and supporters viewed it as a betrayal. But the role of the sheriff was simply to carry out court orders, not to make policy. Hongisto acted with uncharacteristic principle for a public official, though his reluctance was of course a direct result of how much political support the tenants had garnered.

The KDP believed that a solution short of overturning the entire system of capitalist power did indeed exist and that, as a consequence, it was critical that we work with liberals. As I noted earlier, many of the other revolutionaries on the block had already written off the liberals—an assessment that would become self-fulfilling. In practice, this meant that advocates for the I-Hotel often spoke and acted at cross-purposes. For example, at a Chinese Chamber of Commerce meeting, Mayor Moscone publicly charged that some of the hotel's activists had hoped he would become angry enough with their protests to move to doom the hotel. He felt that he was being baited by the anti-negotiation forces and charged that their tactics aimed to embarrass him politically. "In my opinion there are some who would be unhappy if I save[d] the hotel," he said.[11] Earlier, when Moscone refused to meet with the IHTA on June 10, an aide told a sympathizer of the hotel, "The mayor does not meet with Maoists."[12]

Meanwhile, in May 1977, representatives of downtown interests organized a counterattack against district elections. Many cities had such a system of representation, but in the San Francisco context, it was considered part of a "radical takeover." Calling themselves Citizens for Total Representation, these downtown conservatives put Proposition A to repeal district elections on the ballot for a special August 2, 1977, election. The summertime election would favor conservatives because of low voter turnout; also, their campaign had substantial financial backing. "All the money power is there: the real estate interests, the banks, the insurance companies, the airlines, the heavy contractors, the mercantile firms, friendly Southern Pacific, and so forth and so on," a reporter observed.[13]

These corporate interests were taken by surprise when they found themselves outflanked on their right. Supervisor John Barbagelata, who had lost the mayoral election in a bitter, closely contested runoff with Moscone in 1975, put forward his own convoluted plan to defeat district elections, Proposition B. Opponents of Barbagelata's proposal jokingly named Proposition B the "fire everybody petition" because it demanded the recall of the mayor, the district attorney, the sheriff, the city attorney, the treasurer, and the entire Board of Supervisors, requiring them all to run again in the November 1977 election. It also provided for early ends for the terms of appointed members of the city's Police, Fire, Airports, Social Services, Port, Recreation and Parks, Library, and Public Utilities commissions and of the Board of Permit Appeals. Each new supervisor would be elected by the entire city, but with the requirement that they live in the eleven separate districts designated by the original district-elections proposition. This proposition had even more provisions, which made it exceedingly confusing, and there were different implications depending on whether Proposition A or Proposition B, or both, or neither, won at the polls. From the point of view of the left–liberal alliance, Propositions A and B would have to be defeated to ensure that the district-election "revolution" would not be overthrown.[14]

Many thought that Barbagelata, a realtor from the conservative western part of the city, was only interested in getting back at Moscone for beating him in the mayoral runoff. "There's only one goal in his mind and that's to dump me," Moscone declared. "I just know this plan of his has nothing to do with reform."[15] Others felt that Barbagelata represented something else: the angry middle-class voter who resented the cultural and political changes taking place in San Francisco. As the columnist Herb Caen put it, Proposition B "will give the ultras a chance to come out of the bushes. They can stand up and be counted in the anonymity of the voting booth—the lawnorder types, the gay-haters, the anti-blacks, those who blame all the ills of the city on the bleeding hearts."[16] Barbagelata, who was not a member of the corporate club, infuriated the downtown establishment. His proposition muddied the waters and distracted from the simple repeal of district elections. With every single occupant of City Hall on the executioner's block, every politician, whether for or against district elections, would have to mobilize for the special election. The corporate-based Citizens for Total Representation's hope to take advantage of the summer doldrums went up in smoke as every politician cranked up his or her political machine to defend against recall. Still, not every politician mobilized in the same way. While supporters of district elections mounted a combined "No on A and B" campaign, Moscone ran a separate "No on B" campaign, bringing in supporters from Los Angeles to help walk precincts. Barbegalata may have undermined the downtown interests' program with his ploy, but Moscone felt the pressure from corporate and other conservative forces. He had to separate himself from Barbagelata while distancing himself from the "radical takeover" that the banks and corporations inveighed against. A wedge was forced into the left–liberal alliance, and as the August 2 date of the special elections approached, Moscone cooperated less and less with the IHTA.[17]

The Courts Rule against the International Hotel

As the political drama twisted and turned, the crucial legal battle raged. The courts ruled against the International Hotel at every turn. Each judge assigned to the case ruled on the side of untrammeled property rights—and some without minimal expression of concern for the tenants' human rights. Property rights historically have been protected by the law, so asserting that they could be circumscribed by other factors—notably, human rights—was unprecedented. Only the notion of "public good" involved in eminent domain came close.

In the first court case against Four Seas, the IHTA challenged centuries of Anglo-Saxon law by arguing that housing was a right and that Four Seas had a moral obligation to relocate the tenants if it wished to demolish the I-Hotel. The IHTA also claimed that Four Seas' action to force eviction was a "retaliatory eviction," a legal attempt to bust the strongest tenants' union in the city. After the jury became deadlocked in April 1976, Judge Ira Brown directed the jury to find the tenants guilty and ordered the tenants to pay damages to Four Seas and to vacate the hotel. One juror who learned that the law protected property rights and not human rights commented after the trial, "I guess Judge Brown was against the tenants association the whole time. I guess the law just doesn't have too much concern for human rights."[18]

Judge Brown's directed verdict in April 1976, and his repeated orders for eviction (which he issued five times), made him a hated opponent of the I-Hotel tenants and supporters. Despite the appeals on eminent domain winding through the system to the California Supreme Court, Judge Brown never relented, insisting that the tenants be evicted immediately (with one exception: the time he feared for the safety of law-enforcement officers).

Presiding Superior Court Judge Henry Rolph, the first judge to consider the eminent-domain case, was equally hostile. He even objected to demonstrations outside City Hall during the court cases. Rolph insisted to the mayor, district attorney, sheriff, and chief of police that the I-Hotel tenants and supporters who were demonstrating while court was in session were in "clear violation of Section 169 California Penal Code." Until then, city officials had taken no action against the demonstrators. Quentin Kopp, a conservative member of the San Francisco Board of Supervisors, followed up on Judge Rolph's objection by requesting that the San Francisco Bar Association and the Barristers Club of San Francisco file suit against the City and County of San Francisco to enforce Section 169 of the Penal Code.[19] Demonstrating on the steps of City Hall was a First Amendment right of free speech, a civil-rights issue. Mayor Moscone defended his lack of action against the demonstrators by saying, "We cannot deny a permit on presumption that the law will be violated. Only the court can tell us. If a court tells us there is a violation, then the activity will be stopped."[20] One anonymous defense attorney described Judge Rolph as "the most reactionary and imbecilic judge in the county, if not the state."[21] Rolph reassigned the case to Judge Byron Arnold.

When Judge Arnold took the case, he, too, was bent on evicting the tenants, and the International Hotel lawyers tried to have him disqualified. Throughout the proceedings, Judge Arnold demonstrated his bias against the I-Hotel by making wisecracks and insults. For instance, he once said, "The Bar Association is only using this issue to build their reputation of helping the disadvantaged."[22] Judge Arnold had also presided over the granting of a demolition permit to Four Seas, overriding the veto by the city's Board of Permit Appeals. He reportedly reprimanded Gilbert Graham, the attorney for the I-Hotel legal team, for using court time to delay what he considered the inevitable eviction of the tenants. Eventually, Judge Arnold voluntarily removed himself from the case, after his extensive real-estate dealings, absentee-landlord holdings, and appointment as a Port Commissioner were exposed by a local newspaper.[23] Judge Charles S. Peery replaced Judge Arnold.

On May 27, 1977, Superior Court Judge Charles Peery ruled against the Housing Authority and the IHTA, deciding that the Housing Authority "exceeded its authority and abused its discretion" by agreeing to use eminent domain. The Housing Authority, according to Peery, had no authority "to condemn property for other than its own use"—and selling the property to the IHTA was seen as beyond "its own use." Unfortunately, Judge Peery agreed with the Four Seas Investment Corporation that "such a plan is patently invalid and unconstitutional to attempt to condemn property for resale to a private party (the Tenants Association)."[24] Urban-renewal projects on behalf of city redevelopment agencies had routinely been given the right of eminent domain so they could sell property to private developers, but Judge Peery could not envision eminent domain being used on behalf of an organization such as the IHTA. Despite arguments by attorneys for both Mayor Moscone and the IHTA, selling property to a nonprofit organization—namely, the IHTA—was regarded as illegal.[25] The IHTA's attorneys cited legal precedents to assert that the tenants of the International Hotel, through the IHTA, could receive this benefit because the hotel was deemed low-income housing for the poor, a public purpose.[26]

The Housing Authority appealed the May 27 decision to the State Court of Appeal, and on June 15, 1977, that court stayed all Superior Court proceedings, including the pending eviction. With fewer and fewer options, we considered taking the case to the U.S. Supreme Court, but David Spielberg, attorney for the San Francisco Housing Authority, was pessimistic. "We have considered the question of appealing to the U.S. Supreme Court," he said, "but as far as we know there is no way that the court will hear the case. There is no federal question involved."[27]

On July 28, the California State Supreme Court refused to stay the eviction, even though the appeal on eminent domain had not yet been heard. The vote was 4–2; only Chief Justice Rose Bird and Justice Stanley Mosk favored delaying the decision until the case was settled in the Court of Appeal. This latest legal decision stunned the IHTA legal team. The appeals panel was not expected to rule before the eviction deadline ordered by Judge Brown, which meant that only nine days were left for the sheriff's men to carry out the eviction—no later than August 6. Those who had any belief in the justice of the system thought that the courts would not be so callous as to go forward with the eviction when the appeal had not yet been heard.

It became increasingly apparent that the May 27, 1977, decision by Judge Peery marked a decisive moment in the struggle. While we stalled for time through court appeals, it became evident that the Moscone plan could no longer be used and that, unless the IHTA came up with another plan, there would be no alternative to eviction. Right after the May 27 decision, the tenants and supporters resolved to remain "calm and determined." Nancy Erickson, a lead organizer in the Support Committee, told reporters, "It's the same mood I've seen five or six times this year, when eviction threatened. We've really got ourselves organized. I think there will be ten thousand people in the streets, and I think the eviction will be stopped before the sheriff gets down here."[28]

Members of about two hundred organizations had been contacted through the telephone tree to attend a strategy meeting on May 28. The overall mood at the meeting was expectant, with both dread and cautious hope in the air. Some believed that the presence of so many bodies forming a human chain around the building would prompt a positive response from city officials and prevent the eviction. Others thought that evicting the tenants would be political suicide for liberals such as Moscone and Hongisto, particularly if it happened before the August 2 election, because members of the broad coalition that supported them were part of the anti-eviction movement. Some still held on to the belief that the city leaders would not be so callous as to allow the eviction to happen to the old and poor. A belief in America's principles of fairness to all kept many thinking that justice would prevail on behalf of the tenants. Margaret Muyco, former owner of the Lucky M pool hall, which had closed before the eviction, echoed these sentiments. Shocked after the eviction, she said, "No one believed this would happen. They didn't think that this could happen in America."[29]

The IHTA's New Plan

After the court rejected the original eminent-domain plan, the IHTA presented a new eminent-domain proposal. The plan was developed by a group of consultants, including Chester Hartman, Edward Kirshner, Joel Rubenzahl, and Vivian Tsen of the Community Ownership Organizing Project, who had worked since February to develop an alternative that would satisfy the court. Basically, the plan was to have the Housing Authority take the property under a new eminent-domain case, but in this plan the IHTA would lease the property from the Housing Authority and not buy it.[30] The IHTA would become a nonprofit organization representing the tenants, and the IHTA would manage the hotel on behalf of the Housing Authority. The arrangement would circumvent the court's objection that the Housing Authority could not sell the property to a third party.[31]

Moscone shunned the tenants at a June 10 meeting to discuss the new plan. Instead of attending the meeting, he issued a press statement stating his commitment to the old plan and vowing to appeal the May 27 court decision, as well as the impending eviction notice. He elaborated that the residents of the International Hotel would be "cared for whatever happens."[32] In a veiled warning, as if to wash his hands of the fiasco, Moscone stated, "I want to re-iterate so there is no mistake: I have taken this action [contingency plans for relocating the tenants] in the event the courts rule against us. It should be clear that there is no action which can be taken by the Mayor, nor any other City official, to withdraw final order of the court."[33] The KDP I-Hotel team and the IHTA were convinced that the mayor had deserted the I-Hotel front. After June 10, the anti-eviction struggle entered its final stage.

The tenants would be provided a full list of referrals to rental units that were available and within their ability to pay, the mayor explained in his press statement. In addition, he promised rental-supplement payments, reimbursement for the cost of moving, social-service assistance, and escort service for the physically disabled. The IHTA knew that these promises could not be kept, especially the mayor's commitment to finding equivalent replacement housing, because there was no referral list for units comparable to the accommodations at the International Hotel. Preserving the hotel really was the best choice for the tenants.

Supporters and tenants still had a small ray of hope, even though the mayor seemed to be preparing for the worst. On June 15, a stay of eviction was granted. The next day, the hotel was officially placed on the National Register of Historic Places. The official designation was another effort to prevent Four Seas Investment Corporation from demolishing the building, even if the tenants were evicted.[34]

On July 13, 1977, Mayor Moscone formally presented his objections to the new IHTA plan. By then, the August special election loomed, and he was under increasing pressure from the right-wing offensive. He insisted that the buy-back plan was the only plan that voters would accept. He rejected the IHTA plan out of hand, reaffirmed his commitment to the old plan, and said he still hoped that his plan would be validated by the Court of Appeal. He also mentioned that he would withdraw litigation if the IHTA did not obtain additional funding for the old plan according to the indemnification agreement of December 20, 1976.[35]

Moscone's objections to the second eminent-domain plan appeared to be based on minor legal technicalities, all of which were refuted by the IHTA and its housing consultants. Moscone's first criticism was that the plan would require a new resolution by the Board of Supervisors to allow hotel-tax money to be used to help pay for the hotel. The IHTA pointed out that no action by the Board of Supervisors' would be called for at that time and, assuming that Propositions A and B were defeated in the August 2 election, the attitude of the new, district-based Board of Supervisors was likely to be favorable to the new plan. Moscone's second objection was the filing of a new eminent-domain case would void the stay of eviction. The IHTA lawyers explained that filing a new case would be the basis for another stay to be granted. Moscone further objected to the fact that the Housing Authority would have to get permission from the voters to buy the hotel. The IHTA stated that that the bond issue would not have to be started until the following year—time enough to gain more support. "If necessary," Emil de Guzman wrote to the mayor, "we would be happy to take the matter to the people of San Francisco, in full confidence that we would win. And that election of course does not have to be held until the bonds are to be floated, which can be many months off."[36] Finally, Moscone feared that, if the Housing Authority owned the I-Hotel, priority for its rooms would go to those on the city's waiting list, not to the hotel's current residents. The IHTA responded that the lease the tenants would enter into with the Housing Authority would define who would live at the hotel and who would not. Regulations would be negotiated between the two bodies, with the tenants as the decision-making body.[37]

In response to these inquiries about the new plan, Mayor Moscone requested City Attorney Thomas O'Connor's counsel. O'Connor explained, first, that a two-thirds vote of the electorate and an amendment to the code would be required before the City and County of San Francisco could use funds from the hotel tax to support bonds issued by the Housing Authority. Second, a majority vote would be required before the Housing Authority could enter lease financing arrangements with the IHTA. Third, the city and county could use community-development funds to acquire and rehabilitate the I-Hotel. Fourth, only the Housing Authority could determine the priority that could be given to the hotel's current residents and what was necessary to provide safe and sanitary accommodations to the occupants.[38]

The IHTA's housing consultants were optimistic, since the proposal had been researched extensively and was sound and reasonable.[39] Winning two-thirds of the vote would be difficult, but winning a majority vote on the lease was definitely possible, particularly if other funding sources could be found and the two-thirds bond vote could be avoided. "Moscone is very pressurable because of Barbagelata's move to have a vote to re-call Moscone and to defeat District Elections," the IHTA's board reasoned.[40] In any case, the effort would provide yet one more delay of the eviction, and winning some future election was conceivable, particularly if the conservative counterattack was beaten back and the progressive insurgency continued in city politics. Political support was necessary for any proposal that needed the city government's approval. The IHTA and the KDP, along with many other progressive and leftist activists, were willing to fight to build such support again. Our eminent-domain proposal was not far-fetched; similar tenant-management corporations had been employed in St. Louis, Boston, and Newark, New Jersey.[41] But we realized we would have a tough fight, needing alternately to battle and to cooperate with the mayor and supervisors along the way. We also knew the unfavorable court rulings allowed us very little political breathing space.

The KDP pressured the city government to be responsible to its citizens and criticized Mayor Moscone when he refused to support the IHTA's new eminent-domain plan. "The stand the Mayor has taken against the hotel can only suggest that he has traded off the issue of the hotel for his security as a politician in this city," Jeanette wrote. "With the upcoming August 2nd special election the reasoning behind this is simple; in order to get the vote and confidence of Chamber of Commerce and Downtown (where the money is) Moscone has moved to the side of some of the major landowners in San Francisco." Jeanette went on to identify the old enemy of the I-Hotel tenants: "Walter Shorenstein, once the landlord of the International Hotel, is also on the Chamber of Commerce. All of these people control the economic life of S.F. and they all have advocated the demolition of the building and eviction of the tenants for 9 years."[42]

The Barricades

Editorials in local newspapers increasingly called for the eviction of the tenants, forcing Moscone's and Hongisto's hands. No longer were the tenants treated as courageous elders in need of low-income housing. Most of the editorials and columnists at the *San Francisco Chronicle* and *San Francisco Examiner* depicted the I-Hotel as a "flophouse," a "fleabag" hotel. It seemed that opposition to the I-Hotel movement had indeed become a political crusade by propertied elites and pro-growth Democrats.[43] Discrediting the movement's supporters through red-baiting; characterizing the tenants as pawns of violent radicals; denigrating the I-Hotel as a dilapidated place unfit for human habitation—all of these tactics were deployed in the media's rhetoric. "Emotions and sentimentality must yield on occasion to realism and law and order," wrote one editorialist. "The hotel, on the edge of Chinatown, is a dangerous fire trap. Condemnation is legally in order."[44] Moscone and Hongisto were depicted as lawless politicians: "There is no such thing as legal-lawlessness in the books but the term may make an appearance any year now. It's the only way to describe the process by which law is used successfully to do what is solemnly declared to be illegal."[45] Both Moscone and Hongisto were urged by local newspapers to evict. Two days before the eviction, a *San Francisco Chronicle* editorial put it very bluntly:

> The court completely vindicates the right of the owners of the hotel to have their property back. If that requires the physical eviction of a small group of tenants who have unlawfully detained it for many months while pursuing ill-starred, radical tactics of political browbeating designed to palm the hotel off on the city, then let them suffer physical eviction. . . . It is of course high time for Sheriff Hongisto to do his duty and enforce [the court rulings]. . . . Naturally, one would not expect the sheriff to act before Tuesday's election, in which his office is on the line; but he would do well to go about the duty early Wednesday morning.[46]

Moscone apparently got the message, as did Sheriff Hongisto, who gave orders to Undersheriff Denman to evict as planned.

Early on Wednesday, August 3, the news reporter Geraldo Rivera leaked the information to supporters and tenants that the sheriff might be coming that night. Many rumors had circulated throughout the day. Tenants and supporters did not know whether to believe this latest rumor, since five other eviction deadlines had passed. Each time, the sheriff had had to back down. People's power had stopped each threat. Some believed, however, that this might be the time. It was a surprise to us that it had come so soon—barely a day after the defeat of Propositions A and B in the special election.

On August 2, both Propositions A and B were handily defeated. Proposition A, which called for the repeal of district elections, lost by a 58–42 percent margin, while Proposition B went down 64–36 percent.[47] Moscone and his allies thus had won with a comfortable margin. Many of us still held hope that the eviction once again might be averted at the last minute, and these hopes were boosted when representatives of San Franciscans for District Elections, fresh from their victory against Propositions A and B just the day before, met with tenant leaders that evening. The same forces who had come to the rescue of Moscone, walking precincts and getting out the vote, declared that they would now direct their efforts to backing the tenants' fight. Tenants and some supporters, including the KDP team, were encouraged by this support, and we thought that a last-ditch effort to save the I-Hotel was still possible.

But according to housing advocates inside City Hall, Moscone and the Board of Supervisors lacked the political will to prevent the eviction. Perhaps Moscone no longer believed that the I-Hotel was worth saving. After Moscone defeated the right-wing's attack on him and his coalition in the special election, he may have felt that his political future depended on isolating and defeating those farther to his left, and his margin of victory was comfortable enough to carry that out. The timing of the eviction, the very next day after the election, suggests that Moscone wanted to take advantage of the momentum the election had generated to trade his support for the I-Hotel for his security as a politician. For Moscone to prosper politically in San Francisco, especially to consolidate the backing of mainstream Democratic Party figures, he had to side with major landowners and party stalwarts such as Shorenstein. Although the recall movement had been defeated for the moment, Moscone nonetheless feared more attacks from the propertied and political elites, as well as from neighborhood conservatives such as Barbagelata. The I-Hotel became a liability to Moscone, an albatross around his neck, and his refusal to meet with the tenants just before the eviction was a clue that he had moved decisively in the wrong direction.[48]

Meanwhile, repeated demonstrations to prevent eviction had buoyed I-Hotel organizers—but it had also worn us out. Earlier demonstrations in front of the hotel with thousands of people had indicated the movement's strength. On January 12, 2,500–3,000 supporters, complete with a human barricade, had vowed to stop eviction, and the January 16 demonstration of 5,000–7,000 was the biggest San Francisco had seen since rallies against the Vietnam War. Support had come from the Garment Workers, Retail Clerks, United Farm Workers, Steelworkers, Mailhandlers, ILWU, and other unions, as well as from communities of color and progressive activists of all backgrounds.

At another demonstration on June 12, which mobilized 1,500–2,000 people in front of the hotel, Walter Johnson of Retail Clerks Local 1100 and president of the San Francisco Labor Council said, "It's always a privilege to be on the side of the people. I'm concerned about the tenants of the hotel, but also I'm concerned about the attitude of politicians who could buy this hotel so that tenants wouldn't have to worry any more."[49] Also at the June 12 demonstration, David Prowler, a member of the Human Rights Commission staff, charged, "It is an outrage that we have to be here today to protest for a basic human right—the right to live. Today San Francisco is up for sale, and a city that sells itself to the highest bidder cannot survive!"[50]

The imminent danger facing the I-Hotel by August set the tone for unity to prevent eviction despite the conflicts among the tenants, the supporters, and the left. Sympathizers within the city government told organizers that Sheriff Hongisto would conduct a surprise attack in the middle of the night, when people were asleep. His purpose would be to avoid as much confrontation with supporters as possible. In contrast, we wanted to dramatize the eviction for maximum political effect. To provoke greater sympathy from the public, the organizers felt, any protest during an eviction attempt must be highly organized; it must be peaceful, and it must show the callousness of evicting elderly tenants. On the night of August 3, it looked like eviction was imminent.

The coalition believed that the protests should be nonviolent and as orderly as possible. We planned a traditional passive-resistance strategy. Frances Peavey, a teacher and therapist known among tenants and supporters by the nickname "Finley," was the lead organizer for security preparations, or the "eviction response system." She was an experienced nonviolent activist in her thirties, and she beefed up twenty-four-hour internal-security teams in expectation of intruders—especially for a surprise eviction.

Militant and daring nonviolent actions were the order of the day, and the tenants were not squeamish about them. However, to safeguard the health and welfare of the tenants, the anti-eviction coalition united on nonviolent actions to dramatize the political message. This point was stressed by all three key organizations in the anti-eviction fight—the IHTA, the Support Committee, and the Workers Committee. At the same time, activists realized how difficult it would be to control individuals who might be frustrated by the setbacks, and we wanted to redirect the frustration and rage. I attended meetings led by Finley to orient supporters about the nonviolent stand of the anti-eviction movement.[51]

Support Committee organizers had a color-coded system that alerted supporters to the different levels of danger. A red alert meant that the sheriff and police were coming to evict the tenants. A yellow alert meant to stand by and watch for new developments because eviction was imminent. The information then was disseminated throughout a telephone tree of about three hundred supporters, who would then each call several other supporters. At a moment's notice, thousands could be mobilized.[52] A color-coded armband system made it easy to identify hall monitors, medical teams, news media, and others inside the hotel.

These elaborate systems had been prepared to avoid confusion among the organizers and to make sure that resistance to eviction would be organized and peaceful. To prevent violence and to avoid unforeseen incidents, supporters were screened to make sure no provocateurs or police agents infiltrated the security system. Hundreds of people who volunteered to help the tenants conceded to pat-down searches.

Preparing for security was a defensive action, an act of civil defense. Nevertheless, the tension these preparations generated had a contradictory effect on those who participated: Security issues were frightening yet empowering at the same time. It seemed gruesome to anticipate a police action against the frail tenants and their supporters. Hundreds of people were involved, and the large number of people encouraged the tenants and gave them hope that, with such broad public support, compassion would prevail. To the demonstrators who came out repeatedly, Manong Wahat said, "You are my bread and butter. You have really touched my heart, and I'm thanking you for your sympathy, for my dignity."[53]

The civil-rights movement provided our main example. Passive resistance would dramatize that eviction was inherently violent, and any violence in carrying it out would be meted out by the sheriff and the Police Department, not by the resistance of the tenants or their supporters. We did not want a single blot against the tenants and organizers. "Our aim is to keep the situation as under control as possible to avoid panic and to avoid incidents. We want to make sure that any violence that occurs is not of our making," said one security-team leader.[54]

The situation was delicate because the elderly were frail, and, frankly, supporters did not know if the tenants could physically endure the stress. Some had already succumbed to serious medical conditions, and a few, such as Claudio Domingo, had lost their lives under the strain of the eviction threats. The medical-team volunteers were especially helpful to the tenants and ready for the day of the eviction. Counseling teams had been meeting with tenants to prepare them for the coming emotional stresses. Members of the press were invited to come inside the building to witness the eviction. A legal team had been organized to document any "harsh actions done to tenants or supporters."[55] As noted earlier, when a local news reporter asked Wahat Tompao what he was going to do during the eviction, he said perhaps he would chain himself to his bed. Then he replied more tentatively, "Many of us are old people. We don't have the strength or the agility. Most of us are counting on supporters to defend us. It's up to them, really. If they come out in mass, then we can turn them back like we did in January. If not, I don't know."[56]

Every window and door was securely fixed. Plywood two-by-fours barricaded each window and door. Rooms were bolted, making it physically difficult for the sheriff to get inside. It looked as if the building was under siege and the people inside were bracing themselves for a fight. Members of the Support Committee believed that protecting the building from any destruction was necessary, since the next stage of the fight would be for the tenants to return to their homes. In any event, eviction would be difficult because the sheriff's deputies would have to break through the barricades and remove each tenant from each room, one by one.

Tenants and organizers had mixed emotions about, and different positions on, boarding up the building. It created a sense of futility, a gloomy atmosphere that the eviction was inevitable. The KDP team members thought it gave the impression that saving the building was more important than preventing the eviction of the tenants. There were disagreements within the coalition about how the building should be defended. Some argued that stopping the police from occupying the building and removing its tenants and supporters should be undertaken at all costs because it was the most important and concrete way to prevent the eviction: Resistance, short of initiating violence, should be "by any means necessary," as Malcolm X had said. Once the building was relinquished, they reasoned, it would be harder to gain it back, and the building would be demolished.

The KDP thought that the building itself was primarily a political symbol and that it should not to be confused with the eviction of the tenants or the issues of low-income housing and human rights. Escalating the resistance to more militant tactics could be an excuse for the police to initiate violence. Militant tactics had to be balanced against the health of tenants who were already frail. Even some key supporters of the KDP disagreed with our strategy that the building was principally a political symbol; they argued that once the building was lost, it would be hard to regain political support for the tenants. Chester Hartman, for example, felt that the tactics of civil disobedience should have been escalated—preferably by finding a tactic that would have prevented the police physically from entering the building. He argued that such a scenario could have led the police chief, the sheriff, and the mayor to decide to retreat. Given the political consequences of unrestrained brute force (media coverage was extensive), the thousands of supporters outside the building could have been used for more militant measures to resist intrusion by the police to evict the tenants. All agreed, however, that the "human barricade" would serve as another deterrent to evicting the tenants.[57]

The serious implications of what was at stake in these discussions should be underscored. Several organizers advocated that the International Hotel take on the character of a siege similar to the resistance of Wounded Knee on the Pine Ridge Reservation in South Dakota a few years earlier. In other words, some believed that the time had come for armed defense in support of a just mass demand and that the confrontation would expose the violent nature of the capitalist state. Many leading tenants were so militant that they firmly and quietly, without bravado, declared to Jeanette, Emil, and me that they would be willing to die for the hotel if that was what it would take to stop the eviction and defend the rights of poor people, and that if the KDP decided to take that stand, they would follow its leadership without hesitation. However, Bruce Occena, meeting with the KDP I-Hotel team, explained that risking death was not the point; he also pointed out the huge differences between Wounded Knee and the I-Hotel. Political ends could be gained more effectively through symbolic resistance rather through militarized resistance. In fact, Occena argued, an overly militarist defense was not only likely to result in injuries and possible loss of life; it was defeatist because it reduced a fight that was inherently political to a simple struggle over bricks. The issue of low-income housing, human rights, and even the fate of the building itself would take on new and different forms after a symbolic, nonviolent resistance. Organizers needed to have confidence that, even with a major setback, the battle would continue.

Emil, Jeanette, and I were horrified at the prospect of violence. We did not want anyone's death—particularly that of any of the tenants—to be on our hands. The declaration by tenants of their willingness to die moved us deeply, but our emotional and our political instincts told us that escalating tactics and risking a massive outpouring of violence would be a mistake. The situation, particularly with supporters ranging from nonviolent Christian activists to militant anarchist street fighters, was volatile enough. Anything could happen, and neither the KDP's I-Hotel team nor the collective leadership of the three anti-eviction groups could exercise control over the growing mass of supporters, much less over the police, once that level of confrontation was reached. Finley agreed with the nonviolent, symbolic-resistance approach, and her firm, steady leadership of security did much to prevent an "armed-struggle" stance from taking hold and leading to a potential bloodbath.

Finally, a nonviolent human barricade of successive layers, like a tightly wound rubber band, was decided on as the best tactic to prevent the police from easily entering the front door. Depending on the number of defenders, each person was to lock arms with each other, thereby providing a human chain around the building, making it difficult to break the human barrier. External security leaders of the Support Committee prepared supporters for the front line of defense. If violence broke out, local team captains were to assess the situation and evacuate the human barricade, as needed. The supporters were given specific instructions during security orientations not to initiate any violence. The human barricade acted both as a physical and symbolic barrier from the police, and care was taken to explain that no supporters or tenants were to be hurt.

A delegation of tenants, along with Finley and other supporters, met with Undersheriff James Denman, whom Sheriff Richard Hongisto designated to coordinate and direct the eviction. Given the volatility of the situation, the delegation asked the sheriff's deputies not to bring sticks and guns. Undersheriff Denman had prepared more than two hundred deputies in a practice run a month earlier at a site in the Bayview/Hunters Point District, and he had prepared a forty-page operations manual titled "Ethics and Conduct" to guide their behavior. The question was when and how to evict. According to Undersheriff Denman, the element of surprise was paramount because of the stiff opposition from supporters and the sophistication of our organization.[58]

Inside the building, tenants were organized into internal security teams. Each tenant was paired with one or two supporters who would stay by his side throughout the process to provide assistance or, if the need arose, protection. Each of the young aides also served as an official eyewitness to insure the safety of the tenants from the Police Department and the Sheriff's Department. The arrangement also dramatized the intergenerational bond between the elderly and the youthful supporters who took care of their immediate needs. The International Hotel was barricaded; security drills were run; and the tenants were readied. We still had hope, but everyone was prepared for the worst.

Terry Bautista, a KDP activist, described the scene as we waited for the attack:

> We all took on any assignments that were needed. Some were needed to work the phones. Some were lookouts on the roof. I remember 20 or more people sleeping on a stage inside the building, while large numbers of other people were helping the tenants. Some would stay with them in their rooms to make sure that nothing happened to them. My job was to be a lookout [for police] at the front door. It was basically sentry duty. The cops could come at any time and we had to be ready. It was like we were getting ready for war.[59]

CHAPTER SEVEN

The Fall of the I-Hotel

Eviction and Demolition, 1977–79

Eviction Night, August 3–4, 1977

On Wednesday, August 3, the IHTA and the KDP team thought that a last-ditch effort to save the I-Hotel was still be possible. Organizers from the campaign to defeat Propositions A and B, fresh from their victory, told us that they were going to turn their energy toward saving the hotel. We received support from community leaders and even a letter from Art Agnos, the majority whip in the State Assembly, to express "strong support for your organization's effort to retain that valuable low-income housing for poor people."[1] Still, as the day wore on, intelligence reports kept trickling in, and they were all bad news. By evening, the signs were all grim. Police officers were training at the Fire Department facility at 19th and Folsom streets; the Police Department was reserving parking spaces at garages throughout the city; an unusual number of officers were gathering at the Hall of Justice; the freeway exit to downtown had been closed; a contingent of mounted police was gathering near Market Street; and the streets surrounding the I-Hotel were blocked off. According to police reports that were revealed later, the eviction was to begin at 12:30 A.M. on Thursday. At that hour, traffic would be minimal. Also, it was just after the midnight change in police shifts, making a maximum number of officers available for duty.[2]

By 10:00 P.M., the signs were too ominous to disregard. Tenant leaders—Wahat Tompao, Nita Rader, Emil de Guzman, and others—set off the "red alert," and the phone tree was activated to summon the members of three hundred Bay Area political organizations, trade unions, and church groups. Demonstrators started gathering about 11:00 P.M., and by 1:00 A.M., nearly two thousand people circled the building and locked arms in a human barricade ten to twelve rows deep. A lock-down in the hotel went into effect, and about two hundred supporters barricaded themselves inside. The internal security team had already boarded up the front door, and now, at the last minute, they added boards, mattresses, and bedsprings on the stairway leading to the second floor, where the tenants' rooms were. Wet towels were placed under the doors to prevent tear gas from entering the rooms. Enough provisions were gathered to survive a four-day siege. About forty young supporters took positions inside, blocking the steps leading to the second floor and waiting for the assault with locked arms. I took my position in the hallway with others, and some people accompanied tenants into their locked rooms to wait for what was to come.

Most of the tenants gave up going to sleep that night. As we waited, Manong Wahat offered those of us inside sliced cantaloupe to calm us down. I cried intermittently as we got ready. As if by magic, the melon did calm my nerves. We could hear chanting outside in staccato and muffled tones, "Stop the Eviction! We Won't Move!" I briefly remembered trying to muster support for our anti-eviction battle when Wahat and I had appeared on the local radio station KPOO that morning. We began that day just like any other by reaching out to the public. As they had many times before, my two sons and daughter played at the hotel, but I had arranged for someone else to take them home. It had been a very long day. It seemed like a bad dream. I still could not believe the eviction would happen.

Outside the building, two hundred fifty police in full riot gear, wearing jumpsuits and helmets with face masks, moved into position for the military-like assault. Along with them came the motorcycle police. Ambulances, paddy wagons, and other law-enforcement vehicles screeched into place. I could hear loud, frightening voices blaring through the loudspeakers. Finley shouted, "They are coming! They are coming!" To keep the crowd's spirits up, the defenders outside sang protest songs made famous by the Civil Rights Movement between the chants. Those of us inside the building felt extraordinary unity and powerful emotions when we heard them sing, "Just like a tree standing by the water / We shall not be moved!" The singing calmed the crowd and gave them courage. We chanted inside, "The people united will never be defeated!"

At approximately 1:00 A.M., the assault began. Police vehicles blocked Kearny Street on both ends to create a wedge in the center of the barricade. The clip-clop of the horses' hooves came as a surprise to the defenders at the front door, who were no match for mounted police wielding clubs. At previous meetings with the police, supporters had been told that, if the eviction were carried out, the police would be armed only with clubs, although they probably would use them to get to the door. They had told the truth. But no one in external security had expected the police to be mounted on horseback. The police used the combined weapons of clubs and horses to drive a path to the door and ordered protestors to leave, but they refused. At the same time, two sheriff's buses deposited sixty deputies onto the streets, who lined up face to face with the protestors. The demonstrators waited, arms locked, for about two hours while the police continued to position themselves.

A little before 3:00 A.M., police on horseback and on foot formed a wedge and rushed toward the door while other officers began pushing the protesters toward Jackson Street, toward the center door. Then the pushing and shoving started, and violence began. In a pincer-like move, the police charged the human barricade from the flank and the center. The police hoped that by jamming their nightsticks into the demonstrators and shoving them into one another, they could force the demonstrators to break away from the pressure and flee. But the protestors had nowhere to go, and most did not want to leave, anyway.

When that failed, San Francisco police waded into the demonstrators from the front, flailing truncheons and shoving people back into the crowd. Eleven mounted police with swinging clubs forced demonstrators against the building's brick wall. Once they were against the wall, several protestors were pounded with police clubs.[3] Douglas Dowd, one of the supporters in the human barricade, described the grim situation: "We found ourselves massed around the hotel, arms linked, as mounted cops drove their horses into our bodies, pushing into the sides of the building. . . . It was a nightmare that went on and on until . . . more and more cops with swinging batons and great muscular horses with sweaty flanks and flashing hooves moved in to crush us always more."[4]

Members of the I-Hotel internal security team and news reporters inside the building watched in horror. One journalist who observed the melee from inside the building reported: "I moved to the second floor window and saw a policeman hitting the head of a person in the crowd lined nine deep around the hotel entrance. Behind me, I heard supporters singing, 'We Shall Not Be Moved.'"[5] People inside began to sing in unison with those outside to brace ourselves and, perhaps, to give those outside more courage.

Police Chief Charles Gain, wearing three generals' stars on the epaulettes of his Eisenhower jacket, watched with binoculars from the eighth floor of the Holiday Inn across the street. The horse patrol lunged at supporters, jabbing them with black nightsticks, unable to get through to the front door. Three waves of riot police attacked on foot. Each wave was repulsed by the persistent defenders. After the third assault failed, Chief Gain ordered his police to hold back. After the fracas, which had lasted two to three minutes, he told a reporter, "Something went wrong, but I don't know what, I put a freeze on things." As Chief Gain was being interviewed, a police officer clubbed a television cameraman's spotlight.[6] Later, the police claimed that a "mix-up" had occurred because one squad of police used Plan A and another used Plan B. The result of the "mix-up" was that people on the human barricade were pushed against one another and against the wall of the building, unable to move even if they had wanted to.[7]

The resolve of the human barricade grew even stronger. One supporter on the front line told the *San Francisco Bay Guardian* afterward, "The police were jabbing and hitting at the same time as the horses were pushing in on us. People were screaming in anguish and fear. There was nowhere to go and they kept hitting. I covered my head and they started beating me in the stomach. I tried to cover my friend's head and they started hitting me again in the face. But nobody broke, people were just incredibly strong."[8] As one reporter observed, "The police tactic seemed aimed more at punishing us than at removing us from the front of the building."[9]

After the third skirmish, the tactical squad regrouped and menacingly stood with batons ready. The police waited for the order to charge the crowd again, with overwhelming force. Several defenders had been bloodied by nightsticks, and one had been arrested.[10] There were twenty reported injuries among supporters; five required hospital treatment. Scores of others on the human barricade suffered bruises from clubbing and jabbing or being trampled by horses' hooves.

At this point, the IHTA and the tactical leadership of the Support Committee inside the building saw that people had been hurt outside, and they ordered the demonstrators to disperse. The RCP-led Workers Committee had not agreed with nonviolence as a tactic. It felt that "people on the human barricade were sitting ducks for the police" because they could not fight back and held to the opinion that "the cops should be made to pay as high a price as possible," which would have meant a military-style resistance. However, the Workers Committee acquiesced to the leadership of the IHTA and did not fight the police. When the order came to withdraw, most of the Workers Committee members left the human barricade and walked across the street.[11]

The rest of the defenders ignored the order. They were not deluded; they knew the police eventually would break through. Yet they argued that, if the human barricade held out until sunrise, the evictions would have to be conducted during the morning rush hour, when people going to work in the nearby financial district would be forced to witness the brutality.[12] But the tenant leadership wanted to avoid violence and ordered the determined crowd to break up again and again. "Peaceful resistance just wasn't the way to deal with the situation," said Mary Sartin, the spokesperson for the tenants. "If people weren't to be killed we had to get them out of there."[13]

Locking arms and preventing the police from opening the front door was a formidable task, but the defenders were ready. With the sixth major skirmish, mounted police and a riot squad on foot were determined to drive a wedge between the demonstrators. With several defenders already hurt, and fearing even more casualties, tactical leadership teams insisted that the supporters abandon the human barricade. Finley, Mary Sartin, and others implored the defenders several times to abandon the line of battle and to go across the street, but without success. The defenders were determined to be strong, despite the jabs and blows by police. A supporter who had been hit below the neck and back legs recalled that he could hear from behind him, "You can handle it, hang tight. We're behind you." The three hundred to four hundred people directly in front of the door had been told again by the tactical leadership of the Support Committee to move out. Many were willing to stay longer. As one supporter wrote in an article for *Common Sense* soon afterward, "I screamed, NO! I want to stay."[14]

The organizers' guidelines followed the strategy of peaceful, civil disobedience. A careful distinction had to be drawn between defending the building and any untoward action that could negatively affect the health and well-being of the tenants. "Our tactics will be guided by the principles of militant non violent resistance," the guidelines explained. "Anyone in the demonstration who attempts to violently confront the police will be treated as an enemy of the hotel."[15] The moral high ground was to demonstrate peacefully against the onslaught and the possibility of violence by the police. Removing the human barricade had one disastrous effect, however; it meant that the police were free to enter the hotel with no further resistance. Reluctantly, many defenders obeyed the tactical leadership teams' orders, but other supporters outside were stubbornly willing to battle it out with police to prevent them from entering the building.[16] Some supporters had argued that defending the building was critical to prevent eviction, and perhaps defending it at all costs could have done just that. The tactical leadership, however, wanted to prevent a bloodbath. How far can a symbolic action go? There were different interpretations—and for some, the battle was far from symbolic. But the final decision, despite the reluctance of defenders, called for a retreat before a political battle turned into a military one that the tenants and their supporters were sure to lose.

At the same time that the melee in front of the building developed, another scene unfolded at the back of the building. A Fire Department hook-and-ladder truck slid into the parking lot at Kearny and Jackson. The whole block was lighted as if it was daylight, and policemen climbed up an aerial ladder to take the roof. About seventeen young tenants and supporters on the roof also locked arms, blocking the stairwell to the second floor, where the tenants were barricaded in their rooms. At first, they tried to repel the police and sheriff's deputies by pushing the aerial ladder away from the roof. Police shouted to them, "Attention, people on the roof. You will be arrested if you continue to resist." The protestors ignored the warning but were quickly restrained by the police. They formed their own human barricade, but they were unlinked one by one with the force of riot clubs. All were handcuffed and left to stay on the roof until the eviction inside was well under way. Tony Goolsby, a young tenant and cousin of Nita Rader, one of the tenant leaders, later complained to the security team that he had been roughed up by the police as he tried to prevent them from getting onto the roof. Goolsby described the ordeal:

> They threw us on the ground, with our arms outstretched and then with one officer holding his stick down against your neck, another one came around and pulled your arms back and handcuffed them. They threw us up against a wall in the middle of the building, after dragging us over there. I saw the badge number of the officer who dragged me and he

> told me, "If you don't move, I'll break your —— neck!" All in all, we were up on that roof, handcuffed, for three hours or so. My neck's still stiff from the club and everything. You know, when I asked for medical attention, they wouldn't get it.[17]

At 4:20 A.M., I could see that policemen had reached one of the rooms from the roof. I could hear them from the hallway as they broke the wood barrier covering Joe Bungayan's window and smashed the glass to small pieces. Manong Joe had been lying on his bed sleeping when the crash of splintering glass startled him awake. A policeman asked him whether he spoke English, and he said, "Yes." The police then told him he was being evicted from the building and asked whether he would go willingly, without police forcing him out. He walked out reluctantly, explaining that he had high blood pressure and a nervous condition. Manong Joe was clearly irritated, and he complained to me that the broken glass that lay on his bed easily could have hurt him. The usually quiet and reserved man was clearly agitated and very angry. Later, he talked about his experience to Ed Diokno of *Philippine News*: "I was lying down and taking a rest. They're not supposed to break the window. What kind of law we got here. They broke the antenna off my TV and I could have been cut with the glass."[18]

After the demonstrators left the front door, the police began to pull away the physical barricades—the mattresses, boards, and tables. The sheriff's deputies walked through the first floor and then proceeded to remove the people on the landing who were blocking the tenants' rooms on the second floor. More policemen and deputies, with helmets and sticks, entered the building. Demonstrators chanted at Sheriff Hongisto, "Where will you live when you get old?" This chant alternated with, "No Evictions. We Won't Move!" louder than ever. We were outraged that police had gotten inside, and it became even more difficult to control the crowd as the frustration mounted. One protestor, enraged by what had happened, picked up a stick to throw at the police. He was quickly reminded that the demonstration was to remain nonviolent. He dropped the stick.[19]

About forty supporters sitting tensely with locked arms blocked the second-floor landing at the top of the stairs. Anticipating violence from the police, they tightly braced their bodies as they sat in a human chain. The technique was to go limp once deputies broke the chain, making it more difficult for the police officers and sheriff's deputies to carry off their dead weight. In a show of force, and perhaps to intimidate the police and deputies, they chanted in unison to their faces, "No Evictions! We Won't Move!" loud enough for the people outside to hear.

Sheriff's deputies came upon Emil de Guzman. They recognized him as chairman of the IHTA and knew that removing one of the leaders would demoralize the rest of the defenders. They yanked at him, but he held tightly and resisted being pulled away from his fellow supporters, which put severe pressure on his neck and arms. The deputies had him in a choke hold and jumped on his knee to break him free. Emil felt that they were trying to choke him to death, but his martial-arts training and college wrestling experience enabled him to prevent them from blocking his windpipe. It took two to three deputies to pull him away and then drag him down the stairs and into the street. He went limp with pain. In a live radio broadcast, Norman Jayo of the local Pacifica station KPFA, told his audience step by step what the police were doing to Emil: "They got him by the neck—they're pulling at him—I think he may be injured."[20] Terrified, I cried uncontrollably as I witnessed the assault. I was still in shock, as were the tenants, unable to believe that the eviction was actually happening.

The plan to block the second-floor hallway leading to the tenants' rooms was symbolic, and the value of resistance again was weighed against the potential violence that could ensue. Although the defenders had hoped to keep the police from entering, most of the young supporters were systematically and forcibly removed from the landing at the top of the stairs. At least two deputies were dispatched per supporter—more if they were given trouble. Six deputies were used to pry off the more difficult protestors. No one was asked to leave, since it was obvious that no one was going to move. The chanting, "We Won't Move! We Won't Move!" was both loud and furious as each supporter was routed out.

As each of the supporters was carried outside by the deputies, the loud chanting reached a crescendo. Their arms and legs went limp, making it more difficult for the deputies to carry out the eviction. Because of the political sensitivity of the eviction, the sheriff's deputies were forced to clear the defenders inside the building with more restraint than the police had handled themselves outside. They employed muscle power rather than swinging clubs, brandishing guns, or issuing threats. The Sheriff's Department had more of a stake in keeping their violence under control in the vicinity of the elderly tenants—especially with the media recording every move. According to official instructions, the deputies were not to construe nonviolent civil-disobedience tactics by the demonstrators as violence.[21] Deputies were ordered to "talk as little and as softly as possible, be cognizant of the fact that they were being watched not only by other deputies, but also by the police, the media and by tenants and supporters. Deputies' conduct must reflect the highest standards of responsibility and dignity."[22] The sharp contrast in conduct between the inside and the outside may have been due to the different roles of the Police Department and the Sheriff's Department. The Sheriff's Department had exclusive jurisdiction over the actual eviction process, and Hongisto had instructed his deputies to maintain an official posture of sympathy and relative respect. The chief of police had control over the riot squad to clear the front doorway and roof and make way for the eviction process, and he felt fewer constraints against using force, perhaps because he had no political flank to protect.[23]

After the deputies unblocked the second-floor landing, they were able to evict the tenants physically. They ignored those of us who had linked arms in the hallway for the time being and went directly to the rooms. I could see that deputies were breaking down tenants' doors one by one with axes and sledgehammers. Each door was barricaded securely, and I could hear the sounds of heavy steel chopping and splintered wood falling to the floor as the deputies broke through. I was terrified, and I know those inside were, too. Sheriff Hongisto, "wielding a sledgehammer, knocked down some of the doors to tenants rooms and said he found elderly Asians crying," reporters wrote.[24] I saw the sheriff dressed in a golden turtleneck sweater and dark brown sports coat instead of a uniform. His dapper appearance and jovial and even casual demeanor seemed odd and in stark contrast to his actions. It was rumored that he was going on a date immediately after the eviction. In my eyes, he seemed to relish crashing through the doors with his sledgehammer. "Don't do it! Don't do it!" I yelled, still crying. After breaking down the doors with great force, he asked in a quiet and polite voice, "Do you speak English? Hi, I'm the sheriff of San Francisco. We're here for the eviction and I'd appreciate it if you would come out so we can empty the hotel. It's time to go. Would you like to come out? OK, thank you. No. I'm afraid you can't come back."[25]

The sheriff, the apparently principled man who had sided with us and had gone to jail for five days, seemed to revel in the actual eviction. Tenants and supporters alike thought that he might defy the law again because of his liberal beliefs and sympathy for the tenants. He ignored his previous statements opposing the eviction, such as "laws in our society are written to protect people with property and money."[26] The fact that he ultimately carried out the eviction in the face of civil disobedience was expected from a sheriff. It was Hongisto's earlier resistance to moneyed interests that was unusual, and what was different in this case was that he and other city officials had not carried out the eviction months, if not years, earlier. The wide support for the tenants was part of the broader progressive trend in San Francisco that constituted a significant part of Hongisto's electoral base. This pushed the sheriff to find some room to resist; he had hoped to delay the eviction until a solution could be found that would not force him to side with private-property forces.

Wahat Tompao had asked Sheriff Hongisto to go to jail again and be beloved by the people of San Francisco. Art Silverman of the *Berkeley Barb* echoed Manong Wahat when he addressed the sheriff in an open letter: "You cast your lot on the wrong side of history. . . . [T]he only honorable course would have been for you to resign, or alternatively, refuse to carry out the eviction and then fight removal from office."[27] But the sheriff had made other calculations. Hongisto explained that, by wielding the sledgehammer, he was actually showing his deputies how to break the doors down in the least destructive way possible so the tenants could return. He justified his decision to go ahead with the eviction as a choice concerning progressive politics: "I did the evictions because I was one of the foremost jail reformers at the time. We were doing exciting things at the county jail and I didn't want to lose all of that. . . . I was pleased that I had done it without anyone getting shot, and the tenants weren't hurt. But I was disgusted that I had to do it."[28] Despite his rationale, Sheriff Hongisto's conduct during the eviction left a deep scar in the memory of the tenants and supporters. Local newspapers immortalized his behavior during eviction night by publishing a picture of the sheriff swinging a sledgehammer against a door. The notorious photograph haunted him for the rest of his political career.[29]

We felt even more betrayed by Mayor Moscone. He had allowed the eviction to happen even though the appeal to the California Supreme Court had not yet been heard. He had promised the tenants that he would not go ahead with the eviction until all court appeals had been exhausted. We assumed that Moscone would not have defied the court-ordered eviction, but the eviction might have been averted if he had called a state of emergency. Were there other measures he could have enacted? Perhaps, but by this point the mayor and his allies had decided to cast their lot with the business elite. Still, the mayor wanted to hide his role, and he did not come to Kearny Street. There would be no politically damaging photos of Mayor Moscone presiding over elderly tenants being thrown into the streets.

Meanwhile, as the eviction proceeded, I watched sheriff's deputies as they carefully knocked at each door, informed each tenant that he was being evicted, and asked him if he would go peacefully to avoid sledgehammers crashing through the door. Each tenant walked out slowly and deliberately instead of being carried out. Led by supporters who acted as escorts and witnesses, each elderly tenant made his way slowly down the stairs and out to Kearny Street, exhausted. Dazed and shaken, some cried, while others glared defiantly at the deputies.

Cheers and applause met each tenant and accompanying supporter as soon as they stepped into the early-morning darkness. They were cheered for their determination and fighting spirit. Wahat Tompao walked out accompanied by Jeanette Lazam; Mr. Yip was accompanied by Ellen Kaiser. They came out pair by pair, some dignified and straight-backed, and others weeping uncontrollably. All of us—tenants and supporters alike—were overwhelmed with shock, outrage, and feelings of betrayal.

In the midst of this operation, the deputies turned to the rest of us who sat with locked arms in the hallway, and I soon found myself on the street. There, in the chilly early-morning air and in front of the blindingly bright spotlights, sheriff's deputies had summarily deposited each of the tenants. Each one was taken down the street to the wooden police barricades and put on the other side. The deputies were methodical, almost clinical, in the way they conducted the eviction.

The tenants, who had been assured by the deputies that they could return to the hotel in a few days to pick up more of their belongings, had only a few minutes to gather their personal effects. They stood on the sidewalk with no luggage, no bags—just what they had stuffed in their pockets. Finally, the last of the supporters from the roof and from the ACC had been cleared. Chanting from the inside had been silenced.

About a thousand demonstrators stayed across the street as the darkness gave way to daylight. As each tenant stepped outside, the crowd of demonstrators sang, "Just like a tree standing by the water / We shall not be moved." To the police and the Sheriff's Department, the people cried, "Shame! Shame! Shame!" And to Sheriff Hongisto they continued to shout, "Where will you live when you grow old?"

As the last tenants were taken out, police were quickly dispatched to block the doors of the I-Hotel, purportedly to prevent the property from being trashed by intruders. They also may have suspected that supporters and tenants would want to charge back in to retake the building. With riot clubs in hand, they looked menacing as they stood in a line formation.

No other person may have embodied the spirit of resistance as did Felix Ayson that day, and his words echoed the feelings of all the tenants: "I am crippled. I am deaf. I am very old. I'm alone here and they put me out on the street. I will feel solitary and afraid on the street. I want freedom, the principle of American democracy, the richest country in the world. Do you think our mayor has a place for me? No. No, because I was happy here."[30] Despite the horror, he continued to demand his rights. Partially paralyzed and almost totally deaf, he continued to raise his own and others' spirits. Felix Ayson's activist spirit carried to the end, until death muffled his voice a year later.[31]

Meanwhile, the echoes of Mayor Moscone's promises remained. In a previous meeting with tenants, he had said:

> I don't believe there will be any need for police coming into these premises. It's entirely up to you. It's up to you. In terms of eviction, it's always been and will continue to be entirely up to the tenants, the progressive community service groups on the block and the massive support for low-income housing. It's entirely up to them to stop the eviction, to win the use of eminent domain, up to them to put the responsibility of low-income housing, entirely on the shoulders of city government.[32]

It was up to us, and we had done all that we could. We continued to fight the courts; we offered an entirely new and reasonable eminent-domain plan; and we devised imaginative ways for the city government to respond to the needs for affordable housing. But in the end, it was up to the mayor, not the tenants. He refused to keep up his end once he decided the I-Hotel was a political liability. The force of the state, the laws that protect private property, and the pressure from downtown business interests all prevailed over human values. The fact that Moscone understood these forces and the issues that were at stake made the emptiness of his promises even more wrenching for those who believed that city government could be made responsible to all of its citizens. At a safe distance, the mayor judged that all had gone well. "With the exception of the fracas [the police "mix-up"], which lasted two or three minutes," he said, "it went quite peaceably in relative terms."[33]

No Place to Go

The eviction was major, front-page news in the Bay Area. It also made the national news, particularly the violent attacks against the defenders on the outside and the need for low-income housing.[34] However, after the operation was concluded, the media disappeared. Once the tenants had been put out on the street, the story was over—at least, for the moment. It was up to us to take care of the tenants before they suffered from exposure.

The group of heartbroken tenants and dazed supporters decided to move away from the siege. We had assembled on Clay Street and huddled together in the predawn chill to collect our thoughts and decide where to rest and bed down. The Salvation Army and American Red Cross refused to help because of the eviction's political overtones.[35]

Around 7:00 A.M. Emil de Guzman suggested that the tenants regroup at St. Mary's Square, a couple of blocks uphill in Chinatown. The group of refugees spontaneously decided to walk there. Although the square was relatively close by—on California Street between Kearny and Grant streets—climbing up the hill to get there left many of us breathless. When the tenants arrived, they held a short rally to shore up their spirits, but they definitely felt beleaguered; the feeling of loss was overwhelming. It was very early on Thursday morning. The sun was just coming up, and there was no hot coffee or tea to greet any of us. St. Mary's church, one of the few Catholic churches in Chinatown, was not available for the tenants. (We knocked on the door, but the shades had been pulled down, and there was no answer.) St. Mary's had not offered any help to the tenants previously, and, in any case, no one had contacted the church in case the eviction took place.

Wahat Tompao lay down on the pavement and wept uncontrollably for about five minutes. Jeanette, who had been teamed up with him during the eviction, kneeled beside him to offer comfort. For Jeanette, this was the lowest point of the entire struggle. Years later, she described the bitter feelings of the eviction and its aftermath:

> For the first time ever, since I started living and organizing in the Hotel, I couldn't offer the tenants encouragement. I couldn't offer them hope that our Hotel would be saved. I felt so totally helpless. By five o'clock in the morning, it was all over. I walked out of the Hotel arm in arm with Wahat Tompao, leader of the IHTA. We walked out the front door, he turned to look at the Hotel and fell on his knees sobbing like a child.

> Wahat had been one of the strongest people I knew in this struggle. He was relentless and tireless in trying to stave off the eviction. He collapsed again in St. Mary's Square. Wahat was a warrior, and now this warrior, this fierce noble tribesman, wept in my arms.[36]

Although they were together and acted as family, which gave the tenants a small sense of stability, they were psychologically as well as physically devastated. Being evicted and losing a home can have a terrible effect on any family; for the elderly, it can be life-threatening.

It was at this point, with the harsh reality of eviction sinking in, that we realized we had no place to go. The city had just conducted the most elaborate eviction in its history, yet it had no real plans to help the tenants and had failed to provide any temporary housing for them. Supporters had relied on the city government for at least temporary housing, and there was nothing. Days later, Undersheriff Denman apologized for having inadvertently forgotten to hand out to the tenants packets that had been prepared containing information about alternative housing information. When pressed about the cruel oversight at a Board of Supervisors hearing investigating the eviction, Denman testified that he had "goofed" and had failed to ask the deputies to give out the one hundred packets during the eviction.[37]

Before the eviction the Central Relocation Service, an agency of the Mayor's Office, had made a promise: "Because of the special circumstances, the people who [are] evicted will have a free place to stay until we can find them permanent housing."[38] On the morning of the eviction, the *San Francisco Chronicle* incorrectly reported that temporary housing had been offered to the tenants by the Central Relocation Office as they were removed from the building. In actuality, no representatives from any city agency were present other than sheriff's deputies. "Where Have All the Tenants Gone?" asked one newspaper headline after the paper discovered that none of the tenants had registered in the hotels and motels that were supposed to have been offered to them.[39] Representatives of the Central Relocation Service arrived twelve hours later, long after the eviction had ended.

The city had no plans to take care of the tenants. The supporters had no contingency plans, either. In fact, I was responsible for finding emergency housing in case of eviction, but because of the overwhelming daily task of preparing for the night's resistance, I had hardly paid attention to "the day after." Finley, the coalition's internal security officer, insisted that temporary shelter be sought, and I had not followed through—the task got lost in the press of battle. At any rate, more suffering was visited on the tenants in their hour of need. City officials had thrown elderly people out onto the street, knowing that their health and welfare were in jeopardy, with no plans for temporary shelter. We knew the city could not come up with housing comparable to the International Hotel, but we had calculated that it was in the politicians' interests to provide some kind of temporary shelter, at the very least. But we had been lulled by the city's promises, expecting at least minimal aid, and we were wrong. I should have prepared alternatives, and I felt deeply responsible for the tenants' desperate situation.

As the morning wore on, Chester Hartman suggested to Max Elbaum, Jim Shoch, Ann Schwartz, and others that their organization, the Northern California Alliance, could provide temporary space. The NCA ran the San Francisco Liberation School in the Mission District and suggested that the tenants could rest and recuperate from the ordeal there. When we arrived, folded metal chairs were stacked up against the walls and sofa pillows had been strewn on the floor. As unsuitable and clearly inadequate for the elderly as the school was, it would suffice as a refuge for the time being.[40]

About three o'clock in the afternoon on the Friday after eviction, three sheriff's deputies dropped by the San Francisco Liberation School to tender an offer of temporary housing to the tenants. They came with a list of relocation resources and an offer to drive any tenant to one of the places suggested. No one accepted the offer, because each of the suggested places was far too expensive, substandard, and dangerous or did not even exist. The monthly rent at the nine hotels on the city's list averaged \$137—from a low of \$81 to a high of \$292 a month for a substandard one-room apartment—far above the average price of \$50 per month at the I-Hotel. An official Department of Social Services report listed one of the hotels, the Golden Eagle on Broadway, as substandard; two other substandard hotels in the South of Market area were not even included in the Redevelopment Agency's Master List of Standard (i.e., decent) Hotels. One police official told a Human Rights Commission staff member, "If you want to go look at any of those places at night, call and we'll get an officer to accompany you."[41] Even policemen knew that the hotels on the list in that neighborhood were dangerous hangouts for prostitutes and drug addicts.

Not a single one of the hotels on the list was in the Chinatown–Manilatown area, and one of the hotels was even in Daly City, a suburb south of San Francisco. At a press conference the day before, Mayor Moscone said he would put people up at the deluxe Fairmont Hotel or Holiday Inn, if necessary. He also said that any tenant could call him personally, and he would make sure that the tenant had housing for as long as he needed it. This seemed like public-relations talk, particularly when the tenants wanted temporary housing not in an exclusive hotel but in the neighborhood they called home. If anyone had had a doubt before, it became clear to everyone—even to city officials—that there was no housing comparable to the I-Hotel and that the city was desperately short of decent, low-rent housing. The tenants had been telling officials this for almost a decade.[42]

The day after the eviction, the tenants decided that the first step was to retrieve their belongings. On August 7, tenants went to the empty I-Hotel to load their television sets, suitcases of clothes, boxes of old photos, fishing rods, and other possessions on an old green bus donated by the Peoples Food System, one of the organizations in the Support Committee. City officials had not offered any assistance in retrieving their belongings. Quite the contrary: The tenants and their supporters were disappointed and outraged by what they found when they entered the I-Hotel.

The building looked like a war zone. The doors to almost all of the individual rooms had been nearly destroyed by the axes and sledgehammers used to break them down. This seemed unnecessary and wasteful, especially since most of the tenants actually walked out when told to do so. Toilet and sink fixtures had been broken; the floors were covered with debris. Shards of splintered glass, paper, broken furniture, wet towels (which had been placed on the doorsills to prevent tear gas and smoke from entering the rooms), and sleeping bags used by supporters all had been strewn about and jumbled together. The scene was eerie: Although everything else had been broken into, family pictures, calendars, and crucifixes were still affixed to the walls. In other words, remnants of a home were still apparent, despite the chaos.

Even more troubling was that rooms had been ransacked and personal belongings had been looted. Anything that could be moved, such as loose cash, watches, and even fishing polls, had been stolen, despite the presence of police and private security guards, hired by Four Seas, to protect the tenants' belongings. Collectively, the tenants lost thousands of dollars worth of cash and valuables. It was never certain who trashed the hotel or who took the personal property. Although police had been dispatched to protect the building as soon as the hotel was emptied, we were suspicious that they intentionally destroyed the property so the tenants could never return. We also suspected the police because they had assured the tenants that they would protect the valuables, yet belongings were stolen. And, of course, no one believed that Four Seas Investment Corporation was trustworthy. The building was uninhabitable after the police raid.

Wahat Tompao expressed his dismay this way: "They don't even care where they put them—elderly people just dumped in the street at 3 o'clock in the morning. My wristwatch was taken. My television was taken. My two good fishing poles, worth about $200, were taken. I don't know why the sheriff's people had to take all that."[43] Wahat was famous for his fishing, which was both a hobby and source of food.

Yesin Leong, who was eighty-nine and had lived at the I-Hotel for six years, returned to gather his belongings only to find the six hundred dollars he had hidden under some papers was missing. Felipe Daguro said that his life's savings of three thousand dollars had been taken from his room. Other tenants reported losses of televisions and cameras.[44] It was not uncommon for tenants to leave large amounts of money in their rooms, because many of them did not trust banks. They kept their money in books, under the bed, in cardboard boxes.

And because of their mistrust of Joe Diones, and his eventual ouster, the tenants no longer had a manager who would keep their money in a strongbox while they were away. Despite the sadness we felt, the tenants were still determined to get justice from the city. The "little giants" had fought City Hall before. They wanted to be reimbursed for their losses.

Casa de Cambio, a residential drug-rehabilitation facility that was also located in the Mission District, offered its beds to the tenants. After spending a few days at the Liberation School, the tenants moved to Casa de Cambio's Dolores Street house, taking advantage of the organization's hospitality until a long-term solution was found.[45]

In early September, the tenants moved into the Stanford Hotel at 245 Kearny Street, about ten blocks away from the International Hotel. The Stanford Hotel became their residence and command post, but it did not have the same feeling of home as the I-Hotel. Adjusting to the new environment was difficult for many of the tenants because the Stanford was far inferior to the I-Hotel, which had been rehabilitated and filled with life. Their consolation was that they were together in one place—as a family. Rent at the Stanford Hotel began at sixty-five dollars per month, compared to the fifty dollars per month they had paid at the I-Hotel. Unlike the I-Hotel, the Stanford had no kitchen facility; no nearby community groups to help them obtain social services; no recreation spots like Portsmouth Square, a nearby park where they relaxed and played checkers; and no inexpensive restaurants down the block. The I-Hotel tenants at least had the help of people from the Support Committee who went to the Stanford Hotel daily to give them legal, social, and political assistance. Although everyone involved knew that there really was not anything like the I-Hotel, no one was fully prepared for the cruelty of being wrenched from home and of the dispersal of a community.

The IHTA Fights On

On Saturday, August 6, two days after the eviction, the IHTA announced in a flyer to the city and all its supporters that the tenants were still together and described what had happened to them: "We are the International Hotel Tenants Association. We are still together; we are still the IHTA! We are still fighting and we won't stop!"[46] In the flyer, the IHTA made its demands clear to the city administration:

> 1) The City must pay for temporary shelter. . . . We demand that this temporary shelter be for ALL the tenants TOGETHER and that it be situated in the Chinatown/Manilatown area.
> 2) The City must pay reparations for loss of valuables and other belongings.

3) The City must pay for all medical expenses due to the eviction—for medication, doctor visits and hospitalization.
4) The City must account for all police brutality and misconduct.
5) The City must stop Four Seas' demolition of the building and rehabilitate or rebuild the IH for low-income housing.[47]

In a way, it was a concession to the reality of defeat, an acknowledgment that the eviction had indeed occurred. But these demands also showed that the tenants were still willing to fight for justice and to stop the next stage from getting under way—the demolition of the building.

Attorney Bill Carpenter and other supporters, on behalf of the IHTA, filed a claim of 2 million dollars against the City and County of San Francisco on November 3 for damages tenants suffered during the eviction. The claims ranged from small sums for X-rays and medical bills for a cracked rib, a split scalp, and assorted bruises that demonstrators endured to tenants' losses of TV sets, furniture, fishing poles, and a three thousand dollar claim for life savings. The human repercussions of the eviction could not be weighed in terms of money; the tenants' loss of their home could not be quantified.

Tenants and supporters were determined to get justice. In the week after the eviction, they disrupted a regular meeting of the Board of Supervisors, demanding that the board review the eviction procedures, the charges of police harassment and brutality, the lack of relocation housing, and reparations to the tenants for items lost in the eviction. Some supervisors were swayed by bad publicity and even seemed sympathetic to the tenants' situation. Supervisor Terry Francois, a conservative on the board, said, "From all accounts this was one of the worst relocation jobs ever done. These people were just put on the street."[48] After several tenants testified, the request for an inquiry was referred to the Board of Supervisors' Planning, Housing, and Development Committee, which would meet in a week. Soon after the committee met, however, Supervisor Francois abandoned his earlier position after city spokesmen declared that every effort had been made to provide housing for the tenants. Supervisor Ronald Pelosi, the committee's chairman, referred the investigation of the eviction to the City Attorney's Office. With the investigation led by the city attorney, an ally of the mayor, the scandal of how the eviction was mishandled would be quietly buried.

A delegation of supporters visited the Mayor's Office to get Moscone to declare his public opposition to the demolition. A press spokesman stated that the mayor opposed the demolition, and, on August 8, the state Court of Appeal delayed demolition of the hotel, perhaps due to influence from the Mayor's Office. The IHTA hoped that growing national attention could keep the pressure on Moscone. California Senator Alan Cranston spurred the Customs Service to launch an investigation of Supasit Mahaguna to see if he had illegally brought 5 million dollars into the country in 1973, which he had then used to buy the I-Hotel and other properties.[49]

Reading about the eviction in the *Washington Post,* Senator Frank Church (D-Idaho), chairman of the Special Committee on Aging, immediately dispatched two staff members to investigate. After two weeks, Church and the ranking Republican on the committee, Senator Peter Domenici, issued a statement calling for a detailed study of displacement of the elderly from central city areas, along with other issues. As an advocate for the elderly, he said that the eviction proved "the desperate need for adequate housing for the elderly at prices they can afford."[50] Church and Domenici went even further to observe, "For many elderly, the preservation of predominantly ethnic city neighborhoods is not sometimes simply a matter of pride or nostalgia, but a matter of survival."[51]

Five members of the Board of Supervisors—Terry Francois, Dorothy von Beroldingen, Robert Gonzales, John Molinari, and Dianne Feinstein—placed a Voters' Policy Statement on the International Hotel on the November 8 ballot. Proposition U asked San Francisco voters whether the city should buy the I-Hotel, bring it up to code, and turn it over to the Housing Authority for low-rent housing. Even if it won, however, the policy statement had no power to require the city to act. The IHTA and supporters were highly suspicious of the proposition, considering it a trap, a "no-win" set-up. With the exception of Molinari, the sponsoring supervisors had been lukewarm supporters, at best, and we were suspicious of their motives. To our surprise, we discovered that the Workers Committee, once again acting on its own, had lobbied a supervisor to put Proposition U on the ballot. Why would the Worker's Committee seek an electoral mandate when it had previously taken the position that electoral politics was useless? We were perplexed, but the committee's advocacy for the measure made us question its motives.[52]

The IHTA and its supporters had no choice once the proposition had been placed on the ballot, and once again we joined tumultuous city electoral politics by endorsing Proposition U. We had not intended to take the struggle into the electoral arena at this point. On the positive side, the IHTA felt that Proposition U would give us another political opening to garner support for the issue of the I-Hotel and low-income housing.

Two groups formed to support the proposition—the Yes on U Committee and the Workers Committee to Fight for the International Hotel and Victory Building. Characteristically, because of its criticism of the political organizations associated with the Yes on U Committee, the Workers Committee worked on the proposition independently from the Yes on U Committee. Each group won endorsements from organizations and individuals—thirty-five candidates for supervisor supported it, as did Assemblyman (later San Francisco Mayor) Willie Brown—and both committees canvassed in districts with large ethnic-minority populations.[53] The core of the Yes on U Committee, composed of NCA members and the KDP, was allied closely with the IHTA. Directed by Chester Hartman, the campaign concentrated our work in the minority populations in the nine districts. The Workers Committee, composed of members of the ACC and RCP, concentrated its activity in Chinatown and among union groups.

No groups publicly opposed Proposition U until the week before the November 8 election, at which time Four Seas started its own campaign to discredit the proposition. Four Seas purchased radio announcements and sent representatives to public forums. It focused its attack on the condition of the building, saying it was uninhabitable and unfit to live in for people of any age or background. "The present owners bought the hotel *after* it had already been condemned and declared a public nuisance," Four Seas falsely claimed in its campaign literature. The company argued that buying and renovating the property would cost taxpayers 2.5 million dollars, about twice what it actually would cost. Four Seas' representative Robert Jeremiah said, "It will cost taxpayers millions to buy and millions to renovate and at least $100,000 a year to maintain."[54] We sued to prevent the inaccurate figures from appearing in the voter's handbook, but our case was rejected by the courts.[55]

Playing on the fear of excessive taxes, Four Seas' campaign slogan was "Prop[osition] 'U' Means YOU Pay to maintain a SLUM." It also raised the ideological weapon that property owners should have the right to carry out development in their own interests. Four Seas couched these ideas in seemingly reasonable phrases, conceding, "We are in agreement that the public deserves low rent and decent housing. But we just can't agree this location should be sacrificed."[56] In this case, the company argued, the property was better suited to commercial development than low-income housing or residential development. Four Seas appealed to the idea that property owners had the absolute right to dispose of property as they choose.[57]

Proposition U's supporters asserted that the city had an obligation to buy the hotel because it would provide 155 units of desperately needed low-incoming housing in the Chinatown area. Emil de Guzman said, "In the last 20 years, the city has destroyed 10,000 units of housing. We're not just fighting for the I-Hotel. There is a much bigger question of a low-cost housing crisis for Chinatown and Manilatown."[58] The "Yes on U" campaign argued that voting in favor of the proposition would "tell District Supervisors that the housing rights of the people come first," and it would reverse trends of "an acute shortage of decent housing, hiked-up rentals or escalating property taxes."[59] Both "Yes" coalitions mobilized hundreds of volunteers to walk precincts, give out election materials, do phone banking, and mobilize for the "get out the vote" drive.

But on November 8, we were caught by surprise. Voters showed little interest in the election of the new district supervisors or other local issues. Voter turnout had been expected to be 65 percent, but only slightly more than 51 percent actually cast their votes. Many voters were confused by the new district system, in which a total of 130 candidates were running for the board. Further, the large number of liberal and progressive candidates running against each other in several districts dissipated political energy and split the liberal vote. The moderate to conservative elements in city politics had shown up at the polls in large numbers, fearing that district elections would produce an "ultra-liberal" new Board of Supervisors.[60] This skewed section of the electorate voted not only for the six incumbents but also for moderate to conservative newcomers. In the new system, only one member of the Board of Supervisors actually fully supported the new system: Harvey Milk.

Proposition U lost by a margin of more than 2–1. Low voter turnout, which tends to favor conservatives, had a negative effect on Proposition U, and results indicated that voters in the western part of the city, who were predominantly home owners and not renters, had been decisive in the defeat.[61] We were shocked by the wide margin of defeat and concluded that we had overestimated the left–liberal upsurge represented by district elections; counted on far more minority voters turning out in support of the hotel; and underestimated the degree to which our base became confused. We had little experience conducting electoral campaigns and had made mistakes, such as organizing by districts more than throughout the city. At the same time, the conservative "tax revolt" was well under way. The next year, Proposition 13 would win in the California state election, severely cutting property taxes and, as a result, drastically reducing funds for municipal and county governments. In this election, bond measures for the airport and the Fire Department—measures that typically appeal to conservative voters—passed, but funds for low-income housing along with a proposition banning billboards were rejected.

Herb Caen, the *San Francisco Chronicle* columnist, always had a flair for capturing the ironies of city politics. A day before the election, he sarcastically commented about "old San Francisco" as a "repository of freedom, tolerance and understanding." He had discovered an ad for the International Hotel in a guidebook for the city published in 1882, the same year that the Chinese Exclusion Act was passed by the U.S. Congress. Touting the International Hotel as "The Best Hotel in San Francisco," the guidebook listed various amenities that it offered. Caen wryly quoted from the guidebook that the I-Hotel offered "the ultimate inducement to the sophisticated traveler: 'No Chinese Employed In Or About the Hotel.'"[62]

Anti-Demolition Fight

Just days after the eviction, Four Seas continued its assault by hiring Fred Grange, owner of Grange Debris Box Rental in San Rafael, to demolish the hotel. Four Seas, which had an aggressive history of pursuing demolition, was confident that it would be able to evict the tenants and had already filed for a permit to demolish the hotel. The original permit, issued by the Central Permit Bureau on March 10, 1975, had been given with the understanding that Four Seas would either tear down or fix up the I-Hotel, and it was good only for 180 days. If Four Seas had plans beyond demolition, such as commercial development, it would have had to file an Environmental Impact Report, lengthening the process for issuance and opening the possibility that the permit would be denied. The tenants had appealed to the Board of Permit Appeals and lost. But because Four Seas had refused to move, its permit expired before it could begin any demolition.

On February 23, 1976, Superintendent of Building Inspection Alfred Goldberg decided not to cancel Four Seas' permit. The tenants appealed again to the Board of Permit Appeals, and in March the board decided that the original permit had indeed expired. The Board of Permit Appeals treated Goldberg's decision as a new permit. Four Seas went to court in October 1976, and Superior Court Judge Byron Arnold made the invalid permit valid again. But on August 8, 1977, the State Court of Appeal delayed demolition, possibly as a result of pressure from the Mayor's Office. With the eviction already completed and the court having decided against eminent domain, the legal and political prospects seemed dim. Eminent domain was on appeal at the State Supreme Court, but the eviction of the tenants weakened the argument for eminent domain. The building was also in danger of imminent demolition or even arson. Either way, Four Seas was eager to exercise its property rights, legally or illegally.

Twice in September Four Seas made illegal attempts to demolish the hotel. On September 8, the bulldozer operator Fred Grange tried to demolish the hotel, using the 1975 permit to prove the legality of his actions. Fortunately, Patrolman Dennis Meixner of the San Francisco Police Department had been informed that the permit was invalid and that it was being challenged by the city's Board of Permit Appeals at the State Court of Appeal. Only at pistol point did Grange stop his bulldozer.

On September 19, only two weeks later, Grange returned to finish the job. At 7:00 A.M., he brought a crew of eighteen workers, two flatbed trucks, and two heavy-duty tractors to the narrow alley off Columbus Avenue behind the hotel. The tractor, equipped with a clamshell-jaw front blade, tore a gaping twenty-by-thirty-five-foot hole in the rear of the I-Hotel. Water spilled from broken pipes in the two-story hole. By 8:30 A.M., scores of protesters had descended on the site, throwing up a picket line to prevent any more damage. The police then arrived, but they had come too late to prevent the tractor from doing its destruction. Supporters were angered by Grange's action and frustrated that the police had not been alert to his chicanery, and the protestors felt that they were within their legal right to prevent more destruction. Then, according to police, one protestor allegedly loosened one of the wires supporting a plywood section, and a group of protestors had already knocked down an eighty-foot stretch of plywood fencing put up after the eviction. They felt that they were not doing anything illegal—it was Grange who was violating the law. Police Sergeant Salvatore Mrota tried to stop the protestor, and a fracas ensued. Supporters who were angry with the police for apprehending the protestor came to his support while police officers came to the aid of their fellow officer. The police contained the near-riot with brute force, billy clubbing the demonstrators. In the aftermath, ten supporters were arrested. Grange was also arrested and charged for not having a valid permit. He was released on two hundred fifty dollars bail.[63]

Fresh from the melee, tenants and supporters went to City Hall to complain to the Board of Supervisors that afternoon. After some debate, the supervisors agreed to suspend their agenda and quizzed the superintendent of the Bureau of Building Inspection and the city attorney. The superintendent agreed to suspend Grange's license and promised to ask the chief of police to make sure that police were guarding the building. He also sent an order to Four Seas to fix the damaged water main, block up the hole, and inspect and repair any structural damage. The city attorney reported to the Board of Supervisors that there were no legal grounds allowing demolition. The board then voted to request that the mayor and district attorney make sure that the demolition would not be allowed.

On December 8, Four Seas filed a 1.3 million dollar damage claim against the city, naming the Board of Supervisors, the Housing Authority, the Department of Public Works, and the sheriff and asserting that it had been illegally denied the right to use its property since November 1976. The city had asserted its authority to deny a permit to Four Seas while the tenants' lawsuits were being appealed.[64]

On February 22, 1978, Fred Grange was sentenced to fifteen days in jail and fined five hundred dollars after he pleaded no contest to a charge of creating a public nuisance. Four Seas was also fined five hundred dollars and placed on two years' probation by Municipal Court Judge Raymond Arata, who ruled that the corporation did not have a valid permit to demolish the building.[65]

More than a year after the eviction, on September 1, 1978, five justices on the state Supreme Court refused to block a demolition permit, clearing the way for the destruction of the building.[66] On January 10, Robert Levey, director of the Bureau of Building Inspection, refused to issue a stop-work order to Four Seas, even though an appeal was pending on the order with the Board of Permit Appeals. In a last-ditch effort, the attorneys Sue Hestor and John Diamonte protested that Levey should have continued the stop-work order because Four Seas had violated various laws by defying the stop-work order in September 1977. The Board of Permit Appeals had agreed to hear the protest, and on January 15, 1979, it overturned Levey's decision. Although this decision was favorable, it had no effect on the demolition, because Four Seas had already begun the process, and 80 percent of the building had been demolished. The roof and rooms had been torn down; only the second-floor ceiling and the third-floor supports remained. The hotel was just a shell, and Four Seas was given permission by the city to demolish its outer structures, but only on weekends.[67]

Despair and Hope

About a month after the eviction, I collapsed from stress. My children had been taken care of by KDP comrades throughout these intense months, yet they still needed their mother, and the pressure of being a single parent during times of extreme activism had taken its toll. I tried to recuperate by staying home with my children and finding a steady job.

The struggle did not end with the eviction or even with attempts to demolish the building. But the three KDP team members and the leadership had no discussions summing up the conflict and no plans to follow up with the tenants and supporters. The "ultra-left" style of work still dominated the local chapter of the KDP and the region as a whole. Consequently, whenever we attempted to raise issues about the I-Hotel or even meet as a team, we were browbeaten with accusations of "veteranism," or pulling rank because of our mass work experiences. We started to lose contact with the tenants, the housing movement, and one another, and all of us were assigned to other work in the KDP. We had been traumatized, dazed and disoriented, by the eviction—we were pretty much in the same shape as the tenants. But the organization, overwhelmed with other campaigns, did not address our situation and regarded us as three more hands that could be put to better use. I offered to quit the KDP to pull my life and family together, but my resignation was not accepted, so I went on unsanctioned leave instead.

The I-Hotel tenants remained at the Stanford Hotel, and volunteers kept offering what they could. Of the many hundreds who flocked to the International Hotel before the eviction, only a skeleton crew of supporters remained to make meals, keep the tenants up to date on legal matters, and keep them company as the situation became bleaker. A few members of the NCA and the Support Committee kept up much of the work to sustain the tenants, while the center of gravity shifted to the legal work by Bill Carpenter and other lawyers seeking to continue appeals, stop demolition, and pursue other legal avenues.

Chester Hartman's memo to a September 7, 1977, internal meeting of the NCA revealed increasing concerns about the lack of direction for the political struggle. He asked a series of pointed questions, such as:

> [Is the direction or strategy] saving the hotel so that former tenants can move back in? [S]aving the Hotel, independent of whether former tenants can move back in (or de-emphasizing the moveback)? Saving the site only, in order to build new housing? Building a housing movement

in Chinatown/Manilatown, or in the city as a whole? If it's a combination of these, what priority are we giving to each?

To Hartman, it seemed clear that KDP was "pulling back from the Hotel struggle. Emil no longer lives with the tenants and seems to be generally less involved with the day-to-day issues and tenants' needs; Jeanette has been pulled out by the KDP leadership."[68]

Hartman was troubled that the KDP might have developed another "line" about the struggle that it had failed to discuss with allies. But in fact, we were in disarray. The new "line" was to pull the team into other work, although Emil, Jeanette, and I could hardly answer Hartman's and other friends' questions. If, for example, we had decided that the movement would be to save the site to build new housing, we would have to address a variety of concerns: We would need to work more closely with the Chinatown community and the citywide housing movement. How would the Filipino community, now that significant numbers of Filipinos had left the area, relate to such a movement? It would mean that the "socialist" or broader working-class part of the KDP's program would dominate. Logically, it would be more appropriate for KDP team members to join a multiracial, multiclass organization such as the NCA. We were too exhausted and too demoralized to address any of these questions, and clearer, more pressing campaigns that more easily fit into the KDP's program demanded attention.

When Proposition U was suddenly placed on the ballot, we were jolted back into the fray, at least for the duration of the campaign. The KDP's national leadership assigned Trinity Ordona and others to work with the three of us on the election. But after the initiative was defeated, Emil, Jeanette, and I were once again pulled away to other work, still unable to address the kinds of questions Hartman had raised.

The remaining tenants tried to keep their spirits up, but it was difficult. "My life has not changed insofar that I have not left the struggle," Felix Ayson said during the Proposition U campaign. "I have struggled against my enemy for so long and my spirit is so high. I am with oppressed people of all races in the world. Their lives touch my heart and make me cry."[69] Still, the eviction weighed heavily on the tenants' hearts. Within a year, Manong Felix would be dead. Emil continued at the helm of the IHTA alone, although extremely demoralized, working without official KDP sanction. He became more and more isolated, confiding almost exclusively in Wahat Tompao.

The complete demolition of the International Hotel in the fall of 1979 was a key turning point. Soon afterward, the IHTA officially dissolved, although several of the tenants continued to represent the association as part of Manilatown in the Chinatown housing movement. Disunity, suspicion, and distrust grew between tenants and supporters, along with blame for the final eviction and disputes about how much money was actually left in the IHTA's coffers. The money saved in escrow accounts was disbursed to the remaining tenants. When Etta Moon, one of the tenant activists, asked Emil about the prospects for the struggle and the IHTA, he replied, "There is no longer any hope."[70]

Emil was not quite correct. The International Hotel had been placed on the National Register of Historic Places before the eviction, and in 1978 the IHTA joined the Chinatown Coalition for Better Housing and the Chinatown Neighborhood Improvement Resource Center to apply for a grant from the National Trust for Historic Preservation. The grant was to fund a feasibility study of "restoring the International Hotel for housing use," along with community facilities, open space, and other uses on the block bounded by Jackson, Washington, Kearny, and Columbus streets. Mayor Moscone wrote a letter in support of the application, indicating that the city was willing to consider such a proposal seriously, and the grant was accepted. Despite his vacillations and ultimate capitulation, Mayor Moscone still seemed interested in saving the hotel—or, at least, addressing the housing needs in the area. But on November 27, 1978, both he and Supervisor Harvey Milk were assassinated by Dan White, a disgruntled conservative former supervisor, and Dianne Feinstein, president of the Board of Supervisors, inherited the mayor's chair.

Immediately after the assassinations, housing consultants presented the "Chinatown Block Study." This proposal for housing and community development remained part of city politics even after the hotel was entirely demolished.[71] The activism was strong enough to force even Mayor Feinstein (who had not opposed the demolition) to form an ad hoc citizens' advisory committee to consider the fate of the I-Hotel site in 1979.[72] The new mayor mandated the International Hotel Block Development Citizens Advisory Committee (CAC) to monitor any new projects to be built on the old I-Hotel site and the entire block. Feinstein appointed to the CAC tenant representatives from the IHTA, along with Chinese community leaders, ranging from the president of the Chinese Six Companies to members of nonprofit agencies and housing groups in Chinatown. From the Filipino community Feinstein appointed, in addition to former tenants from the IHTA, Al Robles, who represented the Manilatown Senior Center in Chinatown. Eventually, Helen Bautista, a schoolteacher; Wayne Alba, an entrepreneur; and Ed Ilumin, a member of the Human Rights Commission staff, also participated in the CAC.[73]

In December 1979, the Department of City Planning presented the "International Hotel Block Development Plan," which called for a mixed-use project that included low-income housing, commercial space, and underground parking. Four Seas was able to demolish the building in 1979, but it could not begin construction of a parking garage or any other commercial building on the site. The new development plan determined that "eminent domain is a tool which the city could use as a last resort" and that the project could be built without using general-revenue funds from the city.[74] As Chester Hartman noted, "A key to any plan of this type—whether for a single building or a wider area—is the City's willingness to use its legal and financial powers to create and preserve housing and neighborhood, rather than foster 'development,' no matter what the social and human cost."[75] The city had taken the steps to exercise that will. With the major question of public finance addressed and the use of eminent domain back on the table, Four Seas was forced to negotiate. Four Seas' untrammeled use of the property was stymied, and no project could be built until the company relented and made a deal that involved creating low-income housing at the site. Indeed, nothing was built for twenty-five years.

CONCLUSION

The Rise of the I-Hotel

1979–2005

Coming Back Home

On August 26, 2005, I stood with an excited crowd of seven hundred who gathered to cut the ribbon to the new International Hotel Senior Housing. Gordon Chin, executive director of the Chinatown Community Development Center, greeted the throng of people and admitted, "I have waited over 28 years to welcome you back to the new I-Hotel." He was not the only one who had waited a long time, and many of us could not help but remember the eviction in 1977. "We were getting our heads bashed in back then," Emil de Guzman confided to me, "and now we're going inside to drink champagne."

He and I had similar feelings: great joy and bitter sorrow. We were relieved that, after so many twists and turns, so many delays, so many times that the project to rebuild the hotel seemed to teeter on the edge of collapse, a beautiful building stood before us in the very same place as the old International Hotel.

Now a fifteen-story building with 104 studio and one-bedroom apartments for low-income seniors rose up on Kearny Street. After speeches, we joined the mostly Chinese crowd to tour the spacious, clean rooms, and then took the elevator to enjoy the rooftop gardens and the breathtaking panoramic views of Coit Tower, the Golden Gate Bridge, and the bay. In San Francisco's overheated housing market, apartments such as the ones in this building would sell for huge amounts—but now low-income elderly would move in, mostly from Chinatown.

On the building's ground floor is the International Hotel Manilatown Center, a place to pay tribute to those evicted from the original I-Hotel in 1977 and to all of the early Filipino immigrants. The spacious hall has large plate-glass windows looking out on to Kearny and Jackson streets, the same cross streets as before. Sponsored by the Manilatown Heritage Foundation (MHF), the space features a learning center with room for performances and exhibitions. Emil smiled at the familiar photos of the manongs on the center's walls and said, "It's like the phoenix rising up."

Politicians and dignitaries spoke outside at the ribbon cutting in the open space where St. Mary's Catholic school will be built. "I was mayor from 1978 to '88," Senator Dianne Feinstein told the crowd. "My hope at that time was that by 1983 or '84 we would have a building. It's 2005, but there *is* a building."

Those involved in the fight over the vacant Kearny Street site knew how long and difficult it had been to reach this bittersweet moment. After the old building was demolished, the City Planning Commission required that any development on the block include affordable housing and threatened the use of eminent domain if Four Seas did not comply. Mayor Feinstein presented a proposal to Four Seas in 1984 that featured the construction of two towers, one of which would have residential apartments at controlled rents for forty years. In 1986, Four Seas rejected the proposal because the company believed that, with vacancy rates very low in the financial district, the project did not maximize profits.[1] Over the following years, several large-scale plans that combined commercial and retail development with low-income housing were proposed, with Four Seas signing agreements. But the agreements collapsed for various reasons; mostly, the company rejected proposals because they believed they were not economically feasible. The disagreements between Four Seas and the city mostly revolved around the proportion of for-profit commercial use and subsidized low-income housing. In 1991, Four Seas disentangled itself, and a Taiwanese company, Pan-Magna, took over the property but rejected yet another mixed-use plan. Finally, in 1994, Pan-Magna agreed to sell the land for community use to the San Francisco Archdiocese. An 8.3 million dollar grant from the federal Department of Housing and Urban Development was awarded to develop the site for low-income housing. Mayor Willie Brown approved the new proposal, and city monies were designated for the new site.[2] The sale was finalized in 1998.

Under this proposal, the site was split into three separate air parcels so that the housing, parochial school, and an underground garage would own their own sites. St. Mary's parochial school would occupy one side of the block; low-income senior housing would be built on the other side; a parking garage would be located underground; and the Manilatown Heritage Foundation would manage a community center on the ground floor of the senior housing unit.

With the demise of the I-Hotel and the last vestige of Manilatown destroyed, housing activists in the Chinatown community had become the major force to pressure for low-income housing on the site throughout these years. In the 1970s, the Chinatown Coalition for Better Housing aggressively pursued Chinatown's housing problems and joined the Chinatown Resource Center (CRC). In 1978, the CRC formed the Chinese Community Housing Corporation (CCHC), a nonprofit housing-development corporation. This alignment proved to be productive, for more than two thousand units of low-income housing were built in Chinatown and the Tenderloin District. Then CRC and CCHC consolidated to form the Chinatown Community Development Center (CCDC) in 1998. The CCDC's focus, in collaboration with the newly formed Kearny Street Housing Corporation (KSHC) and the Catholic Archdiocese, St. Mary's Catholic Center, and the MHF, was to rebuild the International Hotel.[3] The efforts of progressives such as Linda Wang of Northeast Mental Health Services, committee chair of CAC, and, afterward, chair of KSHC, kept the city focused on proposals for the I-Hotel site. Before the construction of the new building, the KSHC, the CCDC, and the MHF combined to form the new International Hotel Senior Housing Inc. (IHSHI), an independent body to oversee the entire housing component at the site.

When plans to rebuild the hotel were first developed, Al Robles called in veteran activists from the I-Hotel struggle to survey the situation. Robles had been on the CAC from its inception as a representative of the Manilatown Senior Center. He had made a lifelong commitment to the manongs and to the memory of Manilatown, and he felt the urgency to assert a Filipino presence in the new project: There was no longer any Manilatown, and someone had to speak for the manongs. Former Filipino activists in the I-Hotel eviction movement responded to his call. Emil, Bill Sorro, and I joined Robles because we realized that the Filipino community had to become more deeply involved in the new effort or the Filipino presence on Kearny Street would be forgotten and a crucial period of the community's history would be lost. We felt that there should be more than a plaque recognizing the contributions of Filipinos and the legacy of Manilatown. In 1994, the MHF was formed to investigate ways to pay tribute to the manongs and to display Filipino American history in general. In 1996, Sorro was appointed to the CAC to further our aims, but we knew, as before, that we would have to create a movement to sustain such a project. The MHF would be a living institution, a link between generations once again, and we were open to the project's being shaped by the young people who stepped forward to get involved.

The fight to save the International Hotel went far beyond Filipinos. It touched a nerve among an extraordinarily large number of people who flocked to the defense of the elderly victims of the country's colonial and racist past. Supporters came to defend the remnants of a community, to defend "home" and human values rather than "market" values, to advocate broader definitions of civil rights to include the right to affordable housing and of the elderly to live in dignity and not impoverished humiliation. The eviction was a major moment in the fight to allow the "non-rich"—the poor, the working class, and even the middle class—to remain in San Francisco. In the following years, the city would face growing crises in homelessness and gentrification, as well as a vibrant housing movement that won restrictions on demolitions, rent control, linked development, and other concessions.

Edith Witt, a member of the Human Rights Commission staff and a staunch supporter of the I-Hotel, asked a year before the eviction, "Can the system change, according to its own rules, in favor of human values?"[4] The answer—at least as borne out by the legacy of the International Hotel and the city's housing movement—turned out to go far beyond a simple yes or no: Change is possible but at the price of tremendous sacrifice and persistence. The transformation of San Francisco in favor of real-estate and financial interests continues, but not without significant resistance and concessions. The International Hotel was a major force in creating a powerful tenants' movement that for three decades has played a critical role in the city's history. As the housing activist Randy Shaw writes, the housing movement "remains the city's leading opposition to the final transformation of an economically diverse, primarily working-class town into a city for tourists and the economic elite."[5]

Those who attended the ribbon-cutting celebration for the new International Hotel in 2005 were very aware of both the symbolic and the actual role of the new project in creating a space for the "non-rich." The manongs had felt that they were fighting for far more than themselves: They fought for the poor, the working class, the elderly, minorities—or, as Felix Ayson would have said, for all humanity. At last, a victory was achieved. Former tenants were given priority to live in the new building, although very few of the original tenants had survived to savor the joy. Rosalino (Rudy) Daga had lived in the hotel with his father—his hands were burned in the 1969 fire—and he was able to take advantage of the long-awaited triumph.

The others were not so lucky. Wahat Tompao had returned to the Philippines with a broken heart to die. Others, such as Manong Felix Ayson, had died soon after the eviction in lonely hotel rooms. Manong Joe Diones, shunned and isolated after he was ousted as chairman of the IHTA and manager of the hotel, died a lonely man in a nursing home in the 1980s. Luisa de la Cruz longed for a family of her own, but her hope never came to fruition. She died of pneumonia on March 18, 1999, at St. Mary's Hospital in San Francisco.[6] So Chung, who had married Etta Moon, died in 1992.

For many years, Etta (Moon) Chung was one of the last former tenants active in commemorations. Although her eyesight and hearing were impaired, she persevered on the International Hotel Citizens Advisory Committee for more than fifteen years. During the anti-eviction struggle, she translated discussions during meetings from English to Chinese and explained the convoluted political battles for the Chinese tenants. Her life and how she lived it is testimony to one who overcame great odds. She had a congenital deformity that made walking difficult, and she would hobble up and down the hotel's staircase. Like the other elderly at the hotel, she treasured independence. She had struggled hard for it from the beginning, when she labored at the garment factory that was located in the basement of the I-Hotel, until the end, when she reluctantly agreed to move to a nursing home in 2001. She died on June 21, 2004.

"If those tenants could see what has gone up in their old home," Bill Sorro told me during the opening celebration, "they would feel justified for their fight." Now sixty-five, Bill had seen the struggle from its very beginning, but the victory, as satisfying as it was, did not eliminate the pain. "People ask, 'Do you feel vindicated now that they are filling that hole up?' No, we don't," Sorro explained to a reporter. "We don't feel vindicated because justice don't work like that. Justice isn't something simple, so that if you fill the hole up with this much justice then you're equal. The lives of the people who died as a result of the eviction and the trauma of being displaced, these elderly people—is it now OK because we are going to fill it up with 104 units? Is it OK that a community was destroyed and there is no remnant of a Filipino community that thrived there? It is not OK."[7]

The Asian American Left and the KDP

Radical leftists had been in the forefront of the mass movement to defend the I-Hotel. The dedication, energy, and self-sacrifice of all of the different leftist groups and factions gave the struggle much of its dynamic, bottom-up character. The main leadership core composed of the elderly tenants and young KDP activists joined the battle with tremendous commitment and a deep sense of responsibility. This leadership took on the immense challenge of navigating through all the complexities of San Francisco politics, stretching ourselves to find all possible allies while simultaneously having to hold many a politician's feet to the fire. For me, as with the tenants, the I-Hotel struggle was a lesson in dealing with different classes and races and in understanding the nature of political power. We learned to negotiate with city officials, to speak in public, and to organize others to our cause. We learned how established elites could change, despite their power, when confronted with another type of power: the will of masses of people. As a result, we learned that fear could be overcome.

The I-Hotel anti-eviction movement was also a critical site for the development of the various parts of the Asian American movement. It reflected how those parts developed, moving from student activism to the discovery of community struggles; growing from opposition to war and racism during the Vietnam War to identification with anticolonial movements in the Third World; changing from a critique of capitalist exploitation to fully developed Marxist politics, with the aim of overthrowing the capitalist system altogether. Vietnam's resistance of American domination was crucial, especially since Asian Americans identified with the Vietnamese as an Asian people. The successes of the Cuban revolution and the anticolonial movements in Africa and Latin America were also important. Most significant, the People's Republic of China and Mao's leadership had exceptional influence over Asian American activists. Because we did not have full knowledge of the Cultural Revolution and its excesses, Asian American activists in the 1960s and '70s were particularly inspired by the power that young people seemed to possess in China to challenge all forms of class privilege. The upsurge in radical opposition to the war in Vietnam, opposition to racism and the effects of the Civil Rights Movement and Black Power Movement also created a heady atmosphere. Young people sensed that we were part of a worldwide movement for social change. "Be Realistic, Demand the Impossible," said a witty slogan of the 1968 student uprising in Paris, but the impossible—the radical transformation of American politics and the entire world—really did seem to be a realistic goal.

All of the Asian American groups had organic, legitimate ties to the International Hotel. They had all joined the anti-eviction struggle at its start, and the storefront organizations, such as the ACC and the CPA, even had stakes in the struggle as commercial tenants. All of the Asian American organizations, unlike many of the white activists in the New Left, were part of the communities they defended. Although some critics regarded the young leftists as "outside agitators" who had come to stir up the peaceful old folks of Kearny Street, this was not true. The young activists came from Chinatown and other, similar communities themselves. The Chinese and the Filipino activists had a link to the elders, who faced harsh discrimination and exploitation. Making that connection created a deeper need to right historic wrongs.

Commitment to the community was a basic foundation of all the young activists' work, and the I-Hotel was a concrete manifestation of that. But the I-Hotel also became a place where radical politics that went beyond immediate community needs could be developed and tested. The revolutionaries considered all of the concrete goals of the issue in the context of broader analyses, such as how decent housing, along with education, jobs, and health care, should be considered a basic human right; how mass pressure could rewrite the social contract even without complete revolution; how minority communities could demand the right to survive in a pluralistic society; and how the demand for civil rights and integration could erupt into a call for self-determination and political power. Glen Omatsu, an activist and writer, describes the breadth of these transformations and marks the 1960s and '70s as a turning point in the history of Asian Americans:

> The focus of a generation of Asian American activists was not on asserting racial pride but reclaiming a tradition of struggle by earlier generations; that the movement was not centered on the aura of racial identity but embraced fundamental questions of oppression and power; that the movement consisted of not only college students but large numbers of community people, including the elderly, workers and high school youth; and that the main thrust was not one of seeking legitimacy and representation within American society but the larger goal of liberation.[8]

Attempting to find the right relationship between long-term goals and immediate demands was a source of constant debate between the KDP and the other revolutionary organizations involved: the Wei Min Shei/RU/RCP and the IWK. We had significant differences with the IWK, particularly in relation to the tactical use of the Moscone plan to delay eviction, which the IWK rejected. The IWK also saw itself as developing a new, Maoist communist party and tended to regard the KDP as reformists and outside the "vanguard" it was creating. We also differed on how to characterize the anti-eviction movement as the defense of Chinatown–Manilatown—with different understandings of how race and nationality worked as interlinked structures of oppression in the American class context. We emphasized the anti-eviction movement as a struggle for housing as a human right over the racial or national components of the conflict, while the IWK highlighted the defense of a national minority community. The IWK and KDP activists never met to air these differences in a close, trusting manner; instead, our disagreements were argued in meetings of the support coalitions; in leaflets and slogans; and in other contexts. The broader analytical positions were hidden behind seemingly minor tactical issues. These "shades" of Marxist opinions may have weakened our overall unity—particularly if we worked at cross-purposes—but we continued to work together through the support coalitions.

The RCP was a different matter altogether. The RCP-led Workers Committee acted on its own, often oblivious of the IHTA, which created problems with allies and divisions within the IHTA itself. The RCP rejected alliances out of hand, taking the position that the only solution was "mobilization of the masses"—in effect, calling for revolution. It rejected even working with other leftist organizations and regarded itself as having already established the "vanguard" of the working class. This meant that the RCP felt it was the inherent leader of the movement and could operate without the advice or consent of others. The group preferred posturing as revolutionaries and shouting militant slogans to working at practical tasks; its members were quite capable of organizing demonstrations and mobilizing their base, but they saw their role mainly as "exposing" liberals, including supportive politicians, and they denounced elected officials rather than sought alliances with them.

Especially in the anti-eviction movement's last years, politicians and others increasingly perceived the I-Hotel struggle as a "leftist cause." These critics believed that the radicals were not really concerned about the elderly tenants but wanted only to advance their own Marxist agendas and were using the hotel to build a leftist stronghold. This was not true for the most part, but the fact that we could not entirely dispel this image was not solely a result of anti-communist attitudes. The behavior of the RCP no doubt gave credence to such responses. The KDP team was so consumed by day-to-day events, attempting to map out strategy and tactics with the tenants, that we tended simply to ignore disruptions by the RCP. There appeared no way to eliminate the group, yet there was no way to work together except in tacit alliance at certain key junctures, such as during the eviction itself. But by not doing enough to differentiate ourselves, we allowed the entire I-Hotel struggle to be identified with rigid doctrinaire zealots in the eyes of many.

When Mayor Moscone and others eventually withdrew their support, they did so partly due to the barrage of attacks on them, which was at least partially understandable. As the struggle gained the bad reputation of "radical takeover," Moscone, Hongisto, and others took the position that they might as well cut their losses; they abandoned the I-Hotel because, to maintain their credibility with the broader electorate, they had to rid themselves of any radical taint. But after the eviction and demolition, they carried forward the left–liberal alliance to retain support and pursue their own agendas, which meant that they still advocated low-income housing, if not at the I-Hotel itself. For example, Moscone was still willing to support the feasibility study, and Dianne Feinstein, a pro-growth Democrat, installed the International Hotel Citizen's Advisory Committee, which eventually would lead to the new I-Hotel. I felt a deep personal sense of betrayal and, at the time, I did not have the distance to see that these liberals could still be influenced. Only later did I recognize the bind in which the hotel had placed them.

The Asian American leftist organizations evolved in the years after the eviction. In 1978, the IWK merged with other groups to form the League for Revolutionary Struggle as a new communist party, but it dissolved in 1990 in the wake of the collapse of the Soviet Union and the Tiananmen Square incident. Most of the activists became involved in local and national politics, such as Jesse Jackson's Rainbow Coalition, and several became elected officials and community leaders. The RCP has continued on its super-revolutionary path, defending Maoist orthodoxy and remaining a small sectarian group with little influence.

The Kearny Street Workshop (KSW) proved to be one of the most durable organizations to emerge from the I-Hotel struggle. Founded in 1972, the KSW survived the disintegration of many other radical Asian American organizations, and it continues to play a major role in community politics. As an arts group, it was never consumed by Maoist politics but consistently saw itself as an expression of the broader Asian American community. Under the leadership of Nancy Hom, the KSW created a venue for young artists and for community projects such as the Angel Island Project to commemorate the island as the equivalent of Ellis Island for Asian immigrants. It remains active, as it did in its early years when community artists cut their teeth on the I-Hotel struggle.

By the late 1980s, progressive ethnic community politics in the Asian American community were represented mainly through nonprofit organizations, including the CPA, which was still active as a grassroots, membership-based organization promoting justice and equality for all people and, particularly, for low-income immigrants in Chinatown. The acrimony in Chinatown between the pro-China left and the traditional conservative organizations waned as China itself took on more capitalist measures, despite its communist legacy. Animosity still existed, but the Chinese Six Companies no longer held exclusive sway among Chinatown's residents.

The I-Hotel played a similar role for Filipinos that it did for the young Chinese activists who became involved at the beginning of the anti-eviction movement. We were discovering a past that had been covered over and forgotten; we developed ties to that past through relationships with the men who had struggled for dignity as workers; and we learned that radical struggles for equality and justice, such as those of the farm workers and other labor movements in the past and present, were very much a part of the American experience. In the course of the I-Hotel struggle the KDP emerged, joined the fight against the dictatorship of Ferdinand Marcos, and addressed the needs of the newly emerging immigrant community. We grew very quickly from a student or youth movement to a fully developed political organization representing an entire community.

The KDP had a sense of politics as a practical endeavor, and, as I said earlier, we always tried to keep long-range goals such as socialist revolution in realistic perspective. We were open about our views and shared them with "the masses," but we never insisted that our friends agree with us or insulted their beliefs. To us, reforms were possible; they could be stepping stones for the people to gain a sense of their own power; and we did not disdain struggling for immediate, palpable demands. But we were also guided by the experiences of the revolutionary movement in the Philippines, news of which reached us through direct contact with exiles and Filipino Americans who had joined the movement there. For example, Cynthia Maglaya had helped to found Kalayaan and the KDP, applying theoretical and practical political knowledge gained from working with the Philippines' mass student organization Kabataan Makabayan. The arrival of other exiles, such as Rene Cruz, continued the education of the Fil Ams. At the same time, Melinda Paras, who had been a teenage antiwar radical in Madison, Wisconsin, traveled to the Philippines to participate in the movement there, and she was able to apply her experiences when she returned.

Emil de Guzman, Jeanette Lazam, and I first encountered the I-Hotel at early stages in our own development, but when we worked together as the KDP I-Hotel team we were guided by the cumulative perspective gained from the organization's leadership training, as well as our own instincts. Our leadership training included careful understanding of the relationship between reform and revolution: We studied the role of electoral work in a revolutionary struggle; how to evaluate people and parties as political forces and to gauge the balance of power; when to negotiate and when to stand fast. No one simplistically transplanted the analysis of the Philippines to our circumstances in the United States. No one thought that a guerrilla army such as the New People's Army was appropriate in an advanced capitalist country, although we did think that the ruling class would resort to violence once it felt that its interests were threatened, and we would need to defend ourselves. However, the KDP's organizational form—a mass organization that was also democratic centralist and cadre-based—flowed from a perception of increasingly fascist conditions (as existed in the Philippines) and the need to have a more military-like organization. The notion of a highly disciplined yet mass-based organization was probably a mistake, but in the early 1970s there was plenty of concrete evidence that the U.S. government was ready and willing to employ repressive tactics.

Although we were novices, the three of us on the I-Hotel team made judgments based on what we thought were realistic, "materialist" assessments, not fantasies. For example, while some of the I-Hotel supporters thought the anti-eviction movement was an example of class *war,* we never entertained such a notion. We knew, despite the violence, that we were engaged in a class *struggle.* We readily engaged in negotiations with city officials and other liberals, we generally did not attack them, and we thought they could be moved by mass pressure to make decisions in our favor, even though we were well aware that they could be unreliable allies. We also sought real solutions to save the I-Hotel. We did not believe that simply demanding the city buy the hotel and give it to the tenants outright was realistic. The Moscone plan, as flawed as it was, was an attempt to develop a concrete proposal, and we supported it because it gave us some tactical breathing room. Meanwhile, we worked with the housing consultants to develop an alternative plan, even though it was too late. One significant mistake we made was not to seek a new strategy early enough, although we did not realize it at the time.

De Guzman, Lazam, and I worked closely with the tenants, developing strong bonds. When disagreements arose, particularly about the Moscone, or "buyback," plan, the tenants never lost confidence in us, even though our position became isolated. They simply felt that we eventually would come around to the correct view. The fact that de Guzman was elected to chair the IHTA even though he had supported the plan testified to the level of trust in which we were held. Our greatest weakness was that we were not properly "flanked" by other KDP activists, and we were not able to mobilize the broader Filipino community effectively—results of the KDP's application of its "dual program."

As I described earlier, the dual program meant a division in our work that corresponded to the multiple realities of the community in America. On the one hand, we had a responsibility to the broader quest for socialist revolution in the United States, and that meant particular involvement by Filipinos in fighting discrimination, racism, and other issues that pertain to the broader working class in the United States. These issues were not especially "Filipino" except to the degree that one or another part of the community might be involved in something that encompassed or affected many other Americans. On the other hand, we also had a responsibility toward the struggle against dictatorship and for national democracy in the Philippines.

This did not mean an automatic bifurcation in our work. When we engaged in antidiscrimination work, we explained how immigration and racial inequalities were shaped by the development of capitalist empire. When we targeted repression in the Philippines, we underscored how the defense of democratic rights in America allowed us to protest collusion with the Marcos dictatorship. Housing, education, job development, and other needs in the United States were undermined by money spent for military aid to repressive regimes.

The KDP's work in ILWU Local 37 in Seattle offered the most vivid example of the intersection of the "anti-imperialist" and "socialist" programs. Composed mostly of Filipino cannery workers in Alaska (the *Alaskeros*), along with Native Americans, white women, and others, Local 37 served as a hiring hall. In 1981, four years after the eviction of the I-Hotel tenants, two KDP activists, Silme Domingo and Gene Viernes, were elected to union offices. Their program was to wrest away leadership from gangsters who demanded bribes for hiring, among other corrupt dealings; at the same time, Domingo and Viernes campaigned for the international union to condemn Marcos's repression of the trade-union movement in the Philippines. After the election, Tony Baruso, the president of the local, arranged for gangsters to murder both of them. Baruso's goal was to maintain his corrupt control of the union, but further investigations revealed that he had been working in collusion with agents from the Marcos dictatorship. Eventually, the murderers went to jail, and a lawsuit was won charging conspiracy against Ferdinand Marcos and his government. Our goal was to reform the union and stop workers' repression in the Philippines, and Domingo and Viernes knew that they were taking risks. When they were murdered, the mass movement we organized pursued the crimes all the way to the source to illuminate the nexus of class conflict in America and imperialist domination of the Philippines.[9]

The International Hotel was also a site where the social and political currents of the Philippines and the United States intersected and could be played out: elderly workers had been brought from the colonized Philippines to fill in the lowest sectors of the labor market and then cast aside, and now they were not even allowed to grow old with dignity in their own community. We attempted to make the internationalist perspective part of our local housing-rights work. We pointed out how the shape of San Francisco, including its real-estate market, was determined by the imperatives of imperial expansion; how San Francisco would be engineered to become the finance capital of the Pacific rim and not a place where ordinary people, particularly minorities, could find a home; and how colonial empire shaped immigration and labor trends.

However, as I pointed out earlier, we also suffered because of conflicting priorities, along with limited people power. Activists were drawn to the rising new immigrant community rather than to the remnants of a dying one, even though the manongs were involved in a broad class struggle affecting the city's future. The dual program seemed accurate, correct for the time, but our practice often lagged far behind. As a consequence, the KDP I-Hotel team was left to fend for itself, and the I-Hotel struggle as a whole suffered. When we were transferred to work elsewhere after the eviction, I felt that we had simply abandoned the I-Hotel struggle.

The forces driving the dual program created other contradictions. Many in the KDP turned to what we considered the necessity of a new communist party to lead the crucial struggle within the United States. We followed the example of our *kasamas* (comrades) in the Philippines who had set out "to rectify and re-establish" the old pro-Soviet party there. This meant that we considered the established CPUSA as hopelessly mired in ideological corruption. A movement to reexamine and correct its ideological underpinnings, political line, and practice, we believed, would lead to reforming the old party and "reestablishing" it on a sounder basis. If that reform movement failed, we would have to create a new party.

After the eviction, the KDP expanded its work in all arenas at the same time that many of its leaders became involved in the communist reform effort. We collaborated with others in an education program to bolster our ability to engage in Marxist–Leninist theoretical and practical analysis. By 1981, many of us had joined Line of March, an organization that saw itself as part of a "single international communist movement" but was engaged in "rectification and reestablishment" of the existing party. Eventually, Line of March moved entirely away from its Maoist origins to draw far closer to the CPUSA. Within this context, many leaders, such as Bruce Occena, transferred from the KDP to Line of March to take leadership roles in the new communist formation. Many activists now responded to the duality of the immigrant community by participating in a Philippines Commission of Line of March that would lead work in the community but from the vantage point of a multiracial revolutionary organization.

Meanwhile, the left in the Philippines became more fractured, particularly when the Communist Party of the Philippines underestimated the People Power movement, which overthrew the Marcos dictatorship in 1986. These differences changed the relationship between the KDP and the CPP, and the KDP could no longer be seen as the single representative of the revolutionary left in the Philippines. In 1987, the KDP disbanded, weakened by the splits among radicals in the Philippines; in 1989, LOM dissolved after personal and organizational crises combined with disorientation after the collapse of the Soviet Union. Although many former KDP members suffered from "battle fatigue" after pushing themselves beyond their limits as cadres for years, most recovered to play active roles in the community. Our perspective had always been that it was important for activists to be in positions of influence in order to effect change, no matter what realm of endeavor. Today many KDP veterans are active as union leaders, elected officials, government administrators, community nonprofit leaders, academics, and more. Several "exiles" returned to the Philippines to become active in politics there.

After my post-eviction recovery, I resumed working in the KDP chapter, only to collapse again. I had moved away from the Mission District and was renting a small, comfortable house in a neighborhood where my children could play more safely. I had no idea that the owner was selling the house. After I had lived there for about a year, I discovered, without warning, that I had been evicted. Reliving the trauma of eviction was the last straw. I broke down physically and emotionally. I was relieved of all political responsibilities for the KDP. When I completed my recovery a year later, I left the KDP and took on educational tasks in Line of March, away from the stress of day-to-day "combat" in mass work.

When I look back at my involvement in the I-Hotel and in the KDP, I can trace a personal and political development that others also experienced. The radical impulse that moved me to become involved was not originally Marxist or ideological. I felt, in the upsurge of the late 1960s and '70s, that Filipinos had been abused; that we had been wronged in the past and we continued to be wronged in the present, and we were not the only ones. America required fundamental social change. This need to fight for justice was at the root of the I-Hotel struggle—and at the root of the Filipino and other Asian American experiences there. In the course of the struggle, my politics began to change. I became more grounded in Marxist theories, along with others like me, because they provided broader frameworks, wider horizons, with which to fight injustice. The Marxist politics of our generation reached its limits, and the failures of doctrinaire thinking became clear to me and to many others who participated. Even so, anyone who views the history of the I-Hotel—and the gleaming new building now on Kearny Street—will have to acknowledge the participation of the left in a major class struggle. What happened on Kearny Street is part of America's often hidden radical history, including the radical Asian American movement. That fact cannot be erased.

Manilatown and Filipino American Consciousness

"We don't feel vindicated because justice don't work like that," Bill Sorro commented to the newspaper reporter at the ribbon cutting for the new International Hotel. "Is it OK that a community was destroyed and there is no remnant of a Filipino community that thrived there? It is not OK." I understood his anguish and anger. Manong Wahat and Manong Felix and all the rest had been displaced, and an entire community—not just one building—had been destroyed. We would never get that back. But when we founded the MHF we wanted at least to make sure that the history of the manongs would be a part of the communal memory of Filipinos and other Asians in America, as well as of San Francisco broadly.

In a collection of poems and photographs produced just before the eviction, Norman Jayo expressed some of the sense of making history that participants felt during the I-Hotel struggle: "This is part of a vast expanse of struggle / worldwide in force / for some it is a beginning / for others close to the end / for all a recognition of truth." He concluded that "we must leave a strong footprint / for those who will follow."[10] Trying to keep that footprint visible, that sense of historical connection and legacy, has been a difficult struggle in itself, and it is the task to which the MHF has committed itself.

With the opening of the new building, the International Hotel Manilatown Center also opened. The center's goal is to keep alive the memory of the anti-eviction movement, the old Manilatown neighborhood, the manongs, and more. Large, translucent scrims cover the windows with images: Wahat speaking to crowds; a manong dressed up in his suit and tie with a bouquet, dapper and ready to dance; police on horseback charging the human barricade; and other scenes from the movement. One wall is covered in old red bricks from the original International Hotel. Names of donors who "bought" bricks to fund the center are carved into the glass that covers the bricks. In the rear, the Maria and Dado Banatao Education Center is equipped with computers to allow visitors to explore digital archives of photos and documents, and the painstaking process has begun to collect and digitize those archives about the International Hotel, Manilatown, and the history of the first Filipinos to come to America. In the residential part of the hotel, photos have been etched into glass and installed that tell the story of the struggle to defend the International Hotel and achieve the new building.

The Manilatown Center actively engages in making memory a tool for today and for helping to create specifically Filipino American identities. Historical consciousness is cultivated in a community, and it helps people to change or to see the possibilities of change in themselves. The eviction of the I-Hotel and the destruction of Manilatown were cataclysmic events that opened the possibility for new ways to think. If we had forgotten the first Filipinos who came to America, we would be erasing not only their pain but also their triumph. The cataclysm of the eviction would have marked the end, whereas collective memory can now view it as a "footstep" for future generations to follow.

Ruling elites habitually inscribe memory in discourse, and even on material objects, to impose their particular construction of national history and identity. Dominant groups mark out significant events with monuments, commemorations, and museums, and they may not even be aware of (or care about) the negative meanings of those events. For example, in the center of San Francisco's Union Square is a high pillar on top of which stands a statue of Admiral George Dewey, the American hero who defeated the Spanish in the 1898 Battle of Manila Bay, during the Spanish–American War. To Filipinos, the triumphal statue also "commemorates" a darker, unrecognized narrative: the subsequent history of brutal U.S. conquest and colonial domination of the Philippines.[11] For marginalized or minority groups to assert their own "commemorative" acts is to step into an arena that has no "place" for them—except when collective memory becomes an act of resistance and we force ourselves into consciousness. Only recently in American history have groups that have been subordinated or hidden or oppressed asserted themselves to make their presence known—fighting discrimination in social relations and demanding to be included in history. To "write" history in social relations is very different from an antiquarian exercise of collecting amusing bits and pieces of the past. Such history demands the active participation of people.[12]

Emil de Guzman, Al Robles, Bill Sorro, and I contacted others to join us in the Manilatown Heritage Foundation with the same consciousness about mass mobilization that had been at the root of our work in the anti-eviction movement. We knew that the center could thrive only if many people across generations took up its direction as their own. To inspire action, we reached out and encouraged others, particularly young people, to shape the center. It was a challenge to bring young people back to Manilatown and introduce them to that part of our history, to see the I-Hotel as sacred ground on which the foundation for future Filipino immigrants to come to this country was set. It was particularly difficult because nothing was left, and all we could do is conjure up Manilatown in their imaginations.

This is why the work of artists has become particularly important. For example, the Filipina choreographer and dancer Pearl Ubungan directed her dance company to perform a multimedia musical extravaganza for one of our early commemorations, held on August 6, 1997, to mark the twentieth anniversary of the eviction. The troupe danced along Jackson Street to invoke the manongs' past, including taxi dancers, their hard work in the fields, and their resistance. The dance reached its climax with a re-enacted "human barricade" against the fence that stood in front of the hole in the ground. The audience—a thousand people, mostly young, sitting across Jackson Street—got up and joined the dancers to chant, "No eviction! We won't move!" The theatrical dance piece moved the audience to walk through the invisible wall to become participants: A legacy became a living ritual.

The student activists of 1968 and 1977 are no longer young. We are fast becoming honored elders ourselves. Our parents—the aspiring generation squeezed between the gray militants and the young activists—no longer feel shame about the impoverished manongs, the "fleabag" hotel, and the unseemly "radical" struggle. Although they were passive at the time, they could not avoid observing how the fight to stop the eviction came to dominate San Francisco politics, with so many Filipino faces broadcast on the television news. The Filipino community witnessed so many non-Filipinos come to the defense of the manongs, such as sympathizers from civil-rights organizations, churches, trade unions, and other Asian communities. They even saw the county sheriff go to jail on behalf of the rights of the old farm workers, sailors, and veterans, valorizing the struggle in their eyes. Other events also affected the community's perceptions, such as the increasing struggle for democracy in the Philippines that led to the overthrow of Ferdinand Marcos in 1986 and the outspoken defense of Filipino American rights spearheaded by the KDP and others, all of which made the International Hotel a memory that could be entertained with pride, a crucial item in the community's collective inventory of validating memories.

Although the eviction was a defeat, the results could be seen as a vindication, in part because the Filipino American community was able to forge part of its identity through that resistance movement. The anti-eviction movement has taken on a mythic quality involving recognition of the history of colonial domination, racial exclusion, and resistance. It has become one of the founding legends for the community as a whole. Many young activists have joined the MHF, and the sense of family bond, respect, and admiration for the elderly who made sacrifices that animated the I-Hotel struggle continues to be a major component of Filipino American consciousness.

Even in terms of family bonds, it is important to underscore the differences in the Filipino community before 1965 and after. In my generation, the number of families was small, and I never met my maternal or paternal grandparents, who continued to live in the Philippines. Most of my uncles, aunts, and cousins trickled into the United States during the 1980s because family reunification had become a preferential category in the 1965 Immigration Act. At the I-Hotel, Mrs. D and Wahat became the aunt and grandfather I had never had. At the same time, I became their niece and granddaughter. Wahat's warrior character reminded me of my own father, who had fought during World War II and had escaped the Bataan Death March. My father raised me as a disciplined soldier, and Wahat became my chief or general. Mrs. D was the aunt who directed social relations, overcoming language barriers, and she provided the home atmosphere that everyone longed for. These bonds between the manongs and the young were deep, tender, and durable. All of this became far more poignant because of the ways anti-miscegenation laws and other racist impositions had distorted life for Filipinos in America. This bond between young and old—and the act of bonding itself—had become a powerful legacy as a result.

An example of this continuing legacy is the activism starting in the 1990s of many Filipino American students on behalf of the elderly Filipino World War II veterans who have been unjustly denied benefits, despite their valor and service. Again, the elderly Filipino veterans—who have chained themselves to public statues in parks, marched to city halls, and lobbied government representatives—have inspired a new generation of young activists.[13]

Today, the demographic weight of the community tilts toward those who came after the 1965 immigration reforms and their children. As a consequence, a version of Filipino American history could be constructed starting in 1965, effectively forgetting the contributions of the first generation of immigrants. If we did not self-consciously bring this history to light, it could have been lost as an active component in shaping the identity of newcomers and of Fil Ams. However, if the center programmed events at the Manilatown Center only about that past, we would be forgetting the transnational experience of the community today. Consequently, other activities, such as lectures on political and social trends in the Philippines, are also presented, even if the main work of the center remains focused on remembering the significance of the I-Hotel and the manongs.

For the foreseeable future, the Filipino community in the United States will have multiple experiences, and it seems likely that discrimination and the negative effects of globalization will be part of them. The I-Hotel anti-eviction movement will remain as an early expression of those dynamics and a reminder that people can resist. The I-Hotel can be celebrated as a story of how one community asserted its historical agency. In the case of the International Hotel, the expression of ethnic identity went beyond involvement in cultural heritage to include politically conscious resistance to discrimination, racism, and unbridled private-property rights.

NOTES

Introduction: "Coming Home to a Fresh Crop of Rice"

1. During the years of the anti-eviction movement, the International Hotel was also referred to as the I-Hotel, the IH, and the Hotel. Those terms are used interchangeably in this history.

2. A number of terms are used to describe Filipinos. During the 1970s, "Pilipino" became a popular usage, indicating an anticolonialist, nationalist viewpoint. (There is no "F" in any of the Philippine languages.) Eventually, the more customary usage "Filipino" regained currency. I employ that term except when "Pilipino" is historically appropriate. American-born Filipinos and Filipino Americans are often referred to as "Fil Ams."

3. Chester Hartman and Sarah Carnochan, *City for Sale: The Transformation of San Francisco* (Berkeley: University of California Press, 2002), 1–14.

4. Ibid., 337.

5. International Hotel Advisory Committee (Citizens Advisory Committee), 1979–94, Him Mark Lai papers, Ethnic Studies Library, University of California, Berkeley.

6. Connie Young Yu, "A History of San Francisco Chinatown Housing," *Amerasia Journal* 8, no. 1 (1981): 93–109.

7. Al Robles, "Coming Home to Manilatown after a Fresh Crop of Rice," MHF flyer, August 4, 1997, MHF Archive.

Chapter One: Manilatown, Manongs, and the Student Radicals

Epigraph: Philip Vera Cruz, "Profits Enslave the World," song lyrics, in "Makibaka: The KDP's Experience, 1973–1987, Songs of Struggle from the Philippines and America," KDP Reunion, Oakland, Calif., July 10–12, 1998, MHF Archive.

1. Carol Deena Levine, "The City's Response to Conflicting Pressures—A Case Study: The International Hotel" (master's thesis, San Francisco State University, 1970), 2; "The Old International Hotel," *San Francisco Independent,* May 24, 1989, 8.

2. Paul Groth, *Living Downtown: The History of Residential Hotels in the United States* (Berkeley: University of California Press, 1994), 158–59.

3. John M. Sanger Associates (John M. Sanger, Paula Collins, Dennis G. Houlihan, and Darla Hillard), Mui Ho, Samuel Dyer, and Community Economics (Joel Rubenzahl and Edward Kirschner), "Chinatown Block Study," prepared for Chinatown Neighborhood Improvement Center, Chinatown Coalition for Better Housing, International Hotel Tenants Association, San Francisco, December 1978, 9–17, MHF Archive.

4. See Groth, *Living Downtown,* 159, fig. 5.19.

5. John K. C. Liu, "San Francisco Chinatown Residential Hotels," Chinatown Neighborhood Improvement Resource Center, San Francisco, 1980, 8.

6. According to the poet and oral historian Al Robles, Joaquin Legaspi was one of the first to use the term "Manilatown" to describe the Kearny Street area.

7. Ronald Takaki, *Strangers from a Different Shore: A History of Asian America* (Boston: Little, Brown, 1989), 336. "Little Manilas" cropped up in areas next to Chinese business areas in Stockton, Los Angeles, San Francisco, Seattle, and other cities. Dorothy B. Fujita-Rony describes the geographical relationship between Chinese and Filipinos, as well as other racial and ethnic groups, in Seattle's Chinatown in Fujita-Rony, *American Workers, Colonial Power: Philippine Seattle and the Transpacific, 1919–1941* (Berkeley: University of California Press, 2003), 122–28.

8. Bruno Lasker, *Filipino Immigration to Continental United States and to Hawaii,* repr. ed. (New York: Arno Press, 1969 [1931]), 21. Because of the migratory patterns, these estimates vary widely. Lasker gave an estimate as high as 30,000, while I-Hotel tenants gave an estimate of 10,000 in San Francisco.

9. P. C. Morantte, *Remembering Carlos Bulosan: His Heart Affair with America* (Quezon City: New Day Publishers, 1984), 101.

10. This geography was constructed from the accounts of Ben Abarca, Emil de Guzman, Bill Sorro, and others.

11. Quoted in Walter Blum, "Filipinos: A Question of Identity," *San Francisco Sunday Examiner and Chronicle,* March 21, 1982, 8–10.

12. Juanita Tamayo Lott, "Demographic Changes Transforming the Filipino American Community," in *Filipino Americans: Transformation and Identity,* ed. Maria P. P. Root (Thousand Oaks, Calif.: Sage Publications, 1997), 138.

13. Takaki, *Strangers from a Different Shore,* 336.

14. For an explanation of why there was a weaker Filipino entrepreneurial class, see ibid., 336; Elena S. H. Yu, "Filipino Migration and Community Organizations in the United States," *California Sociologist* 3, no. 2 (Summer 1980): 84.

15. Fred Basconcillo, interview by the author, tape recording, Daly City, Calif., June 26, 1997.

16. Lasker, *Filipino Immigration to Continental United States and to Hawaii,* 24–27.

17. Benicio T. Catapusan, "Filipino Labor Cycle in the United States," *Sociology and Social Research* 19 (1934–35): 61–63; idem, "The Social Adjustment of Filipinos in the United States" (Ph.D. diss., University of Southern California, Los Angeles, 1940), 69; Mae M. Ngai, *Impossible Subjects: Illegal Aliens and the Making of Modern America* (Princeton, N.J.: Princeton University Press, 2004), 103–105.

18. For a description of work life in Alaska salmon canneries, see Chris Friday, *Organizing Asian American Labor: The Pacific Coast Canned-Salmon Industry, 1870–1942* (Philadelphia: Temple University Press, 1994).

19. Manuel Buaken, *I Have Lived with the American People* (Caldwell, Idaho: Caxton Publishers, 1948), 235–36.

20. For pictures of camps and barracks-like housing, see Wallace Stegner, *One Nation* (Boston: Houghton Mifflin, 1945).

21. Lasker, *Filipino Immigration to Continental United States and to Hawaii,* 21.

22. See Buaken, *I Have Lived with the American People.*

23. U.S. Census of Population: 1930, *Population,* vol. 5, chap. 3, "Occupational Statistics, Color and Nativity of Gainful Workers" (Washington, D.C.: U.S. Government Printing Office 1932).

24. Al Robles, "The Manongs of Manilatown: Oral Histories," *City Magazine,* December 1975, 26.

25. Luzviminda Francisco, "The Philippine American War," in *The Philippines Reader: A History of Colonialism, Neocolonialism, Dictatorship and Resistance,* ed. Daniel B. Schirmir and Stephen Rosskamm Shalom (Boston: South End Press, 1987), 5–19; Teodoro A. Agoncillo, *History of the Filipino People* (Quezon City: Garotech Publishing, 1990), 240–97.

26. Jovina Navarro, "Toward a Relevant Pilipino Education," in *Lahing Pilipino: Pilipino American Anthology,* ed. Jovina Navarro (Davis, Calif.: Mga Kapatid, 1977), 104.

27. See Stuart Creighton Miller, *Benevolent Assimilation: The American Conquest of the Philippines, 1899–1903* (New Haven, Conn.: Yale University Press, 1982).

28. Fujita-Rony, *American Workers, Colonial Power,* 84; Dean T. Alegado, "The Filipino Community in Hawaii," *Social Process in Hawaii* 33 (1991): 4.

29. Carey McWilliams, *Brothers under the Skin,* repr. ed. (Boston: Little, Brown, 1964), 234.

30. Idem, *Factories in the Field: The Story of Migratory Farm Labor in California* (Boston: Little, Brown, 1939), 131.

31. Idem, *Brothers under the Skin,* 239.

32. Ibid., 235.

33. See John E. Reinecke, *The Filipino Piecemeal Sugar Strike of 1924–25* (Honolulu: Social Science Research Institute, University of Hawaii, 1996).

34. McWilliams, *Brothers under the Skin,* 235.

35. Ibid., 237.

36. Fujita-Rony, *American Workers, Colonial Power,* 51–61.

37. McWilliams, *Brothers under the Skin,* 243. For a study of Filipino repatriation, see Casiano Pagdilao Coloma, "A Study of the Filipino Repatriation Movement" (master's thesis, University of Southern California, Los Angeles, 1939).

38. See Larry Arden Lawcock, "Filipino Students in the United States and the Philippine Independence Movement, 1900–1935" (Ph.D. diss., University of California, Berkeley, 1975).

39. Quoted in Lillian Galedo, "The Development of Working Class Consciousness" (master's thesis, Goddard College, San Francisco, 1978), 46.

40. Vera Cruz, "Profits Enslave the World."

41. Felix Ayson, tenant leader of the I-Hotel movement, was active in one of these unions. For the application of Asian "blood unionism," see Takaki, *Strangers from a Different Shore,* 150. For studies of Filipinos and organizing unions, see Howard A. DeWitt, "The Filipino Labor Union: The Salinas Lettuce Strike of 1934," *Amerasia Journal* 5, no. 2 (1978): 1–21; Jack K. Masson and Donald L. Guimary, "Pilipinos and Unionization of the Alaskan Canned Salmon Industry," *Amerasia Journal* 8, no. 20 (1981): 1–30; Friday, *Organizing Asian American Labor,* 48–81, 125–148; Craig Scharlin and Lilia Villaneuva, *Philip Vera Cruz* (Los Angeles: UCLA Labor Center, 1992).

42. For a history of Filipinos in the Brotherhood of Sleeping Car Porters, see Barbara Posadas, "The Hierarchy of Color and Psychological Adjustment in an Industrial Environment: Filipinos, the Pullman Company, and the Brotherhood of Sleeping Car Porters," *Labor History* 23, no. 3 (Summer 1982): 349–73. On leftist unions, see Fujita-Rony, *American Workers, Colonial Power,* 164–166. On attacks on possible Filipino Communist Party members in unions, see Arleen de Vera, "Without Parallel: The Local 7 Deportation Cases, 1949–1955," *Amerasia Journal* 20, no. 2 (1994): 1–25.

43. See Howard DeWitt, *Anti-Filipino Movements in California* (San Francisco: R and E Research Associates, 1976). For an analysis of how "ideas about gender, sexuality, class, and colonialism intersected in violent ways," see Ngai, *Impossible Subjects,* 109–16.

44. Yen Le Espiritu, *Asian American Women and Men: Labor, Laws, and Love* (Thousand Oaks, Calif.: Sage Publications, 1997), 17–18.

45. Takaki, *Strangers from a Different Shore,* 59.

46. Ibid., 330.

47. See Lott, "Demographic Changes Transforming the Filipino American Community," 13, table 2.1.

48. Stegner, *One Nation,* 19–43.

49. Basconcillo interview.

50. Lott, "Demographic Changes Transforming the Filipino American Community," 15.

51. From 1941 to 1959, about 6 percent of Filipinos held semiskilled jobs or were in the Armed Forces: see ibid., 13.

52. Takaki, *Strangers from a Different Shore,* 357–67.

53. Ibid., 361.

54. Ibid., 331–33, 362.

55. Catherine Ceniza Choy, *Empire of Care: Nursing and Migration in Filipino American History* (Durham, N.C.: Duke University Press, 2003), 64–93.

56. Ngai, *Impossible Subjects,* 237–39.

57. For a study of these demographic trends in one community, Salinas, see Edwin B. Almirol, *Ethnic Identity and Social Negotiation: A Study of a Filipino Community in California* (New York: AMS Press, 1985).

58. For more on the reforms and the restrictions of the Immigration Act of 1965, see Ngai, *Impossible Subjects,* 258–64.

59. U.S. Senate Special Committee on Aging, *Housing for the Elderly: A Status Report* (Washington, D.C.: Government Printing Office, 1973).

60. Harry Johanesan, "Forgotten Filipino Poor Huddle in San Francisco Manilatown," *San Francisco Chronicle,* July 10, 1966.

61. For more on Filipino and Chinese families left behind, see Espiritu, *Asian American Women and Men,* 16–41.

62. Mildred Hamilton, "The Filipinos among Us: A Silent Minority on the Move," *San Francisco Examiner,* January 13, 1970, 18.

63. Al Robles, telephone interview by the author, September 1, 2002. I spent time with Robles in countless meetings as he gave many accounts of the manongs.

64. When a reporter asked Ayson whether student radicals were influencing him, he retorted, "No way. I'm influencing them!" See David Prowler, "International Hotel Study," unpublished ms., San Francisco, ca. 1981, n.p., MHF Archive.

65. Bill Sorro, Al Robles, and Emil de Guzman and various supporters told me about their reactions to tenants they had known.

66. Quoted in Roberto V. Vallangca, *Pinoy: The First Wave (1898–1941)* (San Francisco: Strawberry Hill Press, 1977), 111–117.

67. Antonio Gramsci, "The Intellectuals," in *Selections from the Prison Notebooks,* ed. and trans. Quintin Hoare and Geoffrey Nowell Smith (New York: International Publishers, 1989), 3.

68. Stanley Garibay, a labor organizer, poet, writer, and lifelong activist, wrote to a *Philippines News* columnist about accomplishments among the first generation that had been largely forgotten by the public, including the Filipino community. In his letter, Garibay highlighted that Filipinos had been successful labor organizers: "The AFL [American Federation of Labor] did not want us to join them so we helped organize the CIO [Congress of Industrial Organizations]. Filipinos also fought for the civil rights of minorities." Further, he said, Filipino student groups "helped to educate the American public about the issues of Philippine Independence. Most of our Filipino student debaters had won all the debates with Americans on the issue of Philippine Independence long before Carlos Romulo and his team came to debate the issue": Rodel Rodis, "Letter from Stanley," *Philippine News,* August 8, 1989.

69. Bill Sorro, interview by the author, San Francisco, September 18, 2003.

70. Navarro, "Toward a Relevant Pilipino Education," 101–102.

71. Student Support Committee, "Save the International Hotel: I Am Old, I Am Poor, I Am Tired, I Don't Want to Move," broadside, UC Berkeley, February 1970, MHF Archive.

72. Quoted in Karen Umemoto, "On Strike: San Francisco State College Strike, 1968–1969: The Role of the Asian American Students" *Amerasia Journal* 15, no.1 (1989): 15–19.

73. Ibid., 17.

74. Third World Liberation Front, "Scope and Structure of Ethnic Studies Examined in Final TWLF Proposals," leaflet, UC Berkeley, 1969.

75. For a description of the AAPA, see Floyd Huen, "The Advent and Origins of the Asian American Movement in the San Francisco Bay Area: A Personal Perspective," in *Asian Americans: The Movement and the Moment,* ed. Steve Louie and Glenn K. Omatsu (Los Angeles: UCLA Asian American Studies Center, 2001), 276–83; Bruce Occena, interview by the author, tape recording, San Francisco, May 5, 1991.

76. Occena interview.

77. Ibid.

78. For oral histories of war brides, see Fred Cordova, *Filipinos: Forgotten Asian Americans* (Dubuque, Iowa: Kendall/Hunt, 1983), 223–27.

79. For a description of war veterans, see Ronald Takaki, *Double Victory: A Multicultural History of America in World War II* (Boston: Little, Brown, 2000), 120–24; T. Feria, "War and the Status of Filipino Immigrants," *Sociology and Social Research* 31 (1946–47), 50–53.

80. For more on this generation of immigrants, see Antonio Pido, *Pilipinos in America: Macro/Micro Dimensions in Immigration and Integration* (New York: Center for Migration Studies, 1985).

81. For an explanation of why English is the mother tongue for Filipinos and the effects of colonization, see Renato Constantino, "Miseducation of the Filipino," in *Vestiges of War: The Philippine–American War and the Aftermath of an Imperial Dream, 1899–1999,* ed. Angel Velasco Shaw and Luis H. Francia (New York: New York University Press, 2002), 177–92; Eric Gamalinda, "English Is Your Mother Tongue/Ang Ingles Ay an Tongue ng Ina Mo," in Shaw and Francia, *Vestiges of War,* 247–59. For further analysis of the effects of assimilation and identity from the point of view of colonization, see Oscar Campomanes, "The New Empire's Forgetful and Forgotten Citizens: Unrepresentability and Unassimilability in Filipino American Postcolonialities," *Critical Mass* 2, no. 2 (Spring 1995): 145–200; Yen Le Espiritu, "The Intersection of Race, Ethnicity, and Class: The Multiple Identities of Second-Generation Filipinos," *Identities* 1, nos. 2–3 (November 1994): 249–74; idem, *Home Bound: Filipino American Lives across Cultures, Communities, and Countries* (Berkeley: University of California Press, 2003).

82. Liz Abello Del Sol, interview by the author, tape recording, Milipitas, Calif., November 25, 1997.

83. For a case study of the expulsion of left-leaning leaders from the union movement in Seattle, see Arlene de Vera, "An Unfinished Agenda: Filipino Immigrant Workers in the Era of McCarthyism, a Case Study of the Cannery Workers and Farm Laborers Union, 1948–1955" (master's thesis, University of California, Los Angeles, 1990); idem, "Without Parallel," 1–25.

84. Carlos Bulosan, *America Is in the Heart* (Seattle: University of Washington Press, 1973), 139.

85. Quoted in E. San Juan Jr., *Writing and National Liberation: Essays in Critical Practice* (Quezon City: University of the Philippines Press, 1991), 61.

86. See Jose Rizal, *Noli Me Tangere* (London: Longman Group, 1986).

87. See Jessica Hagedorn, *Gangster of Love* (Boston: Houghton Mifflin, 1996). Hagedorn draws on this type of identity in her fiction. The protagonist's brother wears native clothes and copies Jimmy Hendrix's music. See also the main character, Darius, who dons a G-string for everyday wear, in Rod Pulido, dir., *The Flip Side: A Filipino American Comedy* (Puro Pinoy Productions, Chicago, 2002).

88. See Teodoro Agoncillo, *The Revolt of the Masses: The Story of Bonifacio and the Katipunan* (Quezon City: University of the Philippines Press, 1956).

89. For a breakdown of occupations and the small number of professionals, see Royal F. Morales, *Makibaka: The Pilipino American Struggle* (Los Angeles: Mountainview Publishers, 1974). The late Morales was the founder of SIPA in the Los Angeles area, and he taught Filipino American courses at UCLA for many years.

90. See UCLA Asian American Studies Center, *Letters in Exile: An Introductory Reader on the History of Pilipinos in America* (Los Angeles: ULCA Asian American Studies Center, 1976). Liwanag Collective, *Liwanag: Literary and Graphic Expressions by Filipinos in America* (San Francisco: Liwanag Publications, 1975), was a local publication of poetry and short stories produced mainly by San Francisco State students. Philip Vera Cruz composed "Profits Enslave the World," a poem that was put to music by Chris Bautista. During student conventions, various plays and songs highlighted the manongs' struggles. *Isuda Ti Imuna* and *Mindanao* were a few of the plays produced by the KDP that incorporated such themes during the 1970s.

91. Al Robles, *Looking for Ifugao Mountain* (San Francisco: Children's Book Press), 1977.

92. Idem, telephone interview by the author, September 8, 2002.

92. Idem, *Rapping with Ten Thousand Carabaos in the Dark* (Los Angeles: UCLA Asian American Studies Center, 1993), 30–33.

Chapter Two: A Home or a Parking Lot?

1. George Murphy, "Filipinos March for Their Home," *San Francisco Chronicle,* November 28, 1968, 5.

2. Bill Sorro attended this demonstration and commented to me on the attitudes of the tenants at the time.

3. Levine, "The City's Response to Conflicting Pressures," 29.

4. Ibid., 29.

5. "Support the International Hotel," UC Berkeley students' leaflet, ca. Summer 1971, MHF Archive.

6. Levine, "The City's Response to Conflicting Pressures," 33–35.

7. Fred Basconcillo, interview by author, Daly City, Calif., June 1, 1997.

8. For more on the Lucky M Pool Hall and Tino's Barber Shop, see Curtis Choy's documentary film *Fall of the I-Hotel* (Chunk Moonhunter Productions, Oakland, Calif., 1983; Moonwalk Productions, National Asian American Telecommunications Association, San Francisco, 1993).

9. Bruce Occena, interview by the author, San Francisco, May 30, 1991. Also noted in Hamilton, "The Filipinos among Us," 18.

10. Ibid.

11. Quoted in Levine, "The City's Response to Conflicting Pressures," 37. Luisa Castro, interview by the author, tape recording, San Mateo, Calif., September 4, 1997.

12. Jeanette Lazam recalls that others who may have been on the board of the UFA were Pete Marasigan and his wife, Violeta; Conchita [last name unknown]; and the Reverend Antonio (Tony) Ubalde, a Presbyterian minister: Jeanette Lazam, e-mail to the author, March 28, 2003; Frank Celada, interview by the author, tape recording, Berkeley, June 1, 1999.

13. This elitist attitude as a general phenomenon was highlighted in my personal interviews and conversations with Al Robles, Emil de Guzman, Jeanette Lazam, Bill Sorro, and others.

14. Morales, *Makibaka,* 138.

15. For tactics on how to fight evictions, see Chester Hartman, Dennis Keating, and Richard LeGates, *Displacement: How to Fight It* (Berkeley: National Housing Law Project, 1981).

16. See Chester Hartman, *Yerba Buena: Land Grab and Community Resistance in San Francisco* (San Francisco: Glide Publications, 1974).

17. Luisa Castro, interview by the author, tape recording, San Mateo, Calif., September 4, 1997.

18. Ibid. Sources suggest that Ness Aquino is living in the Bay Area, but I could not locate him.

19. Ibid.

20. Bruce Occena, interview by the author, tape recording, San Francisco, May 25, 1991. Lazam confirmed these observations of his organizing skills, making alliances when necessary. When I worked as a bookkeeper for the IHTA, I also witnessed all aspects of his organizing style.

21. Joaquin Legaspi, "Forays," in Liwanag Collective, *Liwanag,* 69.

22. Ibid., 68–71; for a photograph of Legaspi, see "Dedication," Liwanag Collective, *Liwanag,* 8.

23. Bruce Occena, interview by the author, tape recording, San Francisco, September 10, 1991.

24. "A Reprieve for the International," *San Francisco Chronicle,* December 3, 1968, 5.

25. Dick Halgreen, "Rights Unit Jumps into Two Fights," *San Francisco Chronicle,* December 6, 1968, 6. Notably, at the same meeting, the Human Rights Commission gave support to the Third World Strike at San Francisco State.

26. The property was owned by the Estate of Gertrude Meyer, Maxine Silberstein, and Nancy J. Constine. The manager of the property was Milton Meyer and Company: Teri Lee, "The International Hotel: One Community's Fight for Survival" (master's thesis, University of California, Berkeley, 1976), 13–14.

27. Ibid., 14.

28. For a report on areas considered blighted, see San Francisco City Planning Commission, *The Master Plan of San Francisco: The Redevelopment of Blighted Areas, a Report on Conditions Indicative of Blight and Redevelopment Policies* (1945).

29. For an excellent analysis of the tensions between the Democratic Party's federal urban policy and minority neighborhoods, see John H. Mollenkopf, *Contested City* (Princeton, N.J.: Princeton University Press, 1983), 139–212.

30. UFA, newsletter, ca. 1969, MHF Archive.

31. "Fire Results in Three Deaths," *San Francisco Examiner,* March 17, 1969, 1, 30; Elmonte Waite, "People Were Berserk: San Francisco Hotel Fire Leaves Three Dead," *San Francisco Chronicle,* March 17, 1969, 1, 3.

32. Hartman et al., *Displacement,* 40–54.

33. Maitland Zane, "City Office Wrangle: Hotel Fire Dispute Grows," *San Francisco Chronicle,* March 19, 1969.

34. "Filipino Hotel Tenants Set to Fight," *San Francisco Chronicle,* March 27, 1969, 6. For testimony of the fire chief and the Community Design Center regarding the condition of the I-Hotel after the fire, see Levine, "The City's Response to Conflicting Pressures," 92–93.

35. "No One Wants to Move: Hotel Fire's Old Twist," *San Francisco Chronicle,* March 20, 1969.

36. "Filipino Hotel Tenants Set to Fight," 6.

37. Levine, "The City's Response to Conflicting Pressures," 24.

38. Emil de Guzman, telephone interview by the author, July 10, 2000.

39. Quoted in "Filipino Hotel Tenants Set to Fight," 6.

40. Frank Celada, interview by the author, tape recording, Berkeley, December 21, 1997.

41. Quoted in Lee, "The International Hotel," 28.

42. Sidney Wolinsky, interview by the author, Oakland, Calif., August 31, 2004.

43. "Federal Judge Dismisses Suit to Save Hotel," *San Francisco Chronicle,* May 9, 1969, 29.

44. "Mayor's Advisors: Another Plea to Spare Hotel," *San Francisco Chronicle,* April 19, 1969, 3. Both the Mission Coalition and the Western Addition Community Organization were natural allies in the fight against dispersal. Redevelopment had successfully dispersed the black community in the Fillmore and Western Addition areas, displacing more than 10,000 people.

45. Wolinsky interview.

46. Scott Blakey, "A Bitter Exchange on S.F. Hotel," *San Francisco Chronicle,* April 24, 1969, 2.

47. Dale Champion, "Critical Look at International Hotel," *San Francisco Chronicle,* June 13, 1969, 2.

48. Quoted in "Family Life Plea for Old Hotel," *San Francisco Chronicle,* April 30, 1969, 6.

49. Quoted in ibid.

50. Madeline Hsu, "Gold Mountain Dreams and Paper Son Schemes: Chinese Immigration under Exclusion," *Chinese America* (1997): 46–60.

51. Quoted in Levine, "The City's Response to Conflicting Pressures," 85.

52. For how a sense of home can produce urban social change, see Michael P. Smith and J. R. Feagin, *The Capitalist City: Global Restructuring and Community Politics* (Oxford: Basil Blackwell, 1987), 87–110.

53. This analysis of "home" versus "commodity" was articulated in discussions with Emil de Guzman, Jeanette Lazam, and Bill Sorro.

54. Levine, "The City's Response to Conflicting Pressures," 19.

55. Ibid., 26.

56. For more on Mayor Alioto, see Hartman and Carnochan, *City for Sale,* 24–32.

57. "Alioto Will Meet Tenants Anew on Hotel Row Solutions," *Philippine News,* May 8–14, 1969, 1.

58. See Hartman, *Yerba Buena.*

59. "International Hotel—The Mayor's Idea," *San Francisco Chronicle,* May 6, 1969, 5.

60. Crime statistics from the San Francisco Police Department showed that, from January to April 1969, there were twenty arrests for possession of drugs, five hundred arrests for prostitution, seventy-two reported incidents of and thirteen arrests for grand theft, fifty-one reported incidents of and twelve arrests for armed robbery, and forty reported incidents of and twenty arrests for muggings and aggravated assaults after dark: Levine, "The City's Response to Conflicting Pressures," 52.

61. "Alioto Will Meet Tenants Anew on Hotel Row Solutions," 1.

62. Susan Almazol, "Old Hotel Protesters Ruffle Mayor," *San Francisco Chronicle,* May 11, 1969, 3.

63. "$50,000 from Ford to Save International Hotel," *San Francisco Chronicle,* May 24, 1969, 28.

64. "Hotel Holds Party to Defy Eviction," *San Francisco Chronicle,* June 2, 1969, 3.

65. "New Plea to Save Hotel," *San Francisco Chronicle,* June 12, 1969, 44.

66. Levine, "The City's Response to Conflicting Pressures," 8.

67. Quoted in Chester Hartman, *The Transformation of San Francisco* (Totowa, N.J.: Rowman and Allanheld, 1984), 62.

68. Lee, "The International Hotel," 9.

69. "International Hotel Showdown Expected: Alioto Aide Explains Controversy, Cites City Hall Proposals," *Philippine News,* June 17, 1969, 1.

70. Quoted in Lee, "The International Hotel," 26.

71. Levine, "The City's Response to Conflicting Pressures," 59, 73, 74.

72. Lee, "The International Hotel," 28.

73. Student Support Committee, "Fight for the International Hotel: Asian Tenants Struggle to Keep Their Homes," broadside, International Hotel, ca. 1972, MHF Archive.

74. Scott Blakey, "Victory Reported for Filipino Hotel," *San Francisco Chronicle,* June 25, 1969, 6.

75. Occena interview, May 25, 1991. Aquino made this known to many of the student activists at the time.

76. "Filipinos Win a New Lease on Life at International Hotel," *San Francisco Examiner,* 23 July 1969, 11.

Chapter Three: "Peace with a Lease"

1. Racism Research Project, *Critique of the Black Nation Thesis* (Berkeley: Racism Research Project, 1975). The project included Gary Achziger, Linda Burnham, Harry Chang, Neil Gotanda, Paul Liem, Belvin Louie, Bruce Occena, Smokey Perry, Barbara Pottgen, Pat Sumi, and Bob Wing. The analysis put forward in the critique saw the intersection of class and race in the liberation of black people—that is, with the exception of Native Americans, minorities' conditions are better understood through racial categories than national minority oppression. This became the main outlook of the radical Filipinos involved in the I-Hotel fight.

2. See Community Design Center, *Chinatown: An Analysis of Population and Housing* (Berkeley: Community Design Center, UC Berkeley, 1969), MHF Archive.

3. For a description of the youth scene in Chinatown during this period, see Stanford Lyman, "Red Guard on Grant Avenue: The Rise of Youthful Rebellion in Chinatown," in *Asian Americans: Psychological Perspectives,* ed. Stanley Sue and Nathaniel N. Wagner (Ben Lomond, Calif.: Science and Behavior Books, 1973), 20–44.

4. Emil de Guzman, interview by the author, San Francisco, February 20, 2004.

5. Johanesan, "Forgotten Filipino Poor Huddle in San Francisco Manilatown."

6. Quoted in Mark Schwartz, dir., *Dollar a Day, Ten Cents a Dance* (Gold Mountain Productions, Capitola, Calif., 1984).

7. "Appeal for Help to Restore Hotel," *San Francisco Chronicle,* September 12, 1969, 47.

8. Student Support Committee, "Save the International Hotel."

9. Jeanette Lazam, interview by the author, tape recording, San Francisco, May 30, 1990.

10. Ed Ilumin, telephone interview by the author, August 10, 2004.

11. Quoted in Larry R. Salomon, *Roots of Justice: Stories of Organizing in Communities of Color* (San Francisco: Jossey-Bass, 1998), 98.

12. Quoted in Lee, "The International Hotel," 30. Emil de Guzman conveyed the same sentiments to me: interview by the author, tape recording, San Francisco, September 8, 1995.

13. Quoted in Katy Butler, "Inside the International Hotel Furor," *San Francisco Chronicle,* February 21, 1977, 4.

14. Quoted in Salomon, *Roots of Justice,* 103.

15. Maxi Villones, interview by the author, tape recording, San Jose, Calif., May 27, 1992; Cynthia Bonta, e-mail to the author, September 2004.

16. Project Manong, flyer, ca. 1972, MHF Archive.

17. Student Support Committee, "Fight for the International Hotel."

18. For an example of community service learning applied to a contemporary writing curriculum, see Marjorie Ford and Elizabeth Schave, *Community Matters: A Reader for Writers* (New York: Longman, 2002).

19. Student Support Committee, "Fight for the International Hotel."

20. Katy Butler and Steve Rubenstein, "International Hotel: Cautious Joy among the Tenants," *San Francisco Chronicle,* January 18, 1977, 2.

21. The San Francisco Foundation, a nonprofit organization, funded many of these programs during this stage.

22. Carl Regal, interview with the author, San Francisco, ca. 1971.

23. Quoted in Prowler, "International Hotel Study."

24. Student Support Committee, "Fight for the International Hotel."

25. Emil de Guzman, telephone interview by the author, January 2, 2005.

26. Prowler, "International Hotel Study," 67–68; Vivian Tsen, "The International Hotel: Anatomy of a Housing Issue" (master's thesis, University of California, Berkeley, 1977), 36–37.

27. Emil de Guzman, interview by the author, San Francisco, December 28, 2002.

28. Jeanette Lazam, telephone interview by the author, December 27, 2002.

29. Ibid.

30. "Political Program of the KDP," First Congress pamphlet, KDP, Oakland, Calif., July 1975, appendix, MHF Archive.

31. Beverly Kordziel, "To Be a Part of the People: The International Hotel Collective," in Louie and Omatsu, *Asian Americans,* 241–47.

32. Manong Frankie Alarcon showed pictures of his many girlfriends at the different ports around the world in Choy, *The Fall of the I-Hotel.*

33. Virginia Cerenio, "Dreams of Manong Frankie," in *Making Waves: An Anthology of Writings by and about Asian American Women,* ed. Asian Women United of California (Boston: Beacon Press, 1989), 228–35.

34. Jessie Quinsaat, "An Exercise on How to Join the Navy and Still Not See the World," in *Letters in Exile: An Introductory Reader on the History of Pilipinos in America,* ed. Jessie Quinsaat (Los Angeles: UCLA Asian American Studies Center, 1976), 97–105.

35. See Sr. Mary John Mananzan, OSB, "The Filipino Woman: Before and After the Spanish Conquest of the Philippines," in *Essays on Women,* ed. Sr. Mary John Mananzan (Manila: St. Scholastica's College, 1991), 6–35.

36. Lazam interview, December 27, 2002.

37. Luisa de la Cruz, interview by the author, tape recording, San Francisco, May 1, 1995. Alfredo de la Cruz had passed away by the time the interview took place.

38. Ibid. When I interviewed Luisa de la Cruz, she was shy and said she did not want unnecessary attention and asked me to turn off the recorder. I took notes for the rest of the interview.

39. Frances Peavey (Finley), telephone interview by the author, March 20, 1999.

40. "An Emerging Alternative," editorial, *Kalayaan International,* June 1971, 1.

41. See Rene Cruz, "The KDP Story: The First Ten Years," *Ang Katipunan,* vol. 9, no. 8, September 1983. For the situation in the Philippines, see Jose F. Lacaba, *Days of Disquiet, Nights of Rage* (Quezon City: Rapid Lithographics, 1982).

42. Linda Basch, Nina Glick Schiller, and Christina Szanton Blanc, eds., *Nations Unbound: Transnational Projects, Postcolonial Predicaments, and Deterritorialized Nation States* (New York: Gordon and Breach, 1994), 254–55.

43. Transnationalism as a theoretical concept best describes a phenomenon that affects many immigrant groups. For a general theoretical framework, see ibid. For the broad effect on American studies, see Shelley Fisher Fishkin, "Crossroads of Culture: The Transnational Turn in American Studies—Presidential Address to the American Studies Association, November 12, 2004," *American Quarterly* 57, no.1 (2005): 17–57. For applications of transnational historical frameworks to

Filipino American studies scholarship, see Choy, *Empire of Care*; Espiritu, *Home Bound*; Fujita-Rony, *American Workers, Colonial Power*; Augusto Fauni Espiritu, *Five Faces of Exile: The Nation and Filipino American Intellectuals* (Stanford, Calif.: Stanford University Press, 2005); Catherine Ceniza Choy, "Towards Trans-Pacific Social Justice: Women and Protest in Filipino American History," *Journal of Asian American Studies* 8, no. 3 (October 2005): 293–307.

44. Leni Marin, interview by the author, San Francisco, May 5, 1991.

45. Emil de Guzman, interview by the author, tape recording, San Francisco, September 5, 1997.

46. For a critical review of changes in Filipino American attitudes, see Oscar Campananes, "Filipinos in the United States and their Literature of Exile," in *Discrepant Histories: Translocal Essays on Filipino Cultures,* ed. Vincent Rafael (Philadelphia: Temple University Press, 1995), 159–92. See also Luis H. Francia, "Inventing the Earth: The Notion of 'Home' in Asian American Literature," in *Across the Pacific: Asian Americans and Globalization,* ed. Evelyn Hu-DeHart (Philadelphia: Temple University Press, 1999).

47. Filipino youth argued about whether they should identity themselves as American Filipino, hyphenated "Filipino-Americans," or Pilipino. Many preferred "Pilipino" as a diasporic term that encompasses all deterritorialized Filipinos, regardless of birthplace, and its usage became the chosen form of identification for radicalized Fil Ams. They argued there was no "F" in Tagalog and, thus, that "Filipino" would be continuing the inscription of colonial consciousness.

48. Luzviminda Francisco, "The Philippine American War, 1899–1902," in Quinsaat, *Letters in Exile,* 1–22.

49. Bruce Occena, interview by the author, San Francisco, May 5, 1995.

50. This term was explained to me in a conversation with Carmen Chow, a leading activist of the IWK, in 1976.

51. For a history of Third World Marxist movements in the United States, see Max Elbaum, *Revolution in the Air: Sixties Radicals Turn to Lenin, Mao, and Che* (New York: Verso, 2002), 41–162.

52. For a description and analysis of the different forces in the anti–Marcos movement, see Madge Bello and Vincent Reyes, "Filipino Americans and the Marcos Overthrow: The Transformation of Political Consciousness," *Amerasia Journal* 13, no. 1 (1986–87): 73–83; Barbara Guerlan, "The Movement in the United States to Oppose Martial Law in the Philippines, 1972–1991: An Overview," *Pilipinas* 33 (Fall 1999): 75–98.

53. Cruz, "The KDP Story," 3.

54. Occena interview, May 5, 1995.

55. Cruz, "The KDP Story," 2.

56. See Amado Guerrero (a.k.a. Jose Maria Sison), *Philippine Society and Revolution* (Oakland, Calif.: International Association of Filipino Patriots, 1979).

57. John W. Frazier, "Asians in the United States: Historical and Contemporary Settlement Patterns," in *Race, Ethnicity, and Place in a Changing America,* ed. John W. Frazier and Eugene L. Tettey-Fio (Binghamton, N.Y.: Global Academic Publishing, 2006), 275.

58. Cruz, "The KDP Story," 2.

59. Nick G. Benoza, "NCRCLP Unmasked: Filipino Movement in U.S. Exposed as Red-Tainted, Ex-Consul Bares 'Plot' to Senator Cranston," *Philippine News,* September 20–23, 1973, 1, 12.

60. For example, the Plaza Miranda bombing in 1970 was widely regarded as organized by Marcos agents to justify his rule: see Gregg R. Jones, *Red Revolution: Inside the Philippine Guerilla Movement* (Boulder, Colo.: Westview Press, 1989), 59–64.

61. For a review of the organizations and their affiliations, see William Wei, *The Asian American Movement* (Philadelphia: Temple University Press, 1993).

62. Harvey Dong, interview by the author, tape recording, Berkeley, June 1, 1997.

63. Nancy Hom, interview by the author, San Francisco, June 1, 1998.

64. Peter Rubin, interview by the author, San Francisco, August 6, 2000. Miriam Louie analyzes and reflects on the movement in "Yellow, Brown, Red: Towards an Appraisal of Marxist Influences on the Asian American Movements," unpublished ms., Oakland, Calif., May 1991, MHF Archive.

65. Anonymous medical team member, telephone interview by the author, June 1, 1997. The team member was a doctor who volunteered during the anti-eviction period, and he commented that he wanted to be involved with a struggle that seemed so united. He requested anonymity because of his ties with city politics.

Chapter Four: The Tiger Leaps

1. Prowler, "International Hotel Study"; Tsen, "The International Hotel," 36–37.

2. Quoted in Hartman and Charnochan, *City for Sale,* 232.

3. David Johnston, W. A. Van Winkle, William Ristow, Bruce B. Brugmann, and David Hatcher, "The Godfather of the International Hotel," *San Francisco Bay Guardian,* May 19, 1977, 1, 3–5, 8.

4. Lee, "The International Hotel," 15.

5. Johnston et al., "The Godfather of the International Hotel," 1, 3–5, 8.

6. Ibid., 5. The additional properties bought by Four Seas included 1426 Taylor Street, purchased on July 17, 1973; 37 Columbus Avenue (the Bell Hotel), purchased on December 31, 1973; 1–21 Columbus Avenue (the Colombo Building), purchased on October 31, 1974; and 824–836 Kearny Street (the Victory Building), purchased on June 25, 1976. Except for the Taylor Street building, these properties were on the same block as the I-Hotel. The total value of all of the properties was nearly 5 million dollars.

7. Jerry Roberts, "I-Hotel Trial Ends: Shorenstein–Bangkok Connection," *San Francisco Bay Guardian,* May 7, 1976, 6.

8. Lee, "The International Hotel," 31; Prowler, "International Hotel Study," 68; Johnston et al., "The Godfather of the International Hotel," 1, 3–4.

9. Lee, "The International Hotel," 15–16.

10. Calvin Trillin, "U.S. Journal: San Francisco; Some Thoughts on the International Hotel Controversy," *New Yorker,* December 19, 1977, 116–20.

11. After the 1906 earthquake and fire destroyed most of Chinatown, elements of the business elite connived to remove the Chinese community to Hunter's Point, to the Presidio Golf Links, to the mud flats, and to neighboring residential areas. Residents of Telegraph Hill protested that they did not want the Chinese in their neighborhood. But a few Chinese property owners, such as the Chinese Six Companies, intended to rebuild in Chinatown. White property owners who owned most of the buildings that the Chinese leased in Chinatown calculated that the high rate of return from their investments would be lost if the Chinese abandoned San Francisco. The city also would have suffered a heavy loss of revenues from property owners, of taxes paid by Chinese, and of profits from the China trade. So in the end, Chinatown was rebuilt, but the tenements designed for the working-class bachelor society remained the typical type of Chinatown residence: Connie Young Yu, "A History of San Francisco Chinatown Housing," *Amerasia Journal* 8, no. 1 (1981): 100–101.

12. Housing Rights Study Group, "Who's Moving? A Look at the Neighborhoods," Regional Young Adult Project, San Francisco, ca. 1977, 9, MHF Archive.

13. John K. Liu, "San Francisco Chinatown Residential Hotels," Chinatown Neighborhood Improvement Resource Center, San Francisco, 1980, 5, MHF Archive.

14. John M. Sanger Associates, "Chinatown Block Study," 26.

15. Victor G. and Brett de Bary Nee, *Longtime Californ': A Documentary Study of an American Chinatown* (Stanford, Calif.: Stanford University Press, 1986), xxiii.

16. Ibid.

17. IHTA, "International Hotel: Tenants' Struggle—Who Are We?" flyer, October 24, 1974, MHF Archive; Lee, "The International Hotel," 36–38; Prowler, "International Hotel Study," 78–81.

18. Prowler, "International Hotel Study," 79.

19. IHTA, "International Hotel."

20. Ibid.

21. Idem, letter to supporters, July 9, 1975, MHF Archive; Prowler, "International Hotel Study," 81.

22. Prowler, "International Hotel Study," 80; IHTA, "International Hotel."

23. "Tenants of the International Hotel Sue," *San Francisco Chronicle,* October 25, 1974.

24. Prowler, "International Hotel Study," 81.

25. "Directed Verdict against Tenants in Eviction Case," *San Francisco Chronicle,* May 1, 1976; Prowler, "International Hotel Study," 92–94.

26. Quoted in Prowler, "International Hotel Study," 86.

27. Lee, "The International Hotel," 40–41.

28. Ibid., 42; "City Hall Picketed in Eviction Fight," *San Francisco Chronicle,* July 28, 1976, 1, 14; "State High Court Rejects Appeal in Hotel Evictions, *San Francisco Chronicle,* September 4, 1976, 3; "New Order to Evict Hotel Tenants," *San Francisco Chronicle,* December 4, 1976, 30; "Judge Refuses to Stay Hotel Evictions," *San Francisco Chronicle,* December 15, 1976, 58; Harry Jupiter, "Hotel Eviction Case: Hongisto on Trial for Contempt," *San Francisco Chronicle,* December 21, 1976, 1; "Judge to Rule on Hongisto Mistrial," *San Francisco Chronicle,* December 28, 1976, 3; Harry Jupiter, "Hongisto Is Denied a Mistrial," *San Francisco Chronicle,* December 29, 1976, 4; idem, "Hongisto Refuses Call to Testify," *San Francisco Chronicle,* December 30, 1976, 4; idem, "Testimony in Hongisto Case Ends," *San Francisco Chronicle,* December 31, 1976, 10.

29. "Deputies versus Marchers in Hotel Eviction," *San Francisco Chronicle,* January 8, 1977, 2. Supporters contended that the posting was illegal because each tenant, including commercial tenants, had not been individually served.

30. Marc Elliot, "Sheriff, Aide Ordered to Jail," *San Francisco Progress,* January 12, 1977; "International Hotel: Stage Is Set for Eviction," *San Francisco Sunday Examiner and Chronicle,* January 16, 1977, A8.

31. "Sheriff Posts Eviction Order on Hotel," *San Francisco Chronicle,* January 12, 1976; Prowler, "International Hotel Study," 114, 140.

32. Harry Jupiter and George Snyder, "Bid [*sic*] Demonstration at the International," *San Francisco Chronicle,* January 13, 1977, 1.

33. Prowler, "International Hotel Study," 132.

34. Quoted in ibid., 135.

35. Quoted in Harry Jupiter, "Contempt Case: Five Days in Jail for Hongisto," *San Francisco Chronicle,* January 11, 1977, 1.

36. This analysis was derived from discussions with Emil de Guzman, Jeanette Lazam, Bruce Occena, and Bill Sorro.

37. Quoted in Lee, "The International Hotel," 20.

38. The emblem was ubiquitous, posted throughout the city, and was used for commemorations in later years.

39. IHTA, "Partial List of Organizations Supporting the I-Hotel," unpublished document, ca. 1976–77, MHF Archive.

40. "Statement by Supervisor John Molinari," Board of Supervisors, file no. 182-75, March 3, 1975, San Francisco City Hall.

41. Nelson Dong, "'Analysis of Proposed Housing Demolition Ordinance' and 'To Whom It May Concern,'" Morrison and Foerster, San Francisco, 1976; IHTA, letter to friends, July 9, 1975, both in MHF Archive.

42. Quoted in Sherry Valparaiso, "International Hotel Ordinance Defeated," *Ang Katipunan,* January–February 1976, 5.

43. Quoted in Larry Liebert, "Permit Board Meeting: Stormy Debate on Chinatown Hotel," *San Francisco Chronicle,* April 4, 1975, 3.

44. Bob Hayes, "Tenant Replacement Housing—Who's Responsible?" *San Francisco Examiner,* November 3, 1975.

45. Hartman and Carnochan, *City for Sale,* 227–34. As a result of this system, Harvey Milk, the first openly gay elected official in the country, would be elected to represent District 5, which included the gay community of San Francisco's Castro District.

46. State Senator George Moscone, letter to IHTA, January 2, 1975, MHF Archive.

47. "City Hall Picketed in Eviction Fight," 1, 14.

48. Marshall Kilduff, "Moscone Tells Plan to Save Hotel," *San Francisco Chronicle,* July 30, 1976, 3; Prowler, "International Hotel Study," 96–98.

49. Hartman and Carnochan, *City for Sale,* 8, 15–16, 168, 337; Prowler, "International Hotel Study," 96.

50. See *Winkelman v. City of Tiburon,* 32 C.A. 3d 834, and *San Francisco v. Ross,* 44 C.2d 52. Sid Wolinsky and Gilbert Graham, attorneys for the International Hotel, confirmed the use of these court rulings as part of the IHTA's strategy to employ eminent domain.

51. "A Move to Obtain Hotel for Housing," *San Francisco Chronicle,* October 22, 1976, 37.

52. Maitland Zane, "A Victory for the International Hotel," *San Francisco Chronicle,* November 16, 1976, 19.

53. San Francisco Board of Supervisors, file no. 516-76-1, Resolution 946-76; Duffy Jennings, "Board of Supervisors Vote to Save International Hotel," *San Francisco Chronicle,* December 1, 1976, 5.

54. Prowler, "International Hotel Study," 98–99.

55. "Housing Board Calls Hearing in Hotel Dispute," *San Francisco Chronicle,* December 17, 1976, 32.

56. Robert Bartlett, "Victory for Tenants of Embattled Hotel," *San Francisco Chronicle,* December 24, 1976, 1; Housing Commission agenda, quoted in Prowler, "International Hotel Study," 104.

57. Quoted in ibid., n.p.

58. Quoted in Prowler, "International Hotel Study," 106–107.

59. Quoted in ibid., 110.

60. Quoted in ibid., 111.

61. Ibid., 113.

62. Prowler, "International Hotel Study," 113–14.

63. Ibid., 115–16.

64. Ibid., 116–17; Tsen, "The International Hotel," 46.

65. "A Move to Obtain Hotel for Housing," *San Francisco Chronicle,* October 22, 1976, 37.

66. Quoted in Prowler, "International Hotel Study," 118.

67. Quoted in ibid., 5.

68. The biographical information for Felix Ayson was drawn from many conversations with him by Al Robles and the author; from interviews in Choy, *The Fall of the I-Hotel*; and from material in Prowler, "International Hotel Study."

Chapter Five: "*Makibaka!* Dare to Struggle!"

1. Jupiter and Snyder, "Bid [*sic*] Demonstration at the International"; Harry Jupiter, "Judge Blocks Hotel Eviction," *San Francisco Chronicle,* January 18, 1977, 1, 14; Prowler, "International Hotel Study."

2. Harry Jupiter, "Contempt Case: Five Days in Jail for Hongisto," *San Francisco Chronicle,* January 10, 1977.

3. "Sheriff Posts Evict Order on Hotel," *San Francisco Chronicle,* January 12, 1977.

4. Jupiter, "Contempt Case," 1.

5. Butler, "Inside the International Hotel Furor."

6. For a description of the various Igorot tribes in northern Luzon, including the Benguet, see William Henry Scott, *The Discovery of the Igorots* (Quezon City: New Day Publishers of the Christian Literature Society of the Philippines, 1974).

7. "Thousands of Filipinos Join Celebration: National June 12 Events Successful," *Ang Katipunan,* June 15–30, 1977, 8. I attended this celebration and escorted Wahat to the event.

8. Hilton Obenzinger, interview by the author, Palo Alto, Calif., January 3, 2002. Obenzinger helped to organize this event at the Everett Middle School in San Francisco as a supporter of the American Indian Movement.

9. Norman Jayo, "International Hotel," audiocassette of live broadcast, Third World News Bureau, KPFA Pacifica News, Berkeley, May 1977.

10. Jupiter, "Judge Blocks Hotel Eviction," 1, 14.

11. Quoted in ibid., 1.

12. COINTELPRO was the code name for the FBI's domestic Counterintelligence Program. One of COINTELPRO's methods was feeding damaging information to friendly journalists or tying up organizations or individuals in court with frivolous prosecutions. The Black Panther Party and the American Indian Movement were particular targets of the illegal campaign: see Ward Churchill and Jim Vander Wall, *The COINTELPRO Papers: Documents from the FBI's Secret Wars against Dissent in the United States,* 2nd ed. (Boston: South End Press, 2002); David Hilliard and Lewis Cole, *This Side of Glory: The Autobiography of David Hilliard and the Story of the Black Panther Party* (Boston: Little, Brown, 1993).

13. Quoted in Butler and Rubenstein, "International Hotel," *San Francisco Chronicle,* 2.

14. Quoted in Jupiter, "Testimony in Hongisto Case Ends," 10.

15. Prowler, "International Hotel Study," 117. Jeanette Lazam spent a great deal of time with Manong Frankie.

16. Prowler, "International Hotel Study," 143–44.

17. Emil de Guzman, "I-Hotel Tenant Dies at 76: A Courageous Fighter," *Ang Katipunan,* April 1–15, 1977, 6.

18. Quoted in ibid.

19. Quoted in Bill Sing, "We Won't Move: Saga of the International Hotel," *Winds,* vol. 6, no. 3, February 1977, 1, 7, Asian American students folder, Stanford University Archives. *Winds* was the Stanford University student newspaper.

20. Emil de Guzman, Jeanette Lazam, and other activists all spoke about the transformation of the tenants' attitudes, which the tenants articulated in many speeches and confrontations with government officials, particularly during the last period of the anti-eviction struggle.

21. Quoted in "We Want to Restore the Respect for Human Dignity," *Keep Strong,* July 1977, 43.

22. Jeanette Lazam, "Mayor Moscone Shuns Tenants," *Ang Katipunan,* April 1–15, 1977, 6.

23. Quoted in "Remembering the I-Hotel: Our Homes Are Disappearing," editorial, *Common Sense,* September 1977, 2.

24. Quoted in Prowler, "International Hotel Study," n.p.

25. Revolutionary Communist Party, "Build the Fight for the I-Hotel: Position of the Revolutionary Communist Party on Some Recent Questions," position paper, ca. August 1977, MHF Archive.

26. Quoted in Prowler, "International Hotel Study," n.p.

27. Ibid., 119.

28. Ben Abarca, interview by the author, San Francisco, November 22, 1999. Abarca grew up in Manilatown and knew Diones in the community. Abarca thought that Diones was not a good leader because of his confrontational manner, his corruption and backbiting, and his tendency to use violence.

29. Jeanette Lazam, telephone interview by the author, January 4, 2003.

30. Quoted in Prowler, "International Hotel Study," 58.

31. *Ang Aktibista: Theoretical Bulletin of the KDP,* vol. 2, no. 10, July 27, 1976, 7–8.

32. See Wei, *The Asian American Movement.*

33. Coalition to Support I-Hotel, "City Is Playing More Tricks! I-Hotel Struggle Continues! Tenants, Communities, Supporters Unite to Win Greater Victories!" flyer, January 12 1977, MHF Archive.

34. David Owen, "A Working Paper for the I-Hotel Support Committee; Re: Heterosexism, an Obstacle to Marxist/Leninist Thought and Practice," ca. 1976, MHF Archive.

35. For an example of anticommunist attacks, see Benoza, "NCRCLP Unmasked," 1, 12–13.

36. Jeanette Lazam, e-mail to the author, August 17, 2006. For more on her life, see Jeanette Lazam, "The Mighty Manhattan-Born Pinay," in *Seven Card Stud with Seven Manangs Wild: An Anthology of Filipino-American Writings,* ed. Helen Toribio (San Francisco: T'Boli Publishing, 2002), 89–106.

37. For more on my life, see Estella Habal, "How I Became a Revolutionary," in *Legacy to Liberation: Politics and Culture of Revolutionary Asian Pacific America,* ed. Fred Ho (San Francisco: Big Red Media and AK Press, 2000), 197–210.

38. Lazam interview, January 4, 2003.

39. Prowler, "International Hotel Study," 128–31.

40. *Ang Aktibista,* 7–8.

41. Quoted in Jeanette Lazam, "Filipinos Speak Out—I-Hotel Tenants Pledge to Fight!" *Ang Katipunan,* March 16–31, 1977, 10.

42. Quoted in Chester Hartman, "The Struggle for the International Hotel: What We Won, What We Lost, What We Learned," *Common Sense,* September 1977, 2.

43. Lazam interview, January 4, 2003.

44. Ibid., Oakland, Calif., May 4, 2000. On the day of the eviction, the national leadership published an issue of *Ang Aktibista* (vol. 3, no. 1, August 4, 1977), the internal political-education organ of the KDP, devoted entirely to the campaign to overcome restrictions on the immigration status of Filipino professionals and the nurses' licensure campaign. There was no mention of the International Hotel.

45. See Brian J. Godfrey, *Neighborhoods in Transition: The Making of San Francisco's Ethnic and Non-Conformist Communities* (Berkeley: University of California Press, 1988).

46. For an account of the Narciso and Perez campaigns and the KDP's involvement, see Choy, *Empire of Care,* 139–65.

47. Chris Braga, interview by the author, Oakland, Calif., July 3, 1998. Braga, who was working with farm workers, resigned from the KDP as a result of his disagreements with its priorities in political work.

Chapter Six: People's Power versus Propertied Elites

1. For a version of the internal dynamics of the I-Hotel struggle, see Wei, *The Asian American Movement,* 23–24. Unfortunately, Wei's description is inadequate and inaccurate, leaving out the role of Filipinos and the KDP, as well as that of the ACC/RCP's rival, the CPA/ IWK.

2. Calvin Trillin, "U.S. Journal: Some Thoughts on the International Hotel Controversy," *New Yorker,* December 19, 1977, 116.

3. International Hotel Tenants Support Committee, "City Government: It's Your Responsibility! Buy and Rehabilitate the I-Hotel!" c. June 1977, MHF Archive.

4. Anonymous, telephone interview by the author, June 3, 1997.

5. Revolutionary Communist Party, USA, "Build the Fight for the I-Hotel: Position of the Revolutionary communist Party on Some Recent Questions," position paper, c. August 1977, 5–6, MHF Archive.

6. "Revolutionary Line on Parliamentary Struggle," *Ang Aktibista,* vol. 1, no. 7, November 6, 1974.

7. Ibid.

8. Leftist groups vied for "advanced workers" to recruit to their organizations. Advanced workers were those who were open to progressive and communist ideas and ripe for recruitment. Usually, they were considered rising stars and promoted during events and demonstrations.

9. Lazam interview, December 27, 2002.

10. Douglas Dowd, *Blues for America: A Critique, a Lament, and Some Memories* (New York: Monthly Review Press, 1997), 237.

11. Quoted in "Moscone Replies to Hotel Critics," *San Francisco Chronicle,* July 12, 1977.

12. Prowler, "International Hotel Study."

13. Dick Nolan, "First You Lose Contact, Then You Lose Control," *San Francisco Sunday Examiner and Chronicle,* June 12, 1977.

14. "What Will Happen if Propositions A, B Win or Lose," *San Francisco Examiner,* August 1, 1977, 4.

15. Quoted in Jerry Burns, "Moscone Angered by 'Radical Plot' Charge," *San Francisco Chronicle,* May 27, 1977.

16. Herb Caen, quoted in Hartman and Carnochan, *City for Sale,* 232.

17. For a brief history of district elections and the Propositions A and B campaigns, see ibid., 227–34.

18. Elaine Herscher and Jerry Roberts, "Urban Renewal: San Francisco Hotel Tenants Insist Housing Is a Right, Not a Privilege," *Seven Days,* February 28, 1977, 34.

19. Gilbert H. Boreman, Clerk of the Board, "Letter to San Francisco Bar Association and Barristers Club of San Francisco," February 23, 1977, file no. 516-76, San Francisco City Hall.

20. Quoted in Abe Mellinkoff, "Old Jail Trail," *San Francisco Chronicle,* June 1, 1977.

21. Quoted in Herscher and Roberts, "Urban Renewal," 35.

22. Sherry Valparaiso, "Eviction in Suspense: Court Battle May Determine International Hotel Fate," *Ang Katipunan,* February 16–28, 1977, 9.

23. "The Case against the I-Hotel Judge," *San Francisco Bay Guardian,* April 28, 1977, 5–6.

24. Quoted in Harry Jupiter, "Purchase Blocked: Hotel Tenants Loses Court Ruling," *San Francisco Chronicle,* May 28, 1977.

25. *Winkelman v. City of Tiburon,* 32 C.A. 3d 834–846; *Redevelopment Agency v. Hayes* 122 C.A. 2d 777, 803–804; *San Francisco v. Ross,* 44 C.2d 52.

26. *Redevelopment Agency v. Hayes.*

27. Quoted in Anne Nakao and Raul Ramirez, "Supreme Court Refuses to Stay Hotel Evictions: Way Cleared for Sheriff's Deputies to Act," *San Francisco Examiner,* July 28, 1977, 1.

28. Quoted in Jupiter, "Purchase Blocked."

29. Quoted in Rod Lew, "Remember the I-Hotel: Eviction's Terror Still Lives On," *Asian Week,* June 13, 1986, 13.

30. Community Ownership Organizing Project (Edward M. Kirshner, Joel Rubenzahl, and Vivian Tsen), "Preliminary Draft: International Hotel Feasibility Study," unpublished study, Oakland, Calif., May 23, 1977, MHF Archive; Tsen, "The International Hotel," 42–51.

31. See IHTA, "A Plan to Save the International Hotel," unpublished document, July 1, 1977, MHF Archive; Tsen, "The International Hotel," 42–51; Prowler, "International Hotel Study," 117–19, 120–22.

32. George R. Moscone, "Statement of Mayor George R. Moscone Re: International Hotel," June 10, 1977, file no. 516-76, San Francisco City Hall.

33. Ibid., 2.

34. George Draper, "Now It's a Landmark," *San Francisco Chronicle,* June 17, 1977, 2; Prowler, "International Hotel Study," 145.

35. Mayor George Moscone, "Letter to Gilbert T. Graham," November 15, 1977, file no. 516-76-2, San Francisco City Hall.

36. Emil de Guzman, chairman, IHTA, "Letter to Mayor George Moscone," July 15, 1977, IHTA, MHF Archive.

37. Ibid.; IHTA press release, July 18, 1977.

38. Mayor George R. Moscone, "Statement regarding International Hotel," June 10, 1977, file no. 516-76-1, San Francisco City Hall; "A Ballot Box Condition for Latest Hotel Plan," *San Francisco Examiner,* July 13, 1977; Jeanette Lazam, "Despite Stay of Eviction, Moscone Deserts I-Hotel Front," *Ang Katipunan,* July 27–August 10, 1977, 9.

39. Tsen, "The International Hotel," 37, 42–51.

40. IHTA Board, "Proposed Tenant Plan," memorandum to tenants, ca. July 1977, MHF Archive.

41. IHTA, "A Plan to Save the International Hotel," 3.

42. Lazam, "Despite Stay of Eviction, Moscone Deserts I-Hotel Front."

43. "Another Municipal Folly," editorial, *San Francisco Chronicle,* December 3, 1976; "The International Hotel—There's a Better Way to Go," editorial, *San Francisco Examiner,* January 16, 1977; "Last Call for Eviction," editorial, *San Francisco Chronicle,* August 1, 1977, 34.

44. "The International Hotel—A Touchy Issue," editorial, *San Francisco Examiner,* July 10, 1977.

45. Abe Mellinkoff, "Legal Dust," *San Francisco Chronicle,* July 14, 1977.

46. "Last Call for the Eviction," editorial, *San Francisco Chronicle,* August 1, 1977, 34.

47. Hartman and Carnochan, *City for Sale,* 232–33.

48. Prowler, "International Hotel Study," 124–25.

49. Quoted in Raul Ramirez and Dexter Waugh, "3,000 Backers Mass at International Hotel," *San Francisco Examiner,* June 13, 1977, 4.

50. Quoted in Sherry Valparaiso, "3,000 Form Human Barricade at I-Hotel: Supporters Pledge to Stop Eviction," *Ang Katipunan,* June 16–30, 1977, 12.

51. Prowler, "International Hotel Study," 128, 131.

52. Raul Ramirez, "International Hotel: Final Siege of Eviction Fight—Tenants Are Ready to Put Their Bodies on the Line," *Sunday San Francisco Examiner and Chronicle,* June 12, 1977, 12–13; Prowler, "International Hotel Study," 128, 131.

53. Quoted in Ramirez and Waugh, "3,000 Backers Mass at International Hotel," 4.

54. Quoted in Ramirez, "International Hotel," 12–13.

55. Coordinating Committee to IHTA, letter, ca. May 1977, Ed Ilumin file, Human Rights Commission, San Francisco, MHF Archive. The letter was signed by members of the I-Hotel Support Committee, including the People's Food System, the KDP, the Northern California Alliance, the Puerto Rican Solidarity Committee, and the Tenants Action Group.

56. Quoted in Ramirez, "International Hotel," 12–13.

57. For another point of view regarding defense of the building and other tactics, see Chester Hartman, "San Francisco's International Hotel: A Case Study of a Turf Struggle," *Radical America* 12, no. 3 (May–June 1978): 47–58.

58. Prowler, "International Hotel Study," 137–39.

59. Quoted in Salomon, *Roots of Justice,* 102.

Chapter Seven: The Fall of the I-Hotel

1. Art Agnos, "Letter to Tenants of the International Hotel," August 3, 1977, MHF Archives.

2. Prowler, "International Hotel Study"; George Snyder and Birney Jarvis, "The Explosive Clash between Cops, Protestors," *San Francisco Chronicle,* August 5, 1977, 1, 3; Katy Butler, "Final Hours Inside," *San Francisco Chronicle,* August 5, 1977, 1. News coverage of the eviction by the mainstream media, as well as by the progressive and radical press, was exceptional, particularly the live broadcasts by KPFA. This account of the night of the eviction is based on this coverage, as well as on my firsthand experience inside the building and discussions with many who participated outside on the "human barricade."

3. Katy Butler, "How They Took the Hotel," *San Francisco Chronicle,* August 5, 1977, 4.

4. Dowd, *Blues for America,* 237.

5. Quoted in Butler, "How They Took the Hotel," 4.

6. "How Cops Routed Tenants: Combined City Force Routs 1,000 International Defenders," *San Francisco Examiner,* August 4, 1977, 1, 18; Snyder and Jarvis, "The Explosive Clash between Cops, Protestors," 1, 3.

7. Robert Levering, "The I-Hotel Evictions: A Report from the Scene—And a Call for Action," *San Francisco Bay Guardian,* August 11, 1977, 9.

8. Quoted in Barry Alterman, "Police Attack I-Hotel, Evict Tenants," *San Francisco Bay Guardian,* August 17, 1977, 1, 5.

9. Levering, "The I-Hotel Evictions," 9.

10. Snyder and Jarvis, "The Explosive Clash between Cops, Protestors," 1.

11. Revolutionary Communist Party, "Build the Fight for the I-Hotel: Position of the Revolutionary Communist Party on Some Recent Questions," position paper, ca. August 1977, 7, MHF Archive.

12. This view was noted in the proposal to make the film that would ultimately be titled *The Fall of the I-Hotel*: Christopher Chow, Emiko Omori, Curtis Choy, and Jack Michon, "Manongs: The Tenants of the I Hotel, Proposal for a One-Hour Film," Chonk Moonhunter Productions, Oakland, Calif., and Los Angeles, September 1977, 2.

13. Quoted in Alterman, "Police Attack I-Hotel, Evict Tenants," 5.

14. "Being There: The Night of the Eviction," *Common Sense,* September 1977, 10–11.

15. IHTA Support Committee, "Factsheet," flyer, ca. August 1977, MHF Archive.

16. For criticism of the abandoning of the human barricade in front of the I-Hotel, see Hartman, "San Francisco's International Hotel," 47–58.

17. Quoted in Charles Rohrbacher, "I-Hotel Tenants Evicted," *East West* 11, no. 32 (August 10, 1977): 1, 6–7.

18. Quoted in Ed Diokno, "Hotel Spirit Still Lingers," *Philippine News,* August 13–19, 1977, 1, 12.

19. Anonymous protestor, telephone interview by the author, San Francisco, May 21, 1989.

20. Norman Jayo, "Live Broadcast from the Eviction," tape recording, Third World News Bureau, KPFA Pacifica News, August 4, 1977.

21. David Prowler, handwritten notes, ca. 1976–77, Human Rights Commission, San Francisco City and County, MHF Archive.

22. Ibid., n.p.

23. Ibid., n.p.

24. Snyder and Jarvis, "The Explosive Clash between Cops, Protestors," 1.

25. Quoted in Mary Ganz, "Old I-Hotel Filling the Gap Left by the Eviction," *San Francisco Examiner,* August 4, 1987, 1, 7.

26. Quoted in Jupiter, "Contempt Case," 5.

27. Art Silverman, "Barb Writer Retorts: You Cast Your Lot on the Wrong Side of History," *Berkeley Barb,* August 19–25, 1977, 7.

28. Quoted in Hartman and Carnochan, *City for Sale,* 338; Bernice Yeung, "The 'I' Is for Irony," *San Francisco Weekly,* June 6, 2001.

29. "Hours of Anxiety and Then the Shout: 'They Are Coming!'" *San Francisco Examiner,* August 4, 1977, 1; Snyder and Jarvis, "The Explosive Clash between Cops, Protestors," 1.

30. Quoted in Diokno, "Hotel Spirit Still Lingers," 1, 12.

31. Felix Ayson died on September 18, 1978, from pneumonia and lung cancer. He was eighty-one years old: "Requiem for Felix Ayson: I-Hotel Leader," *Philippine News,* November 4–10, 1978.

32. Quoted in Prowler, handwritten notes, n.p.

33. Quoted in "How Cops Routed Tenants," 1.

34. Walter Cronkite, "CBS Evening News," television broadcast, August 4, 1977. Newspaper coverage of the eviction included "Police, Protestors Clash of Eviction in San Francisco," *New York Times,* August 5, 1977, 8; "Police Evict Elderly Tenants of San Francisco Hotel," *Washington Post,* August 5, 1977, A1, A3; as well as articles in the *Baltimore Sun* and *Los Angeles Times.* Coverage portrayed the basic political conflict rather than just a "human-interest" story.

35. Lee, "The International Hotel," 45.

36. Jeanette Lazam, interviews by the author, tape recordings, San Francisco, May 25, 1990, October 10, 1990. We were both inside the building during the eviction. I witnessed this episode, and she recounted it for me during these interviews.

37. "Undersheriff Apologizes for Tenant Mixup," *San Francisco Examiner,* August 17, 1977, 10.

38. Quoted in "The Evicted Tenants' Search for New Place to Live," *San Francisco Chronicle,* August 5, 1977, 4.

39. Dan Borsuk, "Where Have All the Tenants Gone?" *San Francisco Progress,* August 5, 1977, 2.

40. In addition to the trauma, one tenant, Romeo de los Santos, was missing in the melee, and the survivors who huddled at the Liberation School were deeply anxious until he was found wandering in Chinatown the next day.

41. Prowler, handwritten notes, n.p.

42. Borsuk, "Where Have All the Tenants Gone?"; idem, "What Housing? Evictees Ask," *San Francisco Progress,* August 7, 1977, 9; "Statement of Chester Hartman, Consultant to International Hotel Tenants Association," unpublished press presentation, August 5, 1977, MHF Archive; Prowler, handwritten notes, n.p.

43. Quoted in Raul Ramirez, "I-Hotel Tenants Count Loses," *San Francisco Sunday Examiner and Chronicle,* August 21, 1977, B8.

44. Carol Pogash and Alice Yarish, "A Sad Return to Pick up Belongings," *San Francisco Chronicle,* August 7, 1977.

45. Borsuk, "What Housing?"

46. IHTA, "To the People of San Francisco from the International Hotel Tenants Association," flyer, August 6, 1977, MHF Archive.

47. Ibid.

48. Quoted in "Supervisors Hear Hotel Eviction Protest," *San Francisco Chronicle,* August 9, 1977, 12.

49. Chester Hartman, "Protecting Housing for the Elderly: San Francisco's International Hotel," unpublished ms., ca. August 1977, MHF Archive; John Fogarty, "Probe of Owner of International Hotel," *San Francisco Chronicle,* August 26, 1977, 2.

50. Quoted in Raul Ramirez, "The Old Come Back—To Get Their Things," *San Francisco Examiner,* August 6, 1977, 4; "The Hotel Eviction Arguments Go On," *San Francisco Examiner,* August 9, 1977.

51. Senate Special Committee on Aging, "Church, Domenici Promise Broadened Senate Housing Investigations," press release, August 26, 1977, MHF Archive.

52. Hartman, "San Francisco's International Hotel," 53.

53. Prowler, "International Hotel Study," 154.

54. Quoted in Jerry Roberts, "Voters' Chance at the Issue: International Hotel on the Ballot," *San Francisco Chronicle,* November 5, 1977, 5.

55. Yes on U Committee, "Controller, Voter Registrar Sued: International Hotel Supporters Seek to Block Voters Handbook," press release, October 3, 1977, MHF Archive; idem, "Proposition U Supporters Lose in Court," press release, October 6, 1977, MHF Archive.

56. Quoted in Roberts, "Voters' Chance at the Issue," 5.

57. Four Seas Investment Corporation, "Proposition 'U' Means YOU Pay: NO on 'U'," election campaign pamphlet, ca. October 1977, MHF Archive.

58. Quoted in Roberts, "Voters' Chance at the Issue," 5.

59. Yes on U Committee, "Yes on U," election campaign pamphlet, ca. October 1977, MHF Archive.

60. Jerry Burns, "New San Francisco District Supervisors—Six Incumbents Are Elected," *San Francisco Chronicle,* November 9, 1977, 1.

61. Jerry Carroll, "Billboard Ban, Hotel Lose—Bonds OK'd," *San Francisco Chronicle,* November 9, 1977, 1.

62. Herb Caen, "My Kind of Thing," *San Francisco Chronicle,* November 7, 1977, C1.

63. Marshall Kilduff, "New Clash at the Hotel—Both Sides Arrested," *San Francisco Chronicle,* September 20, 1977, 4; "I-Hotel Demolition Derby: Contractor 1, Tenants 0," *San Francisco Examiner,* Septermber 19, 1977.

64. "Damage Claim over International Hotel," *San Francisco Chronicle,* December 9, 1977, 2.

65. "Sentences in International Hotel Case," *San Francisco Chronicle,* February 23, 1978, 7.

66. "Court OKs Permit for Razing Hotel," *San Francisco Chronicle,* September 2, 1978.

67. Prowler, "International Hotel Study," 154.

68. Chester Hartman, "To the NCA Community Base Committee," internal memorandum, September 7, 1977, MHF Archive.

69. Quoted in Barry Alterman, "I-Hotel Leader, 80, Fights On," *National Guardian,* October 26, 1977, 6.

70. Etta (Moon) Chung, interview by the author, San Francisco, May 1, 1999. Etta Moon, who was middle-aged at the time of the eviction, was a tenant activist. She married So Chung in 1984. She described the conditions and mood at the Stanford Hotel.

71. John M. Sanger Associates, "Chinatown Block Study"; Hartman, "Protecting Housing for the Elderly."

72. Randy Shaw, "Tenant Power in San Francisco," in *Reclaiming San Francisco: History, Politics, Culture,* ed. James Brook, Chris Carlsson, and Nancy J. Peters (San Francisco: City Lights Books, 1998), 287.

73. San Francisco International Hotel Block Development Citizens Advisory Committee, "Summary of Public Hearing," October 8, 1979, November 17, 1979, December 19, 1979, Him Mark Lai Papers, Ethnic Studies Library, University of California, Berkeley.

74. Department of City Planning and International Hotel Block Development Citizens Advisory Committee, "International Hotel Block Development Plan," December 1979, file no. 96-79-3, San Francisco City Hall.

75. Hartman, "Protecting Housing for the Elderly," 4.

Conclusion: The Rise of the I-Hotel

1. Tim Redmond, "Feinstein's Big Hole in the Ground: The I-Hotel Deal Falls Apart," *San Francisco Bay Guardian,* July 16, 1986.

2. Lloyd Watson, "Big I-Hotel Project Set to Roll—Again," *San Francisco Chronicle,* January 29, 1990, B3; Linda Sherry, "126 Units of Senior Housing for International Hotel Site," *Asian Week,* December 6, 1991, 1, 22; Gerald D. Adams, "Project Set for I Hotel Crater," *San Francisco Examiner,* December 7, 1991, 1, 9; Chinatown Community Development Center, "International Hotel Senior Housing Update," memo, February 2002, MHF Archive; Hartman and Carnochan, *City for Sale,* 338–39.

3. Chinatown Community Development Center, "20–20 Vision: 20 Years of Vision and Action," anniversary, brochure, December 1998, MHF Archive.

4. Edith Witt, "Suspense at the International Hotel," *San Francisco Examiner,* August 6, 1976.

5. Shaw, "Tenant Power in San Francisco," 300.

6. The Manilatown Heritage Foundation held a special memorial for Mrs. D at the Besse Carmichael Elementary School on October 30, 1999.

7. Quoted in Neela Banerjee, "Resurrection of the I-Hotel," *Asian Week,* June 13, 2001, 18.

8. Glen Omatsu, "The Four Prisons and the Movement of Liberation," *Amerasia Journal* 15 (1989): xvi.

9. For an account of the lives of the assassinated Filipino American activists Gene Viernes and Silme Domingo, see Thomas Churchill, *Triumph over Marcos: A Story Based on the Lives of Gene Viernes and Silme Domingo* (Seattle: Open Hand Publishing, 1995).

10. Norman Jayo, "Hard Lines and Shades of Grey Flannel," in *We Won't Move: Poems and Photographs of the International Hotel Struggle,* ed. Asian American Writers Workshop (San Francisco: Kearny Street Workshop, 1977), 35.

11. "As a monument, as a design, if people want to keep the column there, that's fine," said Rene Ciria-Cruz, editor-in-chief of *Filipinas,* a monthly magazine based in San Francisco that circulates nationally and in the Philippines. "I just wish people would clarify the description of what's being remembered. Otherwise, it becomes a monument to the 'white man's burden'": quoted in John King, "Filipinos Speak out for Change: Union Square Memorial Causes Controversy," *San Francisco Chronicle,* March 31, 1997, A13.

12. The MHF is not the only Filipino American organization engaged in this process. Cordova's *Filipinos* portrays the pre–1965 period through oral histories and photographs. After the book appeared in 1982, Cordova and his wife, Dorothy, were instrumental in launching the Filipino American National Historical Society (FANHS), a chapter-based organization to preserve, document, and present Filipino American history to the public. In 1987, FANHS inaugurated its National Pinoy Archives as an accessible, nonprofessional repository of documents relating to the Filipino American experience. Dawn Mabalon has worked to establish the Little Manila Foundation to preserve the memory of Filipinos who gravitated to the Central Valley agricultural community of Stockton, California, starting in the 1920s. Community and labor activists established the Carlos Bulosan Memorial Exhibit in the Historic East Hotel in Seattle; members of SIPA were instrumental in designating a Historic Filipinotown in Los Angeles by erecting a sign on Temple Street, where 6,900 Filipinos currently live, on August 2, 2002. See Deborah Kong, "Activists Aim to Preserve Vestiges of Manilatown," *Palo Alto Daily News,* December 26, 2002; "Carlos Bulosan Memorial Exhibit: Historic Eastern Hotel, Seattle Washington," brochure, n.d.; SIPA, "Letter to Family and Friends," Los Angeles, December 2002.

13. For selections on Filipino veterans, their plight, and student supporters, see "Culture Show Pays Tribute to World War II Vets," *Philippine News,* December 4–10, 1996, 10; Tara Shioya, "The Invisible Veterans," *San Francisco Weekly,* July 16–22, 1997, 1, 10–11, 14–15, 17, 19–20; Ricardo Catahan, "Forgotten Heroes of Bataan and Corregidor: Last Days of the War," *Philippine News,* June 2–8, 1993, 21.

BIBLIOGRAPHY

Primary Sources

Manilatown Heritage Foundation (MHF) Archive

IHTA leaflets, newsletters, and correspondence
UFA newsletters
International Hotel Support Groups, broadsides and flyers
American Indian Movement, Third World Liberation Front, and Project Manong flyers
Ed Ilumin, Human Rights Commission, notes
David Prowler, Human Rights Commission, notes
Edith Witt, Human Rights Commission, notes
"Political Program of the KDP," pamphlet, Oakland, Calif. (1975).
Ang Aktibista (theoretical bulletin of the KDP [vol. 22, no. 10, July 27, 1976, 7–8]).

International Longshoremen's and Warehousemen's Union

Amy Schecter Papers

University of California, Berkeley

"International Hotel Citizens Advisory Committee meeting notes," Him Mark Lai Papers, Ethnic Studies Library
James Earl Wood Papers, Bancroft Library

Stanford University Archives

Asian American Students' file

Interviews, Tapes, and E-mail

Abarca, Ben
Anonymous medical team member
Anonymous protestor
Ayson, Felix
Basconcillo, Fred
Bonta, Cynthia
Braga, Chris
Castro, Luisa

Celada, Frank
Chung, Etta (Moon)
De Guzman, Emil
De la Cruz, Luisa
Del Sol, Liz (Abello)
Diones, Joe
Dong, Harvey
Galedo, Lillian
Graham, Gilbert
Hom, Nancy
Ilumin, Ed
Lazam, Jeanette
Marin, Leni
Obenzinger, Hilton
Occena, Bruce
Peavey, Fran (Finley)
Rader, Nita
Regal, Carl
Robles, Al
Rubin, Peter
Tompao, Wahat
Villones, Maxi
Wolinsky, Sidney

Newspapers

Ang Katipunan (national newspaper of the KDP, 1975–83)
Asian Week (1986–2001)
Berkeley Barb (1977)
Common Sense (newsmonthly of the Northern California Alliance, 1976–77)
East West (Chinese American journal)
Gidra (twentieth anniversary issue, 1970–90)
Kalayaan International (1971)
Keep Strong (1977)
New York Times (1977)
Palo Alto Daily News (2002)
Philippine News (1969–89)
San Francisco Bay Guardian (independent radical newsweekly, 1977)
San Francisco Chronicle (1966–2005)
San Francisco Examiner (1969–89)
San Francisco Independent (1989)
San Francisco Progress (1977)
San Francisco Sunday Examiner and Chronicle (1976–82)
San Francisco Weekly (1997)
Seven Days (1977)
Washington Post (1977)
Winds (Stanford University student newspaper, 1977)

Public Documents

Bloch, Louis. *Facts about Filipino Immigration in California.* State Department of Industrial Relations, San Francisco, April 1930; reprint, San Francisco: R and E Research Associates, 1972.
Board of Supervisors. "Resolution 946-76." File 516-76-1, San Francisco City Hall.
———. "Statement of Supervisor John Molinari," March 3, 1975. File 182-75, San Francisco City Hall.
Boreman, Gilbert H., Clerk of the Board. Letter to San Francisco Bar Association and Barristers Club of San Francisco, February 23, 1977. File 516-76, San Francisco City Hall.
Bulosan, Carlos, ed. *International Longshoremen and Warehousemen Union, Local, 1952 Yearbook.* Seattle: ILWU, 1952.
Chinatown Community Development Center. "20–20 Vision: Twenty Years of Vision and Action." CCDC, San Francisco, December 1998.
Community Design Center. "Chinatown: An Analysis of Population and Housing." Community Design Center, Berkeley, June 1969.
Housing Rights Study Group. "Who's Moving? A Look at the Neighborhoods." Regional Young Adult Project, San Francisco, ca. 1977.

Kirshner, Edward M., Joel Rubenzahl, and Vivian Tsen. "International Hotel Feasibility Study." Community Ownership Organizing Project, Oakland, Calif., May 23, 1977.
Liu, John K. C. "San Francisco Chinatown Residential Hotels." Chinatown Neighborhood Improvement Resource Center, San Francisco, 1980.
Moscone, (Mayor) George. Letter to Gilbert T. Graham, November 15, 1977. File 516-76-2, San Francisco City Hall.
———. Letter to IHTA. July 13, 1977. File 516-76-1, San Francisco City Hall.
———. "Statement of Mayor George R. Moscone Re: International Hotel," June 10, 1977. File 516-76-1, San Francisco City Hall.
San Francisco City Planning Commission. *The Master Plan of San Francisco: The Redevelopment of Blighted Areas, a Report on Conditions Indicative of Blight and Redevelopment Policies.* San Francisco: City Planning Commission, 1945.
San Francisco Department of City Planning. *Land Use Survey.* San Francisco, 1970.
Sanger, John M., and Associates. "Chinatown Block Study." Prepared for Chinatown Neighborhood Improvement Center, Chinatown Coalition for Better Housing, International Hotel Tenants Association, San Francisco, 1978.
U.S. Census of Population: 1930. *Population.* Vol. 5, chap. 3. "Occupational Statistics, Color and Nativity of Gainful Workers." Washington, D.C.: U.S. Government Printing Office, 1932.
U.S. Senate, Special Committee on Aging. *Housing for the Elderly: A Status Report.* Washington, D.C.: U.S. Senate, 1973.

Court Records

San Francisco v. Ross, 44 C.A. 2d 52.
Redevelopment Agency v. Hayes, 122 C.A. 2d 777.
Winkelman v. City of Tiburon, 32 C.A. 3d 834.

Secondary Sources

Books

Agoncillo, Teodoro A. *The Fateful Years: Japan's Adventure in the Philippines, 1941–1945.* Diliman, Philippines: University of the Philippines Press, 2001.
———. *History of the Filipino People.* Quezon City: Garotech Publishing, 1990.
———. *The Revolt of the Masses: The Story of Bonifacio and the Katipunan.* Quezon City: University of the Philippines Press, 1956.
Almirol, Edwin B. *Ethnic Identity and Social Negotiation: A Study of a Filipino Community in California.* New York: AMS Press, 1985.
Ancheta, Angelo N. *Race, Rights and the Asian American Experience.* New Brunswick, N.J.: Rutgers University Press, 1998.
Anderson, Benedict. *Imagined Communities: Reflections on the Origin and Spread of Nationalism,* 2nd ed. New York: Verso, 1991.
Asian American Writers Workshop, ed. *We Won't Move: Poems and Photographs of the International Hotel Struggle.* San Francisco: Kearny Street Workshop, 1977.
Asian Women United of California, ed. *Making Waves: An Anthology of Writings by and about Asian American Women.* Boston: Beacon Press, 1989.
Basch, Linda, Nina Glick Schiller, and Christina Szanton Blanc, eds. *Nations Unbound: Transnational Projects, Postcolonial Predicaments, and Deterritorialized Nation-States.* New York: Gordon and Breach, 1994.
Blauner, Robert. *Racial Oppression in America.* New York: Harper and Row, 1972.
Brook, James, Chris Carlsson, and Nancy J. Peters, eds. *Reclaiming San Francisco: History, Politics, Culture.* San Francisco: City Lights Books, 1998.
Buaken, Manuel. *I Have Lived with the American People.* Caldwell, Idaho: Caxton Publishers, 1948.

Bulosan, Carlos. *America Is in the Heart,* repr. ed. Seattle: University of Washington Press, 1973.

Castells, Manuel. *The City and the Grassroots: A Cross-Cultural Theory of Urban Social Movements.* Berkeley: University of California Press, 1983.

Chan, Sucheng. *Asian Americans: An Interpretive History.* Boston: Twayne Publishers, 1991.

Cheng, Lucie, and Edna Bonacich. *Labor Immigration under Capitalism: Asian Workers in the U.S. before World War II.* Berkeley: University of California Press, 1984.

Choy, Catherine Ceniza. *Empire of Care: Nursing and Migration in Filipino American History.* Durham, N.C.: Duke University Press, 2003.

Churchill, Thomas. *Triumph over Marcos: A Story Based on the Lives of Gene Viernes and Silme Domingo.* Seattle: Open Hand Publishing, 1995.

Cordova, Fred. *Filipinos: Forgotten Asian Americans.* Dubuque, Iowa: Kendall/Hunt, 1983.

Daniel, Cletus E. *Bitter Harvest: A History of California Farmworkers, 1870–1941.* Ithaca, N.Y.: Cornell University Press, 1981.

Davis, Mike, Steven Hiatt, Marie Kennedy, Susan Ruddich, and Michael Spinks, eds. *Fire in the Hearth: The Radical Politics of Place in America,* vol. 4. New York: Verso, 1990.

De Leon, Richard Edward. *Left Coast City: Progressive Politics in San Francisco, 1975–1991.* Lawrence: University Press of Kansas, 1992.

DeWitt, Howard. *Anti-Filipino Movements in California,* reprint ed. San Francisco: R and E Research Associates, 1976.

Dowd, Douglas. *Blues for America: A Critique, a Lament, and Some Memories.* New York: Monthly Review Press, 1997.

Elbaum, Max. *Revolution in the Air: Sixties Radicals Turn to Lenin, Mao, and Che.* New York: Verso, 2002.

Espiritu, Augusto Fauni. *Five Faces of Exile: The Nation and Filipino American Intellectuals.* Stanford, Calif.: Stanford University Press, 2005.

Espiritu, Yen Le. *Asian American Panethnicity: Bridging Institutions and Identities.* Philadelphia: Temple University Press, 1992.

———. *Asian American Women and Men: Labor, Laws and Love.* Thousand Oaks, Calif.: Sage Publications, 1997.

———. *Home Bound: Filipino American Lives across Cultures, Communities, and Countries.* Berkeley: University of California Press, 2003.

Foner, Philip S., and Daniel Rosenberg. *Racism, Dissent, and Asian Americans from 1850 to the Present: A Documentary History.* Westport, Conn.: Greenwood Press, 1993.

Ford, Marjorie, and Elizabeth Schave. *Community Matters: A Reader for Writers.* New York: Addison Wesley Longman, 2002.

Fraser, Ronald, et al. *1968: A Student Generation in Revolt.* New York: Pantheon Books, 1988.

Friday, Chris. *Organizing Asian American Labor: The Pacific Coast Canned Salmon Industry, 1870–1942.* Philadelphia: Temple University Press, 1994.

Fujita-Rony, Dorothy. *American Workers, Colonial Power: Philippine Seattle and the Transpacific West, 1919–1941.* Berkeley: University of California Press, 2003.

Gee, Emma, ed. *Counterpoint: Perspectives on Asian America.* Los Angeles: UCLA Asian American Studies Center, 1976.

Gillis, John R. *Commemorations: The Politics of National Identity.* Princeton, N.J.: Princeton University Press, 1994.

Godfrey, Brian J. *Neighborhoods in Transition: The Making of San Francisco's Ethnic and Non-Conformist Communities.* Berkeley: University of California Press, 1988.

Goodno, James B. *The Philippines: Land of Broken Promises.* London: Zed Books, 1991.

Gramsci, Antonio. 7th ed. *The Modern Prince and Other Writings.* New York: International Publishers, 1978.

Gramsci, Antonio. *Selections from the Prison Notebooks of Antonio* Gramsci, 10th ed., ed. Quintin Hoare and Geoffrey Nowell Smith. New York: International Publishers, 1989.

Groth, Paul. *Living Downtown: The History of Residential Hotels in the United States.* Berkeley: University of California Press, 1994.

Guerrero, Amado. *Philippine Society and Revolution.* Oakland, Calif.: International Association of Filipino Patriots, 1970.

Hagedorn, Jessica. *Gangster of Love.* Boston: Houghton Mifflin, 1996.

Hartman, Chester. *The Transformation of San Francisco.* Totowa, N.J.: Rowman and Allanheld, 1984.

———. *Yerba Buena: Land Grab and Community Resistance in San Francisco.* San Francisco: Glide Publications, 1974.

Hartman, Chester, and Sarah Carnochan. *City for Sale: The Transformation of San Francisco.* Berkeley: University of California, 2002.

Hartman, Chester, Dennis Keating, and Richard LeGates. *Displacement: How to Fight It.* Berkeley: National Housing Law Project, 1981.

Hilliard, David, and Lewis Cole. *This Side of Glory: The Autobiography of David Hilliard and the Story of the Black Panther Party.* Boston: Little, Brown, 1993.

Ho, Fred, ed. *Legacy to Liberation: Politics and Culture of Revolutionary Asian Pacific America.* San Francisco: Big Red Media and AK Press, 2000.

Hu-DeHart, Evelyn, ed. *Across the Pacific: Asian Americans and Globalization.* Philadelphia: Temple University Press, 1999.

Ignacio, Lemuel F. *Asian Americans and Pacific Islanders (Is There Such an Ethnic Group?).* San Jose: Pilipino Development Association, 1976.

Jones, Greg R. *Red Revolution: Inside the Philippine Guerrilla Movement.* Boulder, Colo.: Westwood Press, 1989.

Karnow, Stanley. *In Our Image: America's Empire in the Philippines.* New York: Ballantine Books, 1989.

Kushner, Sam. *Long Road to Delano.* New York: International Publishers, 1975.

Lacaba, Jose F. *Days of Disquiet, Nights of Rage.* Quezon City: Rapid Lithographics, 1982.

Lasker, Bruno. *Filipino Immigration to Continental United States and to Hawaii,* repr. ed. New York: Arno Press, 1969 (1931).

Liwanag Collective. *Liwanag: Literary and Graphic Expressions by Filipinos in America.* San Francisco: Liwanag Publications, 1975.

Louie, Steve, and Glenn K. Omatsu, eds. *Asian Americans: The Movement and the Moment.* Los Angeles: UCLA Asian American Studies Center, 2001.

Mananzan, Sr. Mary John. *Essays on Women.* Manila: St. Scholastica's College, 1991.

May, Glenn Anthony. *Social Engineering in the Philippines: The Aims, Execution and Impact of American Colonial Policy, 1900–1913.* Westport, Conn.: Greenwood Press, 1980.

McWilliams, Carey. *Brothers under the Skin,* repr. ed. Boston: Little, Brown, 1964.

———. *Factories in the Field: The Story of Migratory Farm Labor in California.* Boston: Little, Brown, 1939.

Meister, Richard, ed. *The Black Ghetto: Promised Land or Colony?* Lexington, Mass.: Heath, 1971.

Miller, Stuart Creighton. *Benevolent Assimilation: The American Conquest of the Philippines, 1899–1903.* New Haven, Conn.: Yale University, 1982.

Mirikitani, Janice, Louis Syquia, Bariel Clay II, Janet Campbell Hale, Alejandro Murgia, Roberto Vargos, Jim Dong, and Rupert Garcia, eds. *Time to Greez! Incantations from the Third World.* San Francisco: Glide Publications, Third World Communications, 1975.

Mollenkopf, John H. *The Contested City.* Princeton, N.J.: Princeton University Press, 1983.

Moore, Rebecca, Anthony B. Pinn, and Mary R. Sawyer. *People's Temple and Black Religion in America.* Bloomington: Indiana University Press, 2004.

Morales, Royal F. *Makibaka: The Pilipino American Struggle.* Los Angeles: Mountainview Publishers, 1974.

Morantte, P. C. *Remembering Carlos Bulosan: His Heart Affair with America.* Quezon City: New Day Publishers, 1984.

Munoz, Carlos, Jr. *Youth Identity, Power, and the Chicano Movement.* New York: Verso, 1989.

Navarro, Jovina, ed. *Lahing Pilipino: Pilipino American Anthology.* Davis, Calif.: Mga Kapatid, 1977.

Nee, Victor G., and Brett de Bary Nee. *Longtime Californ': A Documentary Study of an American Chinatown,* repr. ed. Stanford, Calif.: Stanford University Press, 1986 (1972).

Ngai, Mae M. *Impossible Subjects: Illegal Aliens and the Making of Modern America.* Princeton, N.J.: Princeton University Press, 2004.

Omi, Michael, and Howard Winant. *Racial Formation in the United States from the 1960s to the 1990s,* 2nd ed. New York: Routledge, 1994.

Pido, Antonio. *The Pilipinos in America: Macro/Micro Dimensions in Immigration and Integration.* New York: Center for Migration Studies, 1985.

Quinsaat, Jesse, ed. *Letters in Exile: An Introductory Reader on the History of Pilipinos in America.* Los Angeles: UCLA Asian American Studies Center, 1976.

Racism Research Project (Gary Achziger, Linda Burnham, Harry Chang, Neil Gotanda, Paul Liem, Belvin Louie, Bruce Occena, Smokey Perry, Barbara Pottgen, Pat Sumi, and Bob Wing). *Critique of the Black Nation Thesis.* Berkeley: Racism Research Project, 1975.

Rafael, Vicente L, ed. *Discrepant Histories: Translocal Essays on Filipino Cultures.* Philadelphia: Temple University Press, 1995.

Reinecke, John E. *The Filipino Piecemeal Sugar Strike of 1924–1925.* Honolulu: Social Science Research Institute, University of Hawaii, 1996.

Rizal, Jose. *Noli Me Tangere,* repr. ed. London: Longman Group, 1986.

Robles, Al. *Looking for Ifugao Mountain.* San Francisco: Children's Book Press, 1977.

———. *Rapping with Ten Thousand Carabaos in the Dark.* Los Angeles: UCLA Asian American Studies Center, 1993.

Rodis, Rodel. *Telltale Signs: Filipinos in America.* San Francisco: INA Development, 1991.

Root, Maria P. P., ed. *Filipino Americans: Transformation and Identity.* Thousand Oaks, Calif.: Sage Publications, 1997.

Rosaldo, Renato. *Culture and Truth: The Remaking of Social Analysis.* Boston: Beacon Press, 1989.

Salomon, Larry R. *Roots of Justice: Stories of Organizing in Communities of Color.* San Francisco: Jossey-Bass, 1998.

San Juan, E., Jr. *Writing and National Liberation: Essays in Critical Practice.* Diliman, Philippines: University of the Philippines Press, 1991.

Scharlin, Craig, and Lilia V. Villaneuva. *Philip Vera Cruz: Personal History of Filipino Immigrants and the Farmworkers Movement.* Los Angeles: Regents UCLA Asian American Studies Center, 1992.

Schirmer, D. B., and S. R. Shalom, eds. *The Philippines Reader: A History of Colonialism, Neocolonialism, Dictatorship, and Resistance.* Boston: South End Press, 1987.

Scott, William Henry. *The Discovery of the Igorots: Spanish Contacts with the Pagans of Northern Luzon.* Quezon City: New Day Publishers of the Christian Literature Society of the Philippines, 1974.

Shaw, Angel Velasco, and Luis H. Francia, eds. *Vestiges of War: The Philippine–American War and the Aftermath of an Imperial Dream: 1899–1999.* New York: New York University Press, 2002.

Shilts, Randy. *The Mayor of Castro Street: The Life and Times of Harvey Milk.* New York: St. Martin's Press, 1982.

Smith, Michael Peter and Joe R. Feagin, eds. *The Bubbling Cauldron and the Urban Crisis.* Minneapolis: University of Minnesota Press, 1995.

———. *The Capitalist City: Global Restructuring and Community Politics.* Oxford: Basil Blackwell, 1987.

Smith, Paul Chaat, and Robert Allen Warrior. *Like a Hurricane: The Indian Movement from Alcatraz to Wounded Knee.* New York: New Press, 1996.

Stegner, Wallace. *One Nation.* Boston: Houghton Mifflin, 1945.

Sue, Stanley, and Nathaniel N. Wagner, eds. *Asian Americans: Social and Psychological Perspectives.* Ben Lomond, Calif.: Science and Behavior Books, 1973.

Tachiki, Amy, ed. *Roots: An Asian American Reader.* Los Angeles: UCLA Asian American Studies Center, 1976.

Takaki, Ronald. *A Different Mirror: A History of Multicultural America.* Boston: Little, Brown, 1993.

———. *Double Victory: A Multicultural History of America in World War II.* Boston: Little, Brown, 2000.

———. *Strangers from a Different Shore: A History of Asian America.* Boston: Little, Brown, 1989.

UCLA Asian American Studies, *Letters in Exile: An Introductory Reader on the History of Pilipinos in America.* Los Angeles: UCLA Asian American Studies Center, 1976.

Vallanga, Robert V. *Pinoy, First Wave, 1898–1941.* San Francisco: Strawberry Hill Press, 1977.

Wei, William. *The Asian American Movement.* Philadelphia: Temple University Press, 1993.

Weiss, Mike. *Double Play: The San Francisco City Hall Killings.* Reading, Mass.: Addison-Wesley, 1984.

Articles in Books

Cerenio, Virginia. "Dreams of Manong Frankie." Pp. 228–35 in *Making Waves: An Anthology of Writings by and about Asian American Women,* ed. Asian Women United of California. Boston: Beacon Press, 1989.

Chan, Sucheng. "Asian American Movement, 1960–1980s." Pp. 525–33 in *People of Color in the American West,* ed. Sucheng Chang et al. Lexington, Mass.: D. C. Heath, 1994.

Constantino, Renato. "Miseducation of the Filipino." Pp. 45–49 in *The Philippines Reader: A History of Colonialism, Neocolonialism, Dictatorship and Resistance,* ed. Daniel B. Schirmir and Stephen R. Shalom. Boston: South End Press, 1987.

Drew, James. "Call Any Vegetable: The Politics of Food in San Francisco." Pp. 317–32 in *Reclaiming San Francisco: History, Politics, Culture,* ed. James Brook, Chris Carlsson, and Nancy J. Peters. San Francisco: City Lights Books, 1998.

Francia, Luis H. "Inventing the Earth: The Notion of 'Home' in Asian American Literature." Pp. 191–218 in *Across the Pacific: Asian Americans and Globalization,* ed. Evelyn Hu-DeHart. Philadelphia: Temple University Press, 1999.

Francisco, Luzviminda. "The Philippine American War." Pp. 6–19 in *The Philippines Reader: A History of Colonialism, Neocolonialism, Dictatorship and Resistance,* ed. Daniel B. Schirmir and Stephen Rosskamm Shalom. Boston: South End Press, 1987.

———. "The Philippine American War, 1899–1902." Pp. 1–22 in *An Introductory Reader on the History of Pilipinos in America,* ed. Jesse Quinsaat. Los Angles: UCLA Asian American Studies Center, 1976.

Frazier, John W. "Asians in the United States: Historical and Contemporary Settlement Patterns." Pp. 265–86 in *Race, Ethnicity, and Place in a Changing America,* ed. John W. Frazier and Eugene L. Tettey-Fio. Binghamton, N.Y.: Global Academic Publishing, 2006.

Gamalinda, Eric. "English Is Your Mother Tongue/Ang Ingles Ay an Tongue ng Ina Mo." Pp. 247–59 in *Vestiges of War: The Philippine–American War and the Aftermath of an Imperial Dream, 1899–1999,* ed. Angel Velasco Shaw and Luis H. Francia. New York: New York University Press, 2002.

Gramsci, Antonio. "The Intellectuals." Pp. 3–23 in *Selections from the Prison Notebooks,* 10th ed., ed. and trans. Quintin Hoare and Geoffrey Nowell Smith. New York: International Publishers, 1989.

Habal, Estella. "How I Became a Revolutionary." Pp. 197–210 in *Legacy to Liberation: Politics and Culture of Revolutionary Asian Pacific America,* ed. Fred Ho. San Francisco: Big Red Media and AK Press, 2000.

Huen, Floyd. "The Advent and Origins of the Asian American Movement in the San Francisco Bay Area: A Personal Perspective." Pp. 276–83 in *Asian Americans: The Movement and the Moment,* ed. Steve Louie and Glenn K. Omatsu. Los Angeles: UCLA Asian American Studies Center, 2001.

Jayo, Norman. "Hard Lines and Shades of Grey Flannel." P. 35 in *We Won't Move: Poems and Photographs of the International Hotel Struggle,* ed. Asian American Writers Workshop. San Francisco: Kearny Street Workshop, 1977.

Kordziel, Beverly. "To Be a Part of the People: The International Hotel Collective." Pp. 241–47 in *Asian Americans: The Movement and the Moment,* ed. Steve Louie and Glenn K. Omatsu. Los Angeles: UCLA Asian American Studies Center, 2001.

Lazam, Jeanette. "The Mighty Manhattan-Born Pinay." Pp. 89–106 in *Seven Card Stud with Seven Manangs Wild: An Anthology of Filipino-American Writings,* ed. Helen Toribio. San Francisco: T'Boli Publishing, 2002.

Lott, Juanita Tamayo. "Demographic Changes Transforming the Filipino American Community." Pp. 11–20 in *Filipino American: Transformation and Identity,* ed. Maria P. P. Root. Thousand Oaks, Calif.: Sage Publications, 1997.

Lyman, Stanford. "Red Guard on Grant Avenue: The Rise of Youthful Rebellion in Chinatown." Pp. 20–44 in *Asian Americans: Psychological Perspectives,* ed. Stanley Sue and Nathaniel N. Wagner. Ben Lomond, Calif.: Science and Behavior Books, 1973.

Mananzan, Sr. Mary John. "The Filipino Woman: Before and After the Spanish Conquest of the Philippines." Pp. 6–35 in *Essays on Women,* ed. Sr. Mary John Mananzan. Manila: St. Scholastica's College, 1991.

Matsuoka, Jim. "Little Tokyo: Searching the Past and Analyzing the Future." Pp. 322–34 in *Roots: An Asian American Reader,* ed. Amy Tachiki. Los Angeles: UCLA Asian American Studies Center, 1971.

Navarro, Jovina. "Toward a Relevant Pilipino Education." Pp. 101–102 in *Lahing Pilipino: Pilipino American Anthology,* ed. Jovina Navarro. Davis, Calif.: Mga Kapatid, 1977.

Quinsaat, Jesse. "An Exercise on How to Join the Navy and Still Not See the World." Pp. 97–105 in *Letters in Exile: An Introductory Reader on the History of Pilipinos in America,* ed. Jesse Quinsaat. Los Angeles: UCLA Asian American Studies Center, 1976,

Rimonte, Nilda. "Colonialism's Legacy: The Inferiorizing of the Filipino." Pp. 39–61 in *Filipino Americans: Transformation and Identity,* ed. Maria P. P. Root. Thousand Oaks, Calif.: Sage Publications, 1997.

San Juan, E., Jr. "In the Belly of the Monster: Reappraising Carlos Bulosan." Pp. 56–64 in *Writing and National Liberation: Essays and Critical Practice.* Quezon City: University of the Philippines Press, 1991.

Shaw, Randy. "Tenant Power in San Francisco." Pp. 287–300 in *Reclaiming San Francisco: History, Politics, Culture,* ed. James Brook, Chris Carlsson, and Nancy J. Peters. San Francisco: City Lights Books, 1998

Syquia, Louis. "Who Are the Poets?" Pp. 21–22 in *Time to Greez! Incantations from the Third World,* ed. Janice Mirikitani, Louis Syquia, Buriel Clay II, Janet Campbell Hale, Alejandro Murgia, Roberto Vargas, Jim Dong, and Rupert Garcia. San Francisco: Glide Publications/Third World Communications, 1975.

Toribio, Helen. "Dare to Struggle: The KDP and Filipino American Politics." Pp. 31–46 in *Legacy to Liberation: Politics and Culture of Revolutionary Asian Pacific America,* ed. Fred Ho. San Francisco: Big Red Media and AK Press, 2000.

Walker, Dick, and Bay Area Study Group. "The Playground of U.S. Capitalism? The Political Economy of the San Francisco Bay Area in the 1980s." Pp. 3–82 in *Fire in the Hearth: The Radical Politics of Place in America,* vol. 4, ed. Mike Davis, Steven Hiatt, Marie Kennedy, Susan Ruddich and Michael Spinks. New York: Verso, 1990.

Articles in Journals and Magazines

Alegado, Dean T. "The Filipino Community in Hawaii: Development and Change." *Social Process in Hawaii* 33 (1991): 4.

Anthony, Donald Elliott. "Filipino Labor in Central California." *Sociology and Social Research* 16 (1931–32): 149–56.

Bello, Madge, and Vincent Reyes, "Filipino Americans and the Marcos Overthrow: The Transformation of Political Consciousness." *Amerasia Journal* 13, no.1 (1986–87): 73–83.

Campomanes, Oscar. "The New Empire's Forgetful and Forgotten Citizens: Unrepresentability and Unassimilability in Filipino American Postcolonialities." *Critical Mass* 2. no. 2 (Spring 1995): 145–200.

Catapusan, Benicio T. "Filipino Labor Cycle in the United States." *Sociology and Social Research* 19 (1934–35): 61–63.

Choy, Catherine Ceniza. "Towards Trans-Pacific Social Justice: Women and Protest in Filipino American History." *Journal of Asian American Studies* 8, no. 3 (October 2005): 293–307.

De Vera, Arlene. "Without Parallel: The Local 7 Deportation Cases, 1949–1955." *Amerasia Journal* 20, no. 2 (1994): 1–25.

DeWitt, Howard. "The Filipino Labor Union: The Salinas Lettuce Strike of 1934." *Amerasia Journal* 5, no. 2 (1978): 1–21.

Espiritu, Yen Le. "The Intersection of Race, Ethnicity, and Class: The Multiple Identities of Second-Generation Filipinos." *Identities* 1, nos. 2–3 (November 1994): 249–74.

Evangelista, Susan. "California's Third Oriental Wave: A Sociohistorical Analysis." *Philippine Studies* 31 (1983): 37–57.

Feria, R. T. "War and the Status of Filipino Immigrants." *Sociology and Social Research* 31 (1946–47): 50–53.

Fishkin, Shelley Fisher. "Crossroads of Culture: The Transnational Turn in American Studies—Presidential Address to the American Studies Association: Nov. 12, 2004." *American Quarterly* 57, no. 1 (2005): 17–57.

Guerlan, Barbara. "The Movement in the United States to Oppose Martial Law in the Philippines, 1972–1991: An Overview." *Pilipinas* 33 (Fall 1999): 75–98.

Hartman, Chester. "San Francisco's International Hotel: A Case Study of a Turf Struggle." *Radical America* 12, no. 3 (May–June 1978): 47–58.

Hsu, Madeline. "Gold Mountain Dreams and Paper Son Schemes: Chinese Immigration under Exclusion." *Chinese America* (1997): 46–60.

Kotake, Donna. "A View from Nihonmachi." *Gidra* (1990): 12.

Louie, Steve. "William Wei's 'Asian American Movement.'" *Amerasia Journal* 19, no. 30 (1993): 155–93.

Masson, Jack K., and Donald L.Guimary. "Pilipinos and Unionization of the Alaskan Canned Salmon Industry." *Amerasia Journal* 8, no.2 (1981): 1–30.

Omatsu, Glenn. "The Four Prisons and the Movement of Liberation." *Amerasia Journal* 15, no. 1 (1989): xv–xxx.

Posadas, Barbara M. "Hierarchy of Color and Psychological Adjustment in an Industrial Environment: Filipinos, the Pullman Company, and the Brotherhood of Sleeping Car Porters." *Labor History* 23, no. 3 (1982): 349–73.

Posadas, Barbara M., and Roland L. Guyotte. "Unintentional Immigrants: Chicago's Filipino Foreign Students Become Settlers." *Journal of American Ethnic History* 9, no. 3 (1990): 26–48.

Robles, Al. "The Manongs of Manilatown: Oral Histories." *City Magazine*, December 1975, 26.

Silva, John L. "Remembering Ray Gathchalian." *Filipinas* (July 2003): 47–48.

Strobel, Leny. "The Cultural Identity of Third Wave Filipino Americans." *Journal of American Association of Philippine Psychology* 1 (Summer 1994): 37–54.

Toribio, Helen. "We Are Revolution: A Reflective History of the Union of Democratic Filipinos (KDP)." *Amerasia Journal* 24, no. 2 (1998): 155–77.

Trillin, Calvin. "U.S. Journal: San Francisco, Some Thoughts on the International Hotel Controversy." *New Yorker,* December 19, 1977, 166–20.

Umemoto, Karen. "On Strike! San Francisco State College Strike, 1968–69: The Role of Asian American Students." *Amerasia Journal* 15, no. 1 (1989): 15–19.

Yu, Connie Young. "A History of San Francisco's Chinatown Housing." *Amerasia Journal* 8, no. 1 (1981): 93–109.

Yu, Elena S. H. "Filipino Migration and Community Organizations in the United States." *California Sociologist* 3, no. 2 (Summer 1980): 84.

Theses and Dissertations

Catapusan, Benicio T. "The Social Adjustment of Filipinos in the United States." Ph.D. diss., University of Southern California, Los Angeles, 1940.

Coloma, Casiano Pagdilao. "A Study of the Filipino Repatration Movement." Master's thesis, University of Southern California, Los Angeles, 1939.

DeVera, Arlene. "An Unfinished Agenda: Filipino Immigrant Workers in the Era of McCarthyism—A Case Study of the Cannery Workers and Farm Laborers Union, 1948–1955." Master's thesis, University of California, Los Angeles, 1990.

Galedo, Lillian. "The Development of Working Class Consciousness: Three Oral Histories." Master's thesis, Goddard College, San Francisco, 1978.

Jeffs, William G. "The Roots of the Delano Grape Strike." Master's thesis, California State University, Fullerton, 1969.

Lawcock, Larry Arden. "Filipino Students in the United States and the Philippine Independence Movement." Ph.D. diss., University of California, Berkeley, 1925.

Lee, Teri. "The International Hotel: One Community's Fight for Survival." Master's thesis, University of California, Berkeley, 1976.

Levine, Carol Deena. "The City's Response to Conflicting Pressures—A Case Study: The International Hotel." Master's thesis, San Francisco State University, 1970.

Mariano, Honorate. "The Filipino Immigrants in the United States." Master's thesis, University of Oregon, Eugene, 1933.

Tsen, Vivian. "The International Hotel: An Anatomy of a Housing Issue." Master's Thesis, University of California, Berkeley, 1977.

Yip, Christopher Lee. "San Francisco Chinatown: An Architectural and Urban History." Ph.D. diss., University of California, Berkeley, 1985.

Other Media

Choy, Curtis. *Fall of the I-Hotel.* Film. Chunk Moonhunter Productions, Oakland, Calif., 1983; National Asian American Telecommunications Association, San Francisco, 1993.

Cronkite, Walter. "CBS Evening News." Television broadcast, August 4, 1977.

Jayo, Norman. "International Hotel." Audiocassette of live broadcast. Third World News Bureau, KPFA Pacifica News, Berkeley, May 1977.

———. "Live Broadcast from the Eviction." Tape recording. Third World News Bureau, KPFA Pacifica News, Berkeley, August 4, 1977.

Lowe, Felicia. *Chinatown.* Film. KQED Neighborhood Series, San Francisco, 1996.

Pulido, Rod, dir. *The Flip Side: A Filipino American Comedy.* Film. Puro Pinoy Productions, Chicago, 2002.

Schwartz, Mark, dir. *Dollar a Day, Ten Cents a Dance.* Video. Gold Mountain Productions, Capitola, Calif., 1984.

Vera Cruz, Philip. "Profits Enslave the World." Song lyrics published in "Makibaka: The KDP's Experience, 1973–1987, Songs of Struggle from the Philippines and America," KDP Reunion, Oakland, Calif., July 10–12, 1998.

Unpublished Sources

Louie, Miriam. "Yellow, Brown, and Red: Towards a Marxist Appraisal of Influence of the Asian American Movement." Unpublished ms., May 1991, MHF Archive.

Prowler, David. "International Hotel Study." Unpublished ms., ca. 1981, MHF Archive.

———. "International Hotel Notes," 1976–77, MHF Archive.

Torrefiel, Esther. "International Hotel." Student paper. San Francisco State University, 1992, MHF Archive.

INDEX

Note: Page numbers in *italics* refer to illustrations. Page numbers followed by "n." refer to information in endnotes.

ESTELLA HABAL is Assistant Professor of Asian American Studies, Department of Social Science, San Jose State University, and a member of the Board of Directors, Manilatown Heritage Foundation.